GERALD
of WALES
A Voice of the Middle Ages

GERALD
of WALES
A Voice of the Middle Ages

ROBERT BARTLETT

The
History
Press

For my Mother and Father

This edition first published 2006
Reprinted 2008

Reprinted in 2013 by
The History Press
The Mill, Brimscombe Port,
Stroud, Gloucestershire, GL5 2QG
www.thehistorypress.co.uk

British Library Cataloguing in Publication Data.
A catalogue record for this book is available from the British Library.

ISBN 978 0 7524 4031 6

Typesetting and origination by Tempus Publishing Limited
Printed and bound by TJ Books Limited, Padstow, Cornwall

CONTENTS

PREFACE

The prolific output of Gerald of Wales has been quarried for telling anecdotes and quotations by virtually every scholar of late twelfth-century English history, but he has not yet been the subject of a comprehensive study. This book attempts to characterize the ideas and attitudes expressed in Gerald's works. It does not give a narrative of his life and is a biographical study rather than a biography. Gerald's cause célèbre, the St. David's case, and the writings in which he described it, are not treated in great detail as they have recently received scholarly examination by Michael Richter. Gerald's Irish and Welsh works (Topographia Hibernica, Expugnatio Hibernica, Itinerarium Kambriae, Descriptio Kambriae) were his greatest achievements, and they are investigated in detail here; as is the De Principis Instructione, Gerald's account of the last years of Henry II. The intention has been to make Gerald's thought comprehensible both in terms of antecedent intellectual traditions and the contemporary social context.

ACKNOWLEDGEMENTS

I would like to thank all those friends and colleagues who have commented upon parts of this work. I owe a special debt to three scholars: Robert Tannenbaum, who first stirred my interest in this kind of history; Henry Mayr-Harting, whose scrupulous and stimulating editorial advice was of immense help in producing this book; and, most importantly, Sir Richard Southern, who supervised the thesis and provided inspiration, criticism, and standards towards which to aspire.

ABBREVIATIONS

The following abbreviations have been used for Gerald's works. The figures in parentheses refer to the volume number of the Rolls Series edition.

De Reb.	De Rebus a Se Gestis (i)
Symb. El.	Symbolum Electorum (i)
Gemma	Gemma Ecclesiastica (ii)
De Jure	De Jure et Statu Menevensis Ecclesiae (iii)
Vita Dav.	Vita Sancti Davidis (iii)
Spec. Eccl.	Speculum Ecclesiae (iv)
Vita Galf.	Vita Galfridi Archiepiscopi Eboracensis (iv)
Top.	Topographia Hibernica (v)
Exp.	Expugnatio Hibernica (v)
Itin.	Itinerarium Kambriae (vi)
Descr.	Descriptio Kambriae (vi)
Vita Rem.	Vita Sancti Remigii (vii)
Vita Hug.	Vita Sancti Hugonis (vii)
Prin.	De Principis Instructione (viii)

The following works are referred to in other editions:

Vita Ethel.   Vita Ethelberti, ed. M.R. James,
'Two Lives of St. Ethelbert,
'King and Martyr',
English Historical Review, xxxii (1917).
Inv.   Invectiones, ed. W.S. Davies,
Y Cymmrodor, xxx (1920).
Spec. Duorum   Speculum Duorum, ed. Y. Lefevre and
R.B.C. Huygens. General
editor, Michael Richter (Cardiff, 1974).

Other abbreviations are:

AASS	Acta Sanctorum, ed. J. Bollandus, etc. (Antwerp and Brussels, 1643-).
Becket Materials	Materials for the History of Thomas Becket, ed. J.C. Robertson (7 vols., RS, 1875-85).
CSEL	Corpus Scriptorum Ecclesiasticorum Latinorum.
Map	Walter Map, De Nugis Curialium, ed. M.R. James (Oxford, 1914).
MGH	Monumenta Germaniae Historica.
PG	Patrologiae Cursus Completus, series graeca, ed. J.P. Migne (162 vols., Paris, 1857-66).
PL	Patrologiae Cursus Completus, series latina, ed. J.P. Migne (221 vols., Paris, 1844-64).
RS	Rerum Britannicarum Medii Aevi Scriptores (251 vols., London, 1858-96), 'Rolls Series'.

INTRODUCTION

Although the primary purpose of a biographical study is to evoke an individual, this cannot be done without continual reference to the world that individual inhabited. The first priority of such a study remains the investigation of how one man or woman was shaped by and related to that world, but there is a need, in the process, to attempt more general historical statements. The illumination that a detailed biographical study can produce is particularly important for the twelfth century since the nature of the evidence in that period makes prosopographical techniques inappropriate. They can, at best, provide limited generalizations which require the animating touch of individual histories before they become meaningful.

Gerald of Wales (1146-1223) is a good subject for such treatment, not because he was typical, but because his life and writing exemplified so many different trends of the time. Moreover, the flood of vivid and personal prose that he produced gives us a degree of intimacy and acquaintance with Gerald that is not common for figures of the twelfth century. The more usual experience for a historian is to have to coax the words and feelings from the starkness of official documentation or stereotyped formulations. In Gerald's case, we can hear his voice. Indeed, it is sometimes necessary, in order to understand him fully, to refuse to be lured by his eloquent self-presentation and to pay attention instead to what he does not say.

The first part of this book, 'Politics and Nationality', is more strictly biographical, and attempts to analyse Gerald's political position and complex, changing sense of nationality. He has to be located, firstly, in the class into which he was born, the Marcher knights of South Wales.

In the late eleventh and twelfth centuries the knightly classes of western Europe engaged in a series of expansionist enterprises. They provided the military spearhead of the Crusades and the reconquests from Islam in the western Mediterranean. In eastern Europe they fought the Slavs and presided over and profited from an eastward wave of peasant colonization. The knightly families of northern France, especially, seem to have contained a reservoir of restless aristocrats prepared to chance their hand in military gambles. This did not necessarily lead them beyond the borders of Latin Christendom. In 1066 the prospect of rich pickings across the Channel drew many northern French warriors into William the Conqueror's army; a century and a half later knights from the North won land and lordship in the Midi as crusaders against heresy.

The Anglo-Norman knightly and baronial class saw opportunities for conquest and profit in the Celtic countries to the north and west. In the case of Scotland, this expansionism took place with the encouragement of the native dynasty. The lowlands were partially feudalized and Normanized under David I. In Wales and Ireland Anglo-Norman expansion involved military aggression and led to (incomplete) conquest and colonization. New forms of military technology, based on feudal cavalry and the castle, were introduced, so that Ireland, for example, became dotted with motte and bailey castles. English law and feudal forms of land-holding were grafted on to existing native institutions, and extensive settlement took place. The eastern half of Ireland and the lowlands of Wales were manorialized and many towns were founded, and many of the burgesses and some of the peasants who inhabited these new settlements came from England or even further afield.

This process can aptly be called 'feudal colonialism'. The Anglo-Norman knights and barons were fighting for the profits of lordship. They expelled or subjugated the indigenous ruling class, continued to draw on the traditional rents and renders where possible, and simultaneously increased their resources by fostering agricultural and urban development. The peasants and burgesses who came to settle were searching for new opportunities, partly driven, perhaps, by relative over-population at home, partly induced by the favourable legal and economic terms which could often be obtained in new settlements.

The conquest and exploitation of Wales and Ireland by the Anglo Normans was not, initially, a royal project. The first incursions into both countries were organized as private aristocratic enterprises, and it was not until the thirteenth century that an English king seriously undertook a policy of conquest. Nevertheless, kings became involved in the process for two good reasons. Firstly, like any other lord, they wanted their share of available profits and hence staked a direct claim in lordships in both countries. Secondly, the situation demanded general political supervision. Although the Norman and Angevin kings had their eyes turned to France, they could not afford to ignore developments in Wales and Ireland completely, especially when these developments involved the creation of a vigorous, semi-autonomous interest group among their own aristocracy.

Gerald was born into this complex society, where Marcher, native, and royal interests often clashed. He was the spokesman and eulogist of the Marchers, the anatomist and critic of the hybrid society from which he sprang.

In describing twelfth-century Wales and Ireland, however, Gerald brought to bear a literary and intellectual equipment which he had acquired elsewhere. The cultural resources of Ireland and Wales in themselves could not have generated his Irish and Welsh works. It was Gerald's training at Paris, and his acquisition there of the highest learning that the Latin West could offer, that enabled him to articulate and analyse his own society in the way he did.

The education available at Paris in the later twelfth century was diverse and sophisticated. The initial stage, the arts course, provided a training in self-expression and logical thought. It also gave the student a chance to become familiar with a broad range of classical literature, and Gerald's ready use of Roman authors has been frequently commented upon. In this respect he can be characterized as a 'humanist' in the same sense as John of Salisbury. John, Gerald, and other twelfth-century authors wrote fluent, forceful Latin, deeply influenced by classical as well as biblical models. They take their place in the great efflorescence of literary culture, both Latin and vernacular, which occurred in this period.

An education in the schools, however, also had more practical ends than the development of a good literary style. After studying the arts, it was not uncommon for a student to go on to one of the higher studies, and Gerald studied civil and canon law in Paris in the late 1170s. This was a natural choice for anyone intending to use learning as a step to government employment. It was during the twelfth century that the schools began to provide for the needs of government in this way.

This century saw an expansion and diversification of government, as rulers and administrators undertook more business and refined their techniques, and this involved more written documents. Instructions had to be sent by letter; financial and legal records had to be kept. The web of governmental activity was held together by writing and, consequently, the bureaucratic element in administration increased greatly in importance. Bureaucracies had to be staffed by men capable of clear verbal expression and, in the higher ranks, by men trained in law. Such men, in both ecclesiastical and secular government, were recruited from those trained in the schools.

Gerald is a good example of a schoolman who entered royal service. Besides periods as an administrator in the diocese of St. David's, he spent ten years as a royal clerk and was employed as envoy to the Welsh, adviser to Prince John, and companion to Archbishop Baldwin. The variety of his experiences in government service stimulated him to produce the works on Ireland and Wales which he wrote during this period. His intellectual training and his practical experience combined in these vivid literary creations.

It is natural to couple Gerald's name with those of Walter Map and Peter of Blois. All three were roughly contemporary, worked in royal or archiepiscopal service, and, while doing so, produced literary works that were designed to be entertaining and stylistically satisfying as well as edifying. Peter's Letters, Map's De Nugis Curialium and Gerald's Irish and Welsh works emerged from the late twelfth century courts, not the schools or monasteries. Written in Latin, they were not intended for a lay audience, but their first readers (or hearers) would be secular clerks, men with ecclesiastical status but experience of the wider world of affairs.

The careers of the three men have many parallels. They sprang from the lower feudal classes and were educated at Paris before entering government service. They rose to be archdeacons but no further, although this exasperated Gerald more than Peter or Map. Both Gerald and Peter of Blois were, in a sense, outsiders, and this made them insecure. Both were also sensitive to the charge that secular literature was a frivolous pursuit for ecclesiastics, and they both developed theological interests in later life. Map, more genial, wittier, and more assured, has left no evidence of a similar shift.

The works of Gerald, Peter, and Walter Map illustrate both the vitality and the diversity of court culture and Latin writing in late twelfth-century England. But Gerald was not simply a court littérateur. He regarded himself as a historian. Although, to our eyes, only the Expugnatio Hibernica conforms to the standard model of historical narrative, the other Irish and Welsh works attempted to delineate contemporary societies as concrete, historical communities, and 'history' was the only term then available to categorize writing of this kind. Gerald must be viewed in the context of the English historical tradition, one of the strongest elements in English culture at this time.

By the late twelfth century historical writing in England was no longer dominated by the monasteries or by that urge to save the shattered past that had animated historians in the generations after the Norman Conquest. Writers such as William of Newburgh, Roger of Howden, and Ralph of Diceto did not belong to the monastic order (although William was an Augustinian canon), and focused their attention on contemporary political and administrative developments. They drew a vivid picture of England under the rule of the Angevins.

Gerald's talents as an observer of contemporary political events give him a high place on the list of twelfth-century historians. He was unrivalled in his sense of social process and awareness of the coherence of societies; his ethnographic writing was therefore highly innovative. He drew strength from seeing himself in the tradition of Gildas or Bede, yet he was attempting something new. He can be contrasted with Geoffrey of Monmouth, a contemporary man of letters from the Welsh Marches (but one who eventually attained his Welsh bishopric). Both Geoffrey and Gerald were innovative; but Geoffrey's work was, in essence, a national or heroic legend. Gerald presented the material, cultural, and historical realities of his subject in a way that highlights the Historia Regum Britanniae's fancifulness and romanticism.

Gerald's years at Paris and the internationalism of twelfth-century culture in general mean that he cannot be understood by reference to the English (or British) context alone. He must be related to the development of scholasticism and naturalism in the Latin West.

Gerald was at Paris when the schools there were the centre of the evolution of that standardized and systematic intellectual technique known as scholasticism. This had various strands, two of which, in particular, have been isolated. One involved a dry, technical style and was very heavily dependent on Peter

Lombard's Sentences. The other was easier in its style, more humane and concerned with pastoral and moral problems. This latter tendency was represented by Peter the Chanter and his followers.

Gerald was influenced by the Chanter's teaching but cannot be said to have had any part in the development of scholastic method. A comparison between Book I of his Gemma Ecclesiastica, which deals with problems concerning the sacraments, and the Chanter's Summa de Sacramentis, shows the gap that existed between Gerald and even the less technical strand of Paris theology. To turn from Gerald to Peter is to turn from disorder and digressive (if lively) anecdote to clarity. Peter knew what he was doing and had a clear framework in which to do it; Gerald made a half-hearted attempt to arrange his material in quaestio form, but this attempt was always breaking down under the weight of exempla and irrelevancies—it is as if Walter Map had tried to write a Summa. Gerald's formal affinities with scholastic theology were thus slight, despite the influence that the Chanter's programme and sense of mission had on him.

Another development in European culture that is important for understanding Gerald is the rise of a new naturalism. Scientists and cosmologists of the period strove towards systematic, physical explanations. Some writers, including Gerald, show alert and individualized observation of the natural world. The roots of this naturalism are obscure: technological explanations have been advanced but are unconvincing. There is no direct evidence that any of the scientific writers of the period were technologically inspired and their thought tended to be bookish and cosmological, not practical. A new emphasis on rationality emerged in the eleventh and twelfth centuries, but this bore no marks of technological origin. The model at the back of twelfth-century science was the organism, not the mechanism—schools and workshops remained divorced.

This naturalism cannot be explained solely in terms of the influx of new material, either. Greek and Arabic science was absorbed in this period, but a new attitude to the natural world was as much a precondition for the translation movement as a consequence of it. Twelfth-century naturalism remains a problematical phenomenon that must be studied in more detail, as exemplified in the works of individual writers, before it can be understood. Part II of this book, 'The Natural and the Supernatural', attempts to do this in the case of Gerald.

Gerald's enduring intellectual achievement was his ethnographic writing, and Part III, 'Ethnography', attempts to analyse this and place it in its context, but his life and work intersected important twelfth-century developments at many points. He was a child of a frontier society at the edge of feudal Europe, a Paris-trained master, humanist, royal servant, court littérateur, historian, and naturalist. A study of his thought throws light on many of the complex processes of twelfth-century society.

PART I

POLITICS
AND
NATIONALITY

I

'GERALD OF WALES' OR
'GERALD THE WELSHMAN'?

Historians studying Gerald all have, at some stage, to discuss his ambiguous sense of nationality. A straw in the wind is their rendering of the name 'Giraldus Cambrensis'. Is it to be the neutral 'Gerald of Wales' or the more provocative 'Gerald the Welshman'? Two Welsh writers on Gerald, Henry Owen[1] and Thomas Jones[2], have chosen, through the latter option, to stress Gerald's identification with the Welsh. F.M. Powicke, in his essay 'Gerald of Wales', tended to emphasize his Norman connections. He was also aware, however, of the complexities of Gerald's situation. With reference to the suspicions of Gerald's loyalty that some entertained, he wrote: 'Here... is a man of Welsh extraction, but not of Welsh race, who does not know Welsh, and is at the same time supposed to be infected by Welsh national sympathies.'[3] The problem of national identity seems to have assumed a particularly central place for foreign, especially German, historians writing on Gerald. Michael Richter subtitled his book on Gerald 'The Growth of the Welsh Nation', and devoted a section to 'Giraldus' Development into a "Cambrensis"'.[4] W. Berges, discussing the De Principis Instructione in his book on Fürstenspiegel, wrote, 'Gerald the Welshman (Der Waliser Girald), who grew up as an Englishman, can never be at home again... Gerald felt himself to be the victim of national oppositions.'[5] The same point was discussed by Karl Schnith, who made an illuminating comparison with Jonathan Swift, another disappointed man with literary and invective talent who suffered from the ambiguities of his national position.[6]

The problem of national identity is a sensitive and potentially explosive one. Moreover, its terms are intellectually confused, vague, and complex. For, even if it is granted that nationality can be determined by some objective criterion, there are many different criteria which could be applied—race, language, culture, citizenship of a state, for example. Acceptance of any one of these criteria then only leads to further practical difficulties. While it is easy to tell a black man from a white man, the borderline cases may, in some times and places, outnumber those who clearly belong to one group or another. The criteria then have to be further differentiated. Hence we have societies like modern Jamaica where skin colour, and social class, is graded from white to black through eight intermediate shades such as 'dusty', 'fusty', 'tea', and 'coffee'. Or, perhaps, political considerations may give the grading an arbitrary element; for instance in the way that the Japanese were 'honorary white men' in South Africa.

In a more important sense, however, nationality is not a matter of objective classification at all. It is a matter of identification, a human judgement doubtless based on many explicit and implicit material and psychological distinctions, but not reducible to any of them. Also, identification is a social process. Self-identification exists in a close relationship with identification by others and identification of others. The friction between how a man sees himself and how he is seen by others can be particularly important and instructive. This is certainly true in Gerald's case. An examination of his career reveals that his 'Welshness' as seen by others has as much importance as his 'Welshness' in any concrete racial, linguistic, cultural, or political sense.

Medievalists are generally aware of the dangers of anachronism when investigating questions of nationality in their period. Modern nationalism has laden the vocabulary of the subject with many hidden traps and unacceptable implications. Yet this awareness can, in fact, actually deepen the historical discussion of nationality, for it is a recognition that nations are made—created and developed—not a priori categories. If we look back to the twelfth century from the twenty-first, then we do so through the transparent but distorting curtain of modern nationalist thought, past the creation of the nation-state in late medieval and early modern times. But if we do so with self-awareness, then our perception of the twelfth century may also be clarified in the process.

The nation-states that took shape from the fourteenth century onwards were distinguished by the high degree to which they developed various principles of unity. The political basis was sovereign monarchy, which gradually achieved supremacy over rival internal and international jurisdictions. Within these institutional boundaries, there began an unparalleled development of homogeneity of culture. The stress on the vernacular, the spread of 'normative' English, French, or Spanish, assisted by printing and central political authority, led to the idea that membership of a state was equivalent to use of a certain mother tongue. In more general terms, a cultural unity was generated by the metropolitan and educational centres—London and the universities in England, Paris, predominantly, in France. The process was, of course, neither smooth nor everywhere successful. But this rough delineation may help us to see what was new at this period and what we should not look for in the twelfth century.

Europe at that time possessed a greater degree both of internationalism and of provincialism than modern Europe. The dynastic nature of political rule and the importance of the diplomatic marriage could create vast, if often ephemeral, political units. Henry II's possessions are an obvious example. On a smaller scale, the way that the possessions of the kings of Aragon or the counts of Toulouse waxed and waned, flowing across the cobweb 'boundaries' of Spain, France, the Empire, and Italy, show the same process at work. The aristocracies of Latin Europe were linked internationally by social position, by a way of life, and even, to a degree, linguistically and culturally, through the French language. In 1200 a French-speaking upper class could be found not only in France but also in the British Isles and the Levant, while the use of French as a literary medium was increasingly common in Italy too. The spread of French dynasties in the following century continued the process.

The Church, of course, was the other main instrument of internationalism. In its patronage and promotions the Church could transcend political boundaries. The use of an international language and the development of Paris and Bologna as European centres of learning ensured a cultural unity which, in a sense, has never been recovered. Hence both aristocracy and Church, or at least their upper reaches, existed in the context of the Latin West as a whole. Gerald's career illustrates the practical aspects of this fact. Whether he was travelling in England, Ireland, or Wales, studying in Paris or pursuing lawsuits at Rome, he never lacked a cultural context with which he could identify, in the form of French-speaking aristocrats or Latin churchmen. He received hospitality, would probably have had relatives or friends in common with his hosts, and shared many aspects of their way of life or educational background. As a counterpoint to Berges's comment, quoted above, that Gerald 'can never be at home again', it must be added that, from Dublin to Rome, he never had to be a stranger.

Alongside this twelfth-century internationalism, one can see another tendency, deeply rooted and with a long, if hidden, history. This was the feeling of loyalty and solidarity, connected either with the 'country' or with the tribe or racial group. The 'country' was a region of vicinity, acquaintance, common ties and experience; it might take for its focus a local cult or a local dynasty. It generated what have been called 'nationalités provinciales'.[7] It is clear that this sense of provincial separateness could exist independently of linguistic or political identity. When William Marshal defeated the knights of Normandy and Anjou, their complaint was: 'We are humiliated to see an Englishman (uns engleis) overcome us.'[8] Gerald's feeling towards Normans (of Normandy) was no friendlier; he accused them of boastfulness and a tendency towards homosexuality.[9] In these instances a common language and political connection had not overcome the deeper roots of regional loyalties and hostilities. It is also symptomatic that the main evidence for the existence of the loyalties is in the hostilities. We have to infer provincial solidarity from expressions of xenophobia.

Sometimes the boundaries of political geography, language, and culture overlapped. Here something like nationalism could be found. This is particularly noticeable in areas of expansion, invasion, and conflict, such as the Celtic parts of the British Isles. In 1284 it was officially recommended to the English government that no Irishman should be appointed an archbishop in Ireland 'since they always preach against the king... and always provide Irishmen in their churches... so that the election of bishops can be made by Irishmen to maintain their language'.[10] Here political, ethnic, and linguistic criteria, combined to produce clear-cut distinctions.

These preliminary observations may help to make it clear that when examining Gerald's own sense of nationality, we are not looking for one distinct element in his own self-awareness, or for a single explanatory principle for his conduct. He can, on the contrary, be considered from many angles. His genetic background included Norman warriors and a Welsh princely family. His mother tongue was French, his occupational tongue Latin, and he had other languages to take into account too, particularly Welsh and English. His class background was knightly, military, and land-holding. He was a member of a vigorous Marcher clan. His order or status was clerical—a secular cleric, curial and scholarly by turn. All of these descriptions assumed importance at different times in his life. Any attempt to understand their significance and interrelationships must look at them in the context of his political career and the political situation of the period.

Gerald was born into a divided and complicated society, a society in conflict. While the Norman conquest of England was completed within a few years, the Norman conquest of Wales took over two centuries. Owing to the difficulties of the terrain, the stubbornness of the resistance, the decentralized nature of Welsh society, and the casual attitude of the kings of England, the political subjugation of Wales was not fully achieved until the reign of Edward I. The result was that from the late eleventh to the late thirteenth century Wales was a patchwork of Norman lordships and Welsh principalities. The boundaries of political control and settlement were constantly shifting and changing. Llanstephan Castle in Carmarthenshire, for example, a day's journey from Gerald's birthplace, changed hands at least four times in his lifetime.[11] Eastern Wales and the valleys of the south and south-west had been penetrated early by the invaders of Rufus's reign, Bernard of Newmarch, Robert fitzHamon, and the house of Montgomery. These areas were more consistently under Norman control in the twelfth century. The northern principality of Gwynedd remained, after the initial incursions of the 1090s, a bastion of Welsh resistance. Yet the shifting alliances and constant feuding meant that the political map was kaleidoscopic. Processes of conquest, settlement, and recovery went on valley by valley.

The political patchwork was reflected in an ethno-linguistic patchwork. To the various dialects of Welsh the Anglo-Normans had added French and English. Henry I had settled Flemings in Pembrokeshire, and Flemish was still being spoken there in the late twelfth century. Gerald's brother, Philip de Barri, understood it.[12] And, of course, Latin held its place as the language of religion and learning throughout Wales.

Moreover, as Anglo-Norman society expanded into the Celtic lands of the west during the Middle Ages, it not only created new tensions and rifts, but also exported its own divisions. The conditions of the settlement in Wales could underline the distinction between Norman and Saxon which was beginning to be eroded in England itself. Gerald's pride in his Norman, Marcher ancestry had, as its counterpart, a contempt for the English: 'the English people [are]... the most worthless of all peoples under heaven... In their own land the English are slaves of the Normans, the most abject slaves. In our land there are none but Englishmen in the jobs of ploughman, shepherd, cobbler, skinner, artisan and cleaner of the sewers too.'[13]

As a final convolution of this tangled pattern, the invasion of Ireland in 1169 and the subsequent settlement exported the whole chequered society of South Wales into a completely different racial and linguistic framework. A charter of Raymond le Gros, Strongbow's constable and Gerald's uncle, was characteristically addressed to 'all present and to come, French, English, Flemish, Welsh and Irish'.[14]

Persistent warfare in Wales and Ireland did not entirely preclude more peaceful relations. Gerald's anecdotes give occasional glimpses of Welsh princes and Norman lords riding or feasting together,[15] and intermarriage occurred between native and intruding dynasties. The most well-known example of this, and the most relevant to Gerald, was the marriage of Gerald of Windsor, castellan of Pembroke from the 1090s, and Nesta, 'the Helen of Wales', daughter of Rhys ap Tewdr, Prince of South Wales. Nesta's children, by Gerald and by others, dominated the political situation in south-west Wales throughout the twelfth century. Angharad, daughter of Nesta and Gerald, married William de Barri, lord of Manorbier, and was the mother of Gerald of Wales.[16]

Gerald's mixed descent gave him a degree of access to both sides of warring Wales. But his basic alignment, especially before his election to St. David's in 1199, is clear. One indication is provided by the languages he could command. It is probable that, although he knew many Welsh words and was interested in philology,[17] he could not speak Welsh fluently. When he preached the Crusade in Wales in 1188, with Archbishop Baldwin, he spoke in French and Latin. Alexander, Archdeacon of Bangor, had to interpret to the Welsh.[18] Much later in life (c.1208), Gerald referred to Latin and French as 'languages which, for us, surpass all others'.[19]

Gerald's political employment in the years c. 1184-94, when he served as a royal clerk, involved furthering the aims of the kings of England in Wales. Henry II, it seems, appreciated the usefulness of Gerald's local knowledge and connections, and Gerald, in his turn, willingly executed royal policy. He wrote of himself: 'He served faithfully, following the court, for several years and assisted greatly in the pacification of Wales and in keeping it peaceful.'[20] His appointments to accompany John to Ireland in 1185 and Archbishop Baldwin to Wales in 1188 suggest the view of him held by the King and officers of government—he was a capable royal clerk with special knowledge of Wales and Ireland, which made him useful for accomplishing the King's business there. On the death of Henry II Gerald was sent to Wales, at Archbishop Baldwin's suggestion, 'to preserve the peace in Wales because of the change of kings'. In this he was successful: 'by his arrival and intervention he pacified his homeland (patriam) which had been seriously disturbed by the death of the king'.[21] In the early 1190s Gerald was employed on similar missions, under the authority of the Chancellor, Longchamp, and of Queen Eleanor and Walter of Coutances, the Justiciar.[22] In his later life, writing the De Rebus a se Gestis in 1208 or later, he looked back on this work with satisfaction: 'Gerald, single-handed, by his own labour and diligence, in addition to many other great services, had turned aside not a few of Rhys' great armies from the king's land, which the prince was preparing to invade...'.[23]

During his service as a royal clerk, therefore, Gerald was actively involved in the containment of the native Welsh. Some of his writings of this period reflect this. The Descriptio Kambriae of 1194, dedicated to Hubert Walter, contains a long discussion of the best method of conquering the Welsh.[24] This bears some remarkable similarities to the actual tactics of Edward I: the necessity of a prolonged campaign; the relative unimportance of pitched battles; castle-building; blockade; the employment of light-armed troops. In this first edition Gerald, after describing how the Welsh could be forced to surrender by famine and the encouragement of internal discords, went on to talk about what should then be done with the conquered country:

Therefore the king will be able to make Wales a colony, after he has expelled the old inhabitants and deported them to other kingdoms. Moreover, many judge that it would be safer and more advisable for a wise ruler to leave such a rough, trackless land, which can only have unruly inhabitants, as a wilderness for beasts and to make a forest of it.[25]

At this period Gerald was evidently not 'Gerald the Welshman'.

Perhaps the callousness of remarks like this was stiffened by the growing characterization of the Welsh as backward and barbarous. This process, which is very noticeable in the twelfth century, is part of a general shift in the attitude of the men of the rest of western Europe towards the Celtic world. The great artistic and missionary civilization of the early Middle Ages gradually came to be regarded as isolated and corrupt. Partly, of course, this is to be explained in terms of the relative development of the material culture. Twelfth-century Italy, France, and even England supported societies of a wealth and complexity well beyond that possible in the social and economic context of the Celtic world. Yet the change of attitude is also linked with other, less material changes.

The relevance and significance of 'Church Reform' in this context will be discussed below,[26] but there was also the more secular concept, 'barbarousness', and references to this are scattered throughout Gerald's works. St. David's was situated in 'a barbarous and hostile land';[27] the Welsh, through their rebelliousness, bloodthirst-iness, and perjury, exhibited 'barbarous *mores*';[28] the Irish were 'a barbarous nation';[29] the Scots did not escape—a Scots invasion too was 'an incursion of barbarians.'[30] Writing as an Anglo-Norman and a churchman trained at Paris, Gerald viewed the Celtic world as united by, among other things, barbarity.[31] Thus in the 1180s and 1190s Gerald was an active agent of a power hostile to the Welsh and shared some of that hostility himself. He did not speak Welsh, regarded the Welsh as barbarous, and actually gave advice on the conquest and depopulation of Wales.

The evidence for any opposite tendency in his thought is slight. In the Descriptio Kambriae[32] he counterbalanced his chapter 'How that people should be conquered' with a chapter 'How they may resist and rebel', which he justified from his mixed descent: 'just as I am descended from both peo-ples, reason demands that I should argue equally on behalf of both...'. In the Itinerarium Kambriae[33] he also recounted a story which seems to suggest that he sympathized with the wrongs the Welsh had suffered. Gruffydd ap Rhys, heir of the princely house of South Wales, was shown by an omen (the flight of birds) to be 'natural prince of Wales'. When this is reported to King Henry I, Gerald has him say: 'No wonder! For although, through our great power, we have inflicted injury and violence upon that people, nevertheless we know that they have a natural right to those lands.' These passages are significant, in that they hint at a sympathy with the Welsh that Gerald was to express more fully under the impact of the St. David's controversy, but they should not be over-emphasized in this earlier part of his career.

Such statements, however, may have given fuel to the kind of opposition that Gerald was to find he generated. By the early 1190s he had become very dissatisfied with the rewards that royal service had brought him. Moreover, his enemies had found that his family connections made him particularly vulnerable. A clear illustration of his deep sense of frustration can be found in the original preface to the De Principis Instructione, written, probably, in the mid-1190s.[34] He expressed his distaste for the court, 'that image of death and model of Hell', and asserted that he was now returning to the spiritual health of scholarly life. He bewailed the fact that neither Henry II nor Richard I had given him his just rewards. 'Whatever esteem my gravity of manner, literary ability and hard work could bring me was taken away by that suspect, dangerous, hateful name—Wales.' Although he was only a quarter Welsh, this was enough to corrupt him totally in the eyes of a 'hostile people'. His *morum institutio* and *conversatio* (his upbringing and active life) were among the English, his *natio* and *cognatio* (descent and family connections) in Wales. The result, he complained, was that 'both peoples regard me as a stranger and one not their own... one nation suspects me, the other hates me'. He revealed both his own vanity and the suspicious, competitive nature of court life in two rather sad comments. If he said or did anything notable, there would immediately be a sarcastic chorus of 'Can anything good come from Wales?' On the other hand, if he ever made a verbal slip, he would be mocked with a shout of 'A typical Welsh error! [Kambriae vitium]'.

This problem, which irritated Gerald so much, was not a purely individual one. The invasion of Wales and Ireland by the Anglo-Normans had created satellite societies in which the crucial issue was one of ambiguous nationality. In a speech put into the mouth of Maurice fitzGerald, one of the earliest Norman invaders of Ireland, Gerald expressed the dilemma of Marcher society and, in a sense, the dilemma of all colonial societies, in a nutshell: 'What can we expect? Should we hope for any help from our own race? We are in the grip of a law that just as we are Englishmen to the Irish, so we are Irish to the English...'[35] The subsequent course of Anglo-Irish history is prefigured in that insight.

The problems of loyalty and identification created by this situation can be exemplified by the case of Robert fitzStephen, one of Gerald's uncles. A descendant of Nesta like Gerald, his mixed ancestry had led him to an impasse. He had been captured by the Lord Rhys, his cousin, and kept in prison for three years. He was eventually released only on the condition that he should bear arms for Rhys against Henry II. FitzStephen escaped the dilemma by engaging in the Irish expedition:

> Robert saw that he was naturally bound, on his father's side, to fealty to the lord king. For on his mother's side, the noble Nesta, daughter of Rhys the Great, he was a cousin of Rhys ap Gruffydd. He preferred and elected rather to commit his fate and fortune to foreign parts under danger of his life than to risk the accusation of faithlessness before posterity, with loss of reputation and great blame from his own men.[36]

FitzStephen's situation shows the cleft stick that these Norman-Welsh warriors might find themselves in and also, in the light of such motivations, illuminates Henry II's distrust of the Irish expedition.

Amongst fellow Marchers and Geraldines dual descent need not be a matter of shame or anxiety. The oration that Gerald assigned to fitzStephen at the start of the Irish venture is an almost defiant eulogy of his mixed descent: from their Welsh blood the invaders inherit courage, from their Norman descent (ex Gallis) they have skill in arms. 'Since, because of this double nature and noble lineage, we are both brave and skilled in arms, who can doubt that this unarmed people and common mob will be unable to resist us?'[37]

These words sounded less bravely on the other side of the Irish Sea. Here Gerald faced not only sarcasm at court, but, increasingly, a skilful manipulation of his ambiguous position to do him real political harm. Even in the 1190s, before the St. David's case raised the issue to a critical level, Gerald's enemies had learnt the weakness of his position. William Wibert, a Cistercian monk, later Abbot of Biddlesden (in Buckinghamshire), who accompanied Gerald on diplomatic missions to Wales around 1192-3,[38] obviously came to the decision that he could ease the path of his own advancement by denigrating Gerald. He began by denouncing him to 'the great men of the court', insinuating that it was unsafe to send Gerald on such missions unsupervised because of his blood ties with the Welsh princes. 'To cap his malice, he accused me of the crime of treachery... he said that a castle which the Welsh had invested was besieged by my scheming and that whatever evil occurred in the March had been forwarded at my instigation.' Wibert had the favour of Hubert Walter; moreover, we may suspect that his accusations had enough plausibility, in the light of some of Gerald's writings, not to fall on deaf ears. Gerald attributed his disfavour and lack of promotion at court largely to Wibert's slanders. His retirement from court did, in fact, follow soon after these accusations and may be connected with them. His disgrace, however, was not total, as he continued to receive payments from the Exchequer.[39]

As Wibert's schemes drew their strength from Gerald's Welsh connections, so the hostility of Peter de Leia, Bishop of St. David's, exploited the suspicions that the Welsh princes might have of a royal clerk. He suggested to the Lord Rhys and his sons that Gerald had been a prime mover in their excommunication. The result was that they excluded his prebend at Mathry (Pembrokeshire) from the local truce, and Welsh warriors devastated it. Peter de Leia, however, was adept at playing a double game—at least according to Gerald's account. He also warned Henry II and others not to promote Gerald because of his relationship with Rhys. 'Thus he was two-handed in his persecution of me... for to the French he made me a Welshman and an enemy of the kingdom, but to the Welsh he declared me to be French and their mortal foe in all things...'[40]

The vulnerability of Gerald's position was to be highlighted during the controversy over the St. David's election. But before that time, his own self-identification seems not to be as 'Welsh and rebellious' as his enemies portrayed him. Yet the suspicions that were entertained of him were not quite phantasms. For the most important secular group with whom he identified was one which had given, and was again to give, cause for real political concern to the English Crown—the barons and knights of the March.

In his earlier works Gerald frequently appears as the spokesman for the Marchers. He was their eulogist and apologist. The Expugnatio Hibernica is, in many ways, a family epic. The work was dedicated to Richard as Count of

Poitou, but the heroes of the narrative were the descendants of Nesta, Gerald's own kinsmen. His boyhood at Manorbier and his frequent periods in Wales had created close bonds of acquaintance with the Norman Marchers, particularly of south-west Wales. He visited Norman Ireland four times in all, including two visits of up to two years' duration. His first visit was in 1183,[41] when he accompanied his elder brother, Philip de Barri, lord of Manorbier, who was on his way to take possession of lands in south-west Ireland which fitzStephen, his uncle, had granted to him. FitzStephen's charter granted Philip de Barri the cantred of Olethan plus two others to be chosen by lot (and presumably as yet unconquered), for the service of ten knights.[42] Such a sudden augmentation of a family fortune—the de Barris held probably only two knights' fees in Wales[43]—was the primary motivation of the warriors who streamed to Ireland. Among them was another of Gerald's brothers, Robert, and a nephew, Philip's son, Robert junior, who was killed at Lismore in about 1185.[44] If this list was extended to include Gerald's uncles and cousins, virtually all the major figures of the early days of the invasion—fitzStephen, the fitzGeralds, the Carews, Meiler fitzHenry (Justiciar of Ireland 1199-1208)—would have been mentioned.

The Expugnatio Hibernica was written from the viewpoint of the first invaders, and the gallantry of the descendants of Nesta was a recurrent theme. The de Barris, Meiler fitzHenry, Maurice fitzGerald and Raymond le Gros were all praised either in short but recurrent phrases or in the set-piece *descriptiones* with which Gerald adorned this work. Maurice fitzGerald is 'an upright and prudent man, a man notable for loyalty and energy'.[45] Raymond is 'modest... prudent... patient... generous... mild... a man praiseworthy in two things—having much of the warrior but more of the leader'.[46] Meiler is 'brave, competitive first in battle, eager for praise and glory'.[47] Gerald's accounts of Meiler's exploits certainly bear this out: 'surrounded by the enemy and grasped from every side, this brave man drew his sword and opened a path for himself with his strength; here he cut off a hand, there an arm, there head and shoulders; he returned to his own men with three Irish axes stuck in his horse and carrying two in his shield'.[48] The qualities held up for admiration were very straightforward.

This simple pride in the warlike ability of his kin and his pleasure in recounting their conquests stayed with Gerald, despite the complexities of his later political career. In the Itinerarium Kambriae (1191) he mentioned the marriage of Gerald of Windsor and Nesta 'from which, in the course of time, arose a distinguished breed of both sexes, through whom the south Welsh coast was retained for the English and the ramparts of Ireland were stormed'.[49] Much later still, in his autobiography (c.1208), Gerald eulogized the 'sons of Nesta', painstakingly listing their possessions and conquests.[50] Despite the pull of the ecclesiastical and scholarly world, here is one secular, feudal grouping with which Gerald felt a strong identification.

In fact, not only was he the chronicler of the Marchers' achievements, he was also their apologist and mouthpiece. He expressed the grievances that the first invaders of Ireland felt concerning royal interference and the hostility of foreign or curial officials. Despite their great achievements, the Geraldines and their kin considered that they had been held back in the early days of the invasion and treated very cheaply by the royal administrators who were eventually imposed. The eulogies in the Expugnatio Hibernica are always tempered with complaints of the envy that is attacking the Marchers.

In the passage 'Praise of his Family' (Generis Commendatio), Gerald asked what were the deserts of fitzStephen's sons, Maurice fitzGerald, Robert de Barri, Milo of St. David's, Robert fitzHenry, Raymond of Cantiton, Robert de Barri junior, Raymond fitzHugh,

> and many others of the same lineage, whose noble deeds can promise to each of them an eternal memorial of praise; O family, O race! With a twin nature, drawing courage from the Trojans, armed skill from the Gauls. O family, O race! Always suspect for your numbers and inborn energy. O family, O race! Capable of the conquest of any kingdom by yourself alone, if envy, jealous of such vigour, had not descended from on high.[51]

Later he included another passage of rhetoric in which he hinted at the Marchers' resentment towards Henry II:

> This is the nature and condition of this family: always beloved in war, always first, always renowned in military matters for their noble daring. But when the crisis has passed, they are straightaway hateful, straightaway the last, straightaway pressed down to the depths by envy...
>
> Who are those who penetrate to the heart of the enemy? The fitzGeralds.
>
> Who are those who preserve the country (patriam)? The fitzGeralds.
>
> Who are they whom the enemy fear? The fitzGeralds.
>
> Who are those whom envy slanders? The fitzGeralds.
>
> O, if they had found a prince who weighed the merits of their great efforts justly, then how tranquil, how peaceful they would have rendered the state of Ireland. But their efforts were always suspected without reason.[52]

The feeling that Henry II had put a determined check on the first impetus of the invasion was well based. He was extremely suspicious of the venture, especially after Strongbow's landing, and one motive in his own expedition to Ireland was to nip in the bud any possible semi-independent Norman-Irish power. The careers of, for example, William de Breuse and Earl Richard Marshal in the next century show what a danger to royal power the Norman-Irish could be. Henry's foresight, however, seen from the point of view of the invaders, was frustrating and unwelcome. In 1170 he imposed a blockade on Ireland and threatened the invaders with loss of their lands if they did not return. The Pipe Rolls of 1170-1 and 1171-2 show fines being levied on those who had gone to Ireland against the King's command.[53] Ireland would have been completely subdued, wrote Gerald, 'if the royal edict had not stopped others following the first arrival of the pioneers.'[54]

The Geraldines not only felt frustrated by the brake that Henry's intervention placed on their activities. They were critical, too, of the behaviour of the royal officials left in Ireland. Gerald's portrayal of William fitzAudeline, for example, is an echo, in the late 1180s, of the controversies of the 1170s. FitzAudeline was sent to Ireland as procurator after Strongbow's death in 1176. The account of him in the Gesta Henrici II mentions conflicts with his fellow Norman settlers[55] and with the native Irish. In 1179 he fell from favour, for a time, owing to his conduct in Ireland.[56] In the Expugnatio Hibernica we have a dramatic partisan account of the hostility between the Geraldines and fitzAudeline.

It was hatred at first sight. When fitzAudeline landed at Wexford, Raymond le Gros, Meiler fitzHenry, and a great train of young knights came to meet him. They were bravely arrayed and well armed. According to Gerald, FitzAudeline said, in an aside to one of his followers, 'I will soon check this pride and scatter those shields.' He and the other royal officials 'did not cease to harm Raymond, Meiler, the fitzMaurices, fitzStephen and the whole family'.[57] Gerald described various disseisins that the Geraldines and their kinsmen suffered at fitzAudeline's hands.[58] Moreover, he criticized the military slothfulness of the procurator and his deputies: 'it is amazing that such a noble, energetic king has habitually put in command of distant marches such ignoble men, lacking in vigour'.[59] In his characterization of fitzAudeline, Gerald described him as 'a man of the court' (vir... curialis) and 'with ambitions at court' (curialiter ambitiosus).[60] FitzAudeline's fortune did indeed rest entirely on his service as royal steward, justice, envoy, and, later, sheriff. He was the classic 'king's servant'.[61] These criticisms give a first hint of Gerald's anti-curial feeling, which was later to become so strong—a feeling that was nursed by the anti-curialism of his Marcher connections.

The sense of grievance that the Marchers felt and Gerald so explicitly records was generalized in his mind into a contrast between 'the old soldiers' (antiqua... militia) and the newcomers. He stressed the lost opportunities that had resulted from the Angevin kings' reliance on outsiders and foreigners. Ireland should have been handed over to those capable of governing it. Prevarication and vacillations of policy had given the Irish a chance to consolidate their defence.[62] John's followers in 1185 were singled out for particular criticism. One of the reasons for the failure of the expedition was the untactful treatment of the native Irish chiefs 'who were mocked and held in contempt by the newcomers and the Normans on our side'.[63] There is an interesting parallel here with the Crusading states of the Levant, where the modus vivendi that had been established between the Syrian Franks and their Muslim neighbours was being continually disturbed by the intrusions of tactless newcomers.[64]

Gerald distinguished three parties among the invaders: 'the Normans, the English and our men'. The Normans he described as debauched, boastful, blasphemous, arrogant, and very remiss in the military side of the expedition. 'The old soldiers, however, attacked by the ill will of the newcomers, remained silent and withdrawn... waiting with equanimity the eventual result of such intemperance and such a tempestuous storm.' The Geraldines seem to have engaged in a conscious policy of non-co-operation: 'The old soldiers of the land, who had opened the way into Ireland, were despised and out of favour; all counsel was with the newcomers alone, they alone were trusted and deemed worthy of honour. Therefore, since the old soldiers withdrew and, although unwilling, did not engage in any actions, the newcomers achieved little in their affairs.'[65] The Marchers' combination of hatred of 'new men' with a robust xenophobia is a typical attitude of the medieval baronage, which was highlighted during the recurrent crises between king and barons in the thirteenth century.

Just as the thirteenth-century barons claimed that their position as 'natural counsellors' of the king had been ignored, so Gerald, as a spokesman for the late twelfth-century Marchers, asserted that they were the natural choice as governors, counsellors, and warriors in the Marches. Just as an artisan knows his craft best, they had greater acquaintance with the enemy and knew best how to fight them. The new men used inappropriate continental tactics, while the Marchers were more flexible:

> That people raised in the March of Wales, experienced in the hostile conflicts of those parts, is most capable... bold and ready. When they engage in the changes of war they are found now readily on horseback, now agile on their feet; they are not fussy about food or drink and are prepared to abstain from bread and wine if necessary. The beginning of the invasion of Ireland was due to such men; the completion of the conquest will be achieved by such men or by no one.[66]

This passage, taken from the Expugnatio Hibernica, was repeated in the Welsh works, the Itinerarium Kambriae and Descriptio Kambriae. Gerald was thus expressing an attitude which extended beyond the specific situation in Ireland. He wrote that Henry II's three Welsh expeditions were unsuccessful because 'he did not have faith in the proven men of the country and the chief men who knew and were acquainted with that province, but had as his chief counsellors for these affairs only men remote from the March and wholly ignorant of the ways and manner of the people'.[67] The point was repeated, with slight variations, in the Descriptio Kambriae: 'Those regions of Wales inhabited by the English would have been happy if the English kings, for advice and arrangements concerning the government of those regions and defence against the enemy race, had relied more on the Marchers and barons of the country than on Angevins and Normans.'[68] Passages like these show how little the international activities and connections of the Angevin dynasty were reflected in the sympathies of the provincial aristocracies within their territories. The words were written only ten years before the defection of Normandy.

It is already apparent that Gerald's association with the Marchers of Wales and, especially, with those who invaded Ireland, had occasionally led to criticisms of royal policies. The frustration of the invaders was expressed through his pen. Gradually this criticism of the Angevins became a major factor in his outlook. But before discussing Gerald and the Angevin kings, it is necessary to step back a little and attempt to introduce and integrate an ecclesiastical dimension into our picture of Gerald's political world. Gerald was certainly a Marcher and a disappointed courtier but he was also, emphatically, a churchman.

Descendants of NESTA, daughter of RHYS AP TEWDWR

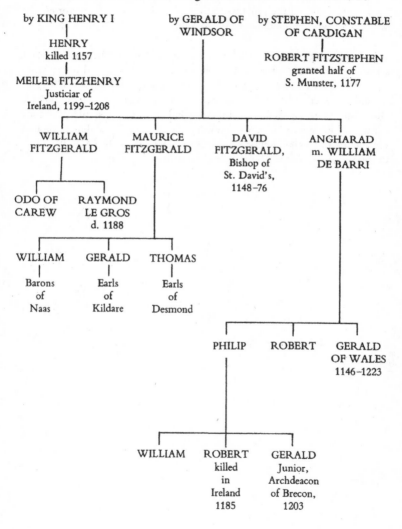

GERALD THE ECCLESIASTIC

The previous chapter attempted to describe the particular feudal grouping into which Gerald was born and to discuss the problems which faced him, in his political career, because of his Marcher connections. But a study of the tensions and interests of lay society alone cannot give us a full understanding of Gerald's position. He was brought up for the Church and given the best clerical education that his age could offer. This left an indelible imprint on him, which it is necessary to characterize.

REFORMER IN WALES AND IRELAND

The changing, varied, and flexible Church of the twelfth century cannot be described simply. Its relationship with lay society was highly complex. In one sense it was congruent with that society—furthering the aims, channelling the feelings, and reflecting the prejudices of laymen. On the other hand, there were ways in which it transcended or cut across lay distinctions and values. Gerald's early career illustrates both these aspects.

His own account of his early life, as given in his autobiography, pictures him marked out from childhood for the service of the Church. Apparently, when his young brothers were building sand-castles, he was busy building sand churches.[1] In debates on the subject of lay and clerical jurisdiction, he would always support the clerical case, 'for he desired nothing so much on earth as the great glory of Christ's Church and its advancement and honour in all things'.[2]

On the other hand, Gerald's own words suggest that he was not entirely immune from the attraction of the secular and military world. He records, for example, how he could be distracted from his studies by the company of his military brothers.[3] Even when he was much older, his shrewd comments on military matters[4] reveal that he maintained an observant interest in such affairs. His description of a tournament which he witnessed at Arras[5] illustrates the two strands in his outlook very clearly. On the one hand he described the scene in detail and, 'observing everything with great attention, was scarcely able to admire everything enough'. On the other, he wrote 'Would that Gerald were strong enough to despise all this as vanity!' There was an unresolved tension here between the scion of the military aristocracy and the ecclesiastic.

In general, however, it is clear that from an early age Gerald saw his own future in a clerical context. He was the youngest son of a knightly family and his predilection for the Church was given every encouragement. His eldest brother, Philip, was to inherit (and augment) the patrimony. Of the other two brothers, one, 'a distinguished knight', was killed in battle, probably against the Welsh.[6] The other sought his fortune in Ireland.[7] They were typical *iuvenes* in Duby's sense.[8] The Church offered a useful and honourable alternative to such a career, and Gerald's father must have felt that his duty of paternal provision had been properly fulfilled as he set his youngest son on the path to clerical preferment. The father's ambitions for Gerald seem to have been quite precise; he used to call him 'my bishop'.[9]

Gerald's appointment as archdeacon of Brecon in about 1175 is another clear case of the way in which lay and clerical interests could prove mutually accommodating. He was appointed to the post by his uncle, David fitzGerald, Bishop of St. David's. Bishop David seems to have been particularly generous in providing for his relatives from Church land. An attack on him, probably written by one of his canons, is extant and gives details of his alienations to his kin[10] and some of these accusations are corroborated by charter material.[11] Gerald's preferment was thus simply another example of the way the bonds of kinship and lay interests could be served by ecclesiastical patronage as well as by secular. South-west Wales was an area in which the fitzGeralds and related families formed a close-knit network of intermarriage, feudal relationship, and political mutual aid. The local Church was incorporated into this network.

Gerald's activities as archdeacon, however, were not to be as customary and accommodating as the circumstances of his promotion might suggest. In part, this was a consequence of the ideals he absorbed during the course of his higher education. After receiving his elementary schooling from Bishop David's clerks and at St. Peter's Abbey, Gloucester, Gerald studied at the schools of Paris for several years (c.1165-72[12] and 1176-9). Here he came into contact with theologians and canon and civil lawyers, some of them committed to high standards in Church life.

The influence of Peter the Chanter was particularly important in shaping Gerald's ideal of 'reform'. Gerald's Gemma Ecclesiastica of 1197 shows a considerable debt to the Chanter's writings[13] and he has been described as one of the Chanter's 'circle'.[14] This circle, it has been observed,[15] 'had a sense of mission. Their role was to lead the clergy in reforming the church and the laity... They were high churchmen.' Immersed in such an environment, Gerald adopted a rigorous moralism, a reforming zeal, and a vocal concern with the pastoral duties of ecclesiastics.

The rhetoric of reform is scattered throughout Gerald's writings but the work where his views are most fully expressed is the Gemma Ecclesiastica. From this digressive and unsystematic book it is possible to abstract Gerald's underlying ideals of reform. These can be grouped under two main heads: the individual moral reform of the clergy, and the freedom of the Church from lay control and interference.

His polemic was at its most exuberant when dealing with issues of clerical continence. Most of the second 'Distinctio' of the Gemma Ecclesiastica is a violent attack on sexual laxity among the clergy. Throughout his life, Gerald waged a vigorous campaign, in word and deed, against clerical concubinage. His attack was given much of its edge by a high ideal of the priestly role. Higher standards were demanded of him who consecrates the host: 'If a priest who is about to celebrate mass is a fornicator,' he wrote, 'although he washes his hands and face, he is unwashed and unclean inside.'[16]

This reverence for the sacramental office of the priest did not lead Gerald to under-emphasize the ecclesiastical duties of teaching and guiding. His idea of the good bishop included a strongly evangelical emphasis. Both higher and lower clergy, in fact, should be learned men and active preachers. He satirized clerical ignorance and insisted that proper examination of ordinands should take place—'with what temerity blind, illiterate bishops ordain blind and completely illiterate priests'.[17] In Gerald one can recognize a conviction that devotion and faith should include a certain degree of consciousness. He disapproved, for example, of the mechanical repetition of certain masses or verses of the Bible as charms to ensure fertility or health.[18]

Gerald's attitude to the worldly rights of the Church was less straightforward. While he sometimes praised poverty, he was also a vigorous champion of the Church's property rights. This latter position fitted in well with the traditional role of abbots and bishops as fierce defenders of the rights of their abbeys and sees. It was an ecclesiastical equivalent of the litigiousness and dynasticism of the lay land-holder. It did not, however, harmonize with an emphasis on poverty and simplicity, and here a latent tension existed between the high clerical assertion of ecclesiastical rights and the moral attack on superfluities and excrescences in Church life.

Gerald's high conception of the dignity of the Church and the sharp line he drew between clerical and lay naturally led him to insist on the freedom of the Church from lay control. The quality of bishops had declined, he thought, because 'as long as God made bishops through canonical election, they were good and holy, but from the time when men and kings, rather than God, made them at their own command, they began to be such as you can see nowadays'.[19] Contemporary elections were purely nominal,[20] just 'a shadow'.[21] 'In the kingdoms of tyrants... bishops are created at the prince's command.'[22] The issue of freedom of election will recur in discussion of both Gerald's own candidacy and his attitude to the Angevins.

His criticism of royal interference in elections is indicative of Gerald's general attitude to the behaviour of the laity in relation to the Church. The Church had its proper dignity, which should be respected. He advocated reverence and orderliness on the part of lay congregations. Laymen should not enter the chancel,[23] for example, and should refrain from dancing in the church-yard to celebrate saints' vigils.[24] This idea of reverence was part of his whole conception of seemliness and Christian order in the Church. Gerald took the trouble to give detailed advice on the proper procedure for administration of the sacraments, backed by the opinions of the Paris masters and extracts from canon law.

This outward order should have, as its counterpart, an inner spiritual order. Gerald quoted with approval a statement of Origen, commenting on St. Paul's exhortation, 'Everything should be done decorously and according to order'. Origen wrote, 'He wished order to be maintained not only in offices and in behaviour, but he also meant some order in the soul'.[25]

This complex of ideals and values is not strikingly original or surprising. The attacks on concubinage and other clerical vices, such as nepotism and simony, which Gerald made, had formed part of the legislation of Church councils during the previous century,[26] while his emphasis on reverence for the sacraments and for the priestly function reflected one of the major theological developments of the twelfth century. Yet when we look at his reforming activities in those regions where he could hope to give them practical effect, his conventional utterances assume a different aspect. As a social programme 'in the field', reform could be more explosive, more divisive, and more dangerous than might appear from sermon or treatise. Beryl Smalley's book on Becket and the schoolmen has shown the intransigence and ideological extremism of some of the Paris-trained clerks around Becket. Gerald's behaviour on his return from Paris in about 1173, as he himself describes it,[27] illustrates the same attitudes. His account of his behaviour in the diocese of St. David's in the years 1174-6 makes clear the very disruptive effects that an active clerical reformer could have.

His first efforts were directed towards enforcing the payment of tithes. In a region as disturbed as south-west Wales after the coming of the Normans it is unlikely that tithes had ever been paid on a regular basis. Gerald, armed with powers delegated from the Archbishop of Canterbury, immediately stirred up trouble. Although the Welsh were compliant, the Flemish settlers in Rhos (west Pembrokeshire) refused to pay, and their position was supported by Henry II. Some of the local magnates, too, were extremely hostile towards Gerald. The sheriff of Pembroke was only subdued by excommunication. The threats made by Richard fitzTancred, another Pembrokeshire knight, had to be silenced by a warning of dreadful vengeance from Gerald's kin. Here, as on other occasions, Gerald's local lay connections proved very useful in the pursuit of his clerical aims. He had a whole range of ecclesiastical sanctions to employ—excommunication, interdict, even a mandate from the Pope—but much of the success of his attempt to enforce payment of tithes was due to these lay connections.

A second aspect of his reforming activity appears in his attempts to regularize clerical life. The aged Archdeacon of Brecon was deposed for keeping a concubine.[28] This was the archdeaconry that was shortly afterwards conferred upon Gerald himself. Upon his appointment he continued his campaign by restoring to the parson of Hay (Brecon) the full revenues from his church, which had been shared with a knight, the parson's brother. In all these activities one can see the traditional goals of Church reform—a pure clergy, sharp division between clerical and lay, and a strict insistence on the Church's rights.

These activities were, of course, disruptive. Disruptive not only of lay interests in the Church, but also of the lives and positions of 'unreformed' churchmen. Many of the local clergy, especially those in more remote areas, had established a quite comfortable, although uncanonical, mode of life. They were married, passed on their benefices to their children, engaged in the minimum spiritual duties, and probably aimed, above all, at being left alone. The arrival of a bishop or archdeacon with rigorous views on the state of the clergy was a disaster; and, as appears in the De Rebus a se Gestis, a disaster they would strive to avert.

In 1176 Gerald undertook an archidiaconal visitation of Elfael and Maelienydd (roughly the eastern half of present-day Radnorshire). The rural dean of the area sent clerics to him as he was about to set out, who urged him not to conduct the visitation in person but, like all his predecessors, to act through officers and messengers. The most natural agent, it was suggested, would be the rural dean himself. Despite this message, and although the clerics held up a crucifix in front of him in an attempt to bar his path, Gerald continued on his way. The next idea of the local clerics was to meet him under the eaves of a great forest through which he had to pass. They claimed that certain chiefs of the region, motivated by an ancient family feud, were lying in wait for him in the forest. Despite the fears of his own followers, Gerald discounted the story and continued on his journey. He eventually arrived at a town (probably Llanbadarn Fawr in Maelienydd) where he intended to hold a chapter. His household, whom he had sent on before him, were driven back from the town by showers of spears and arrows. Gerald, however, entered the town and, finding no other shelter, spent the night in the church. He immediately sent messages to the local chief, Cadwallon ap Madog, who was also related to him. Cadwallon threatened vengeance on Gerald's opponents and came next day in person to support the Archdeacon. The very disruptive nature of active reformers and their dependence on secular support are again well illustrated by these events.

The situation in Pembrokeshire, with the hostility of the sheriff, the threats and counter-threats of the fitzTancreds and de Barris, and the restiveness of the Flemings, must have been highly disturbed, while in Maelienydd open violence broke out. Indeed, reformers, if militant, could not help but disturb vested interests by criticizing long-standing accommodations of clergy and laity.

There is a further, special significance in Gerald's activities. His attempts at ecclesiastical and moral reform took place chiefly in Wales and Ireland, during a period when those regions formed a battleground between indigenous societies and Norman colonizers. Gerald's position was frankly partisan and his rhetoric of Church reform and moralism continually became entangled with the prejudices of national hostility and the calumnies of propaganda. It is true that the Welsh and Irish Churches endorsed many uncanonical practices and that lay society in those countries engaged in customs which were condemned by active churchmen wherever they were found. But the attack on these practices and customs by Anglo-Norman churchmen of the eleventh to thirteenth centuries (among whom Gerald may be numbered) clearly shows, by its hostile, external stance, by its overtones of national prejudice, and by the ease with which it served as justification for Anglo-Norman invasion and colonization, that the moral injunctions of the conscientious pastor and the severe ideals of the reforming churchmen were not without a secular and political edge.

In the Descriptio Kambriae of 1194 Gerald aimed his criticisms at some venerable aspect of the Welsh church—portionary churches and heritable benefices:

> All their churches have almost as many parsons and co-sharers as there are families of chief men in the parish. Also, sons obtain churches through succession to their fathers and not by election, possessing them by hereditary right and polluting the sanctuary of God, since, if the bishop should presume to elect and consecrate any other, the kindred will, without a doubt, avenge the injury on the consecrator or on the man who is consecrated.

He believed that the inheritance of benefices was an ancient characteristic of the British church, being found among both Welsh and Bretons.[29] Much later in his life, in the De Jure et Statu Menevensis Ecclesiae, Gerald urged Archbishop Stephen Langton to visit Wales in order to eradicate three clerical vices—concubinage, portionary churches, and the inheritance of benefices.[30] His treatment of the subject in this work strongly emphasized the innate immorality of the Welsh. The canons of St. David's, he wrote, were divided between the Welshmen, 'greater in number, but less in dignity', and the French and English, who were 'fewer in number but far greater in merit and dignity'[31] and who 'excel in morals and in knowledge'.[32] He claimed that the St. David's canons (particularly the Welshman) were notorious as public fornicators and possessors of concubines. They inherited their benefices and expected to hand them on to their children, and married their sons to daughters of fellow canons. 'Because they know that their way of life is detestable to good, upright, and learned men, both on account of the crime of fornication and incontinence... and because of the stain of clerical inheritance... they wish to have such bishops from their own people who will condemn neither... crime...' Clerical succession was prevalent not only in the cathedrals, Gerald complained, but throughout Wales. 'This, therefore, is the reason why they desire bishops of their own race so much, since such bishops do not condemn these vices, which are innate in them and in their race and which have become second nature (velut in naturam conversa) by long use...'[33] These stern phrases are not generalized criticisms of clerical vices but rather attacks on specifically Welsh vices. Gerald wrote that a Welsh bishop who would not condemn concubinage and hereditary benefices was 'behaving in the manner of his country'.[34] It is true that the Welsh church did possess some distinctive and uncanonical features, such as the portionary church,[35] but clerical marriage and inheritance of benefices were widespread throughout Western Europe in the twelfth and thirteenth centuries—the English examples were numerous.[36] Despite this Gerald chose to write as if they were particularly characteristic of the Welsh church. He even went so far as to appeal to Bishop Iorwerth of St. David's (1215-29) to prohibit hereditary canonries as 'a barbarous practice.'[37] Hereditary benefices were common in England, but were 'barbarous' only in Wales. Here, then, there is a conflation of the concept of 'barbarousness' with the critical rhetoric of ecclesiastical reform.

It is not only when dealing with questions of the clerical life that Gerald mingled moral criticism with a hostile national characterization in this way. He did the same when dealing with lay vices, especially those which came under special ecclesiastical supervision. Perjury is a good example. He thought of this as a characteristically Welsh vice and in the Descriptio Kambriae said that the Welsh would perjure themselves for any material advantage. He contrasted the Welsh, with their frequent oath-breaking, with 'other races for whom sworn agreements are inviolable'.[38] In the Gemma Ecclesiastica, which was written for the clergy of his archdeaconry of Brecon in 1197, he gave examples of divine punishment of perjury and added,

My counsel is to rebuke your parishioners, who are too greatly prone to perjury, at prayers on Sundays and when you preach them sermons, by putting forward to them these and other examples... Also tell them, and propound this forcibly, that there is no doubt that those who presume to perjure themselves on the gospels frequently or irreverently as a matter of course, as they do in those parts more than elsewhere... will not escape the heaviest divine punishment.[39]

The Welsh were 'a people... who do not keep their word and have little respect for promise or oath'.[40] Although Gerald sometimes wrote as if the Welsh were simple, backward people who could be improved by a good teacher, he used the language of innate qualities when discussing their perjury: 'a people naturally mobile and quick, not less in mind than in body; a people truly stable only in instability, faithful only in infidelity'.[41] These passages, from writings spread over a period of twenty years, show the consistent way that Gerald built up a national stereotype of the Welsh based on condemnation of their moral character.

In the case of the Irish, this tendency was much more forcibly and openly expressed. Gerald had Welsh blood and had grown up acquainted with the Welsh; his characterization of them in the Descriptio Kambriae has many sympathetic elements. These modifying influences were not at work in his attitude to the Irish, and his picture of them has made him 'a thorn in the side of Irish nationalists'.[42]

There is another difference between Gerald's criticisms in Wales and in Ireland. In Wales, Gerald had an official clerical position from which to attempt the practical enforcement of reforming ideals; in Ireland he was purely a preacher and a critic. He sometimes had a chance to reach important channels through the spoken word and, for example, he raised his criticisms of the state of the Irish church at a synod in Dublin before Gerard, a clerk of the Roman curia in Ireland on legatine business.[43] But his writings were the chief means by which he disseminated his criticisms. It is the Topographia Hibernica which has preserved his critical comments on the state of religion in Ireland.[44]

Gerald was particularly critical of the bishops. In his view, they had failed in their duties of preaching and moral discipline. The bishops were drawn from the monasteries and were too monkish; it might be true that they followed the path of contemplation, but they were remiss in their pastoral duties: 'They do not preach the word of God to the people, nor proclaim their sins to them, nor root out vice or implant virtue in the flock committed to them.'[45] When Gerald judged the Irish bishops, he was implicitly contrasting them with the model bishop he had presented in such works as the Gemma Ecclesiastica. His attack on their 'monkishness', however, gave his picture a specifically Irish colouring, for it was only during the twelfth century that Irish bishoprics came to be modelled on the European, territorial diocese rather than on the traditional monastic basis.

The failure of the Irish bishops, in Gerald's view, was reflected in several ways. There was, for example, the reproach that Ireland had produced not one martyr, a state of affairs 'which it will be difficult to find in any other Christian kingdom'. This lack of martyrs, especially considering the cruelty and bloodthirstiness of the Irish people, suggested to Gerald the lukewarmness of clerical devotion in Ireland—no one had been willing to risk his neck for Christian beliefs. The Archbishop of Cashel's response may serve as a counterweight to Gerald's prejudices:

> It is true that, although our people seem to be barbarous, rough, and cruel, nevertheless they have always been accustomed to show great honour and reverence to churchmen and have never laid a hand on God's saints. But now a people have entered the land who know how to make martyrs and are accustomed to do so. Henceforth Ireland, like other regions, will have martyrs.[46]

Gerald saw another sign of the failure of the Irish clergy in the religious ignorance of the Irish people. Despite the ancient foundations of the faith in Ireland, 'it is amazing that this people have remained until now so uninstructed in the rudiments of the faith... They do not frequent God's church with due reverence'. Many were not baptized.[47] Other criticisms Gerald made remind one of what he said about the Welsh. Like them, the Irish were characterized as faithless and treacherous: 'they keep their given promise to no man. They have no shame or fear in violating the obligation of promise and oath...'[48] They did not even respect solemn blood-brotherhood.[49] One is reminded of Gerald's efforts to enforce payment of tithes in Pembrokeshire when reading his complaint that the Irish did not pay tithes or first-fruits,[50] and the line between clerical and lay continued to be a matter of importance to him—he added to his account of the religious ignorance of the Irish an indignant description of 'lay ecclesiastics', who had clerical immunity, but married, had long hair, and were in all respects laymen.[51]

Gerald's attacks on clerical marriage, non-payment of tithes, and the monastic character of the Irish Church cannot be characterized simply as the irruption of a new, more rigorous or 'Gregorian' concept of the Church into an ecclesiastical backwater. Twelfth-century Ireland was the scene of vigorous efforts on the part of native reformers.[52] The Irish reformers were, of course, no more successful in the complete eradication of what they saw as vices than clerical legislators have ever been, but they were as active as anywhere in western Europe. Gerald's criticisms were not distinguished so much by the rigour of his principles as by his unsympathetic and external viewpoint. He wrote as a hostile outsider.[53]

One issue, that of marriage and sexual practices, strikingly demonstrates the complex mixture of canon law principles, national prejudice, and political polemic that is revealed in the writings of Gerald and others.[54] The twelfth century was a time when the Church was engaged in an energetic attempt to extend its control over marriage and sexual affairs. Canonists were working out a coherent contractual theory of marriage, while the elevation of marriage to the status of a sacrament and the insistence that a priest should be present at the wedding ceremony represent encroachment by the 'clerical' view of marriage upon the 'aristocratic' (or lay) view. The aristocracy had traditionally held a very casual attitude to dissolving marriages or taking wives within the prohibited degrees, but the moral crusade of high churchmen in the eleventh and twelfth centuries led to a considerable modification of aristocratic practices in these respects.[55]

The Church did not win an outright victory. In some areas it had to modify its claims. The extreme definition of the prohibited degrees, by which marriage was forbidden within seven degrees of consanguinity, proved impracticable for the tangled aristocratic kinship networks of Europe and had to be reduced to four degrees at the Lateran Council of 1215. In the words of the legislators of 1215, 'It ought not to be judged reprehensible if human rulings sometimes vary according to different ages, especially if pressing necessity or evident utility demand it...'[56]

However, the imprecations of twelfth-century moralists and reformers and the legislation of Church councils show that the variation of human rulings was certainly judged reprehensible when the rulings were made by secular communities rather than by churchmen. The Hildebrandine assault on custom on the behalf of law continued in the twelfth-century attack on uncanonical sexual practices. The aristocracy of the whole of western Europe came under attack, but in Wales and Ireland there were special circumstances. In these countries well-defined (often written) bodies of custom existed which expressed the local lay view of marriage. It was only to be expected that Welsh and Irish customs would be subjected to vigorous attacks by clerical critics, of whom Gerald was one of the more vociferous.

According to Gerald, Welsh marriage customs were unsatisfactory in several respects. His critical, celibate finger pointed out three problems in particular: incest, the dissolubility of marriages, and the lack of clear distinction between legitimate and illegitimate children.

'The crime of incest', he wrote, 'is so prevalent among them all [the Welsh], both high and low, that they feel no shame or fear in marrying their cousins in the fourth and fifth degree quite indiscriminately, and often in the third degree also, since the fear of God is not before their eyes.'[57] He was aware of the social functions of these marriage alliances—they served to heal feuds and preserved noble blood on both sides of the family—but would not accept these as excuses.

As well as such generalized complaints he also frequently levelled the charge of incest against individual members of the Welsh princely houses.[58] It does seem as if the Welsh princes paid even less regard to the prohibited degrees than was customary among the aristocracy of the rest of Europe. There are several instances of marriage between first cousins. Owain

Gwynedd, Prince of Gwynedd (1137-70), for example, married his first cousin Christina. The furious criticisms of John of Salisbury, when writing to the Pope about the case on behalf of Archbishop Theobald, show how English churchmen regarded the Welsh, in general, as sexually irregular: 'Despising the law of matrimony, they barter for a price their concubines, whom they have as well as wives; and, ignoring the guilt of incest, they do not blush to uncover the nakedness of those who are their kin by ties of blood.'[59] Owain Gwynedd was eventually excommunicated by Becket and died unreconciled. Gerald reports that in 1188 when Archbishop Baldwin visited Bangor Cathedral, where Owain was buried, he ordered that the body should be removed from the church as soon as the Bishop of Bangor could find an opportunity to do so.[60]

Gerald believed that the Welsh also showed sexual laxity in the habit of cohabitation before marriage and in that of 'purchasing girls on trial'. 'It is an ancient custom of this race', he wrote, 'not so much to marry, as to purchase (non ducere... sed quasi conducere) girls from their parents for a fixed payment and with a decreed penalty for changing their minds.'[61] It seems that Gerald's description of this practice represents a misunderstanding of Welsh divorce arrangements.[62] However, his general point was accurate—the failure of the Welsh to recognize the binding nature of marriage as defined by twelfth-century canon law. The Welsh laws—the so-called 'Laws of Hywel Dda'—contained, in fact, detailed provisions for divorce and remarriage.[63] Such arrangements were obvious targets of ecclesiastical legislation. One of the canons of Archbishop Richard's council of 1175, for example, stated 'the Welsh should not cleave to their cousins nor exchange wives'.[64] Again, it was incest and divorce which were under attack.

The question of inheritance by bastards is a particularly interesting example of the clash between Welsh custom and canon law. Welsh inheritance law declared that all sons should inherit and that the illegitimate had equal right with the legitimate.[65] Gerald mentioned the practice critically and clearly felt that the bishops should take a stand against it.[66] During the course of the thirteenth century some texts of the Welsh laws were, in fact, modified by the canon law. But while certain recensions of the 'laws of Hywel Dda' show considerable ecclesiastical influence, others were revised to counter the Church's claims.[67] The recension most closely associated with the court of Gwynedd includes this passage: 'The ecclesiastical law says again, that no son is to have the patrimony but the eldest born to the father by the married wife; the law of Hywel, however, adjudges it to the youngest son as well as to the oldest; and decides that the sin of the father or his illegal act is not to be brought against the son, as to his patrimony.'[68] Here the struggle between the 'law of Hywel' and the 'ecclesiastical law' was actually being fought out within the text of the laws themselves. There are other instances of such clashes between Welsh customary law, applied under the aegis of the Llywelyns of Gwynedd, and the canon law supported by the bishops.[69]

Archbishop Pecham's visitation of Wales in 1284[70] crystallized many of the tendencies implicit in this clash between native secular custom and the canon law as applied by hostile, often alien, ecclesiastics. Pecham's activities and criticisms can be seen as a fulfilment and development of Gerald's. His archiepiscopal visitation (the first since Baldwin's of 1188 which Gerald recorded in the Itinerarium Kambriae) took place in the wake of the Edwardian conquest of Wales. Indeed, it is unlikely that it could have taken place without English conquest. Pecham's attitude to the laws of Hywel Dda was harsh. He wrote that 'they are said, in many points, to be contrary to the ten commandments',[71] and that 'they contain many irrationalities'.[72] He complained that the Welsh 'regard legitimate marriage so lightly that they do not bar bastards and children born of incest from inheriting; indeed, they divorce their legitimate wives, contrary to the gospel, vindicating themselves by Hywel Dda'. He believed that the laws of Hywel Dda were inspired by the devil.[73] A document probably connected with Pecham's visitation paints a particularly lurid picture of Welsh sexual immorality, mentioning specifically divorce and inheritance by bastards.[74] Pecham's own view of the Welsh, as recorded in visitational documents, was that they were lazy, backward, and sexually immoral. His attitude to the Welsh has been aptly compared to that of a Protestant Ascendancy clergyman to the Irish.[75]

The analogy holds equally well for Gerald. The comparison is, indeed, more than an analogy, for many of the elements which went to make up the later English attitude to the Irish were already present in the clerical complaints of the eleventh to thirteenth centuries. Like the Welsh, the Irish were judged to be guilty of great sexual immorality. The brehon laws, the native secular laws of Ireland dating from the seventh and eighth centuries, permitted divorce and polygamy and had nothing to say on the subject of prohibited degrees, and it seems that Irish marriage customs in the later Middle Ages resembled those presented in the brehon laws.[76] This created a persistent conflict between Irish custom and canon law.

The clash was already apparent in the late eleventh century when Lanfranc and Anselm attacked Irish marriage customs. Lanfranc wrote to Guthric, King of Dublin: 'In your kingdom men are said to marry wives from their own or their dead wife's kindred; others give up those to whom they are legitimately joined at their own choice and will; some give their own wives to others and receive the others' wives in a wicked exchange.' Another letter from Lanfranc, to Toirdelbach Ua Briain, the High King, complained, 'In your kingdom anyone, through his own free will, can leave his lawfully wedded wife, without any canonical cause and marry, with culpable boldness, any other of his own or his dead wife's kindred or someone abandoned by another man

in a similar wicked way through matrimonial—or, rather, fornicators'—law.'
Anselm continued the attack, writing to Toirdelbach's son, Muirchertach, 'We
have heard that in your kingdom marriages are dissolved and changed without
any reason and that cousins are not afraid to join together either under the
name of man and wife or in some other way, openly, without rebuke and
against canonical prohibition.' 'It is said that men exchange wives freely and
publicly, just as one exchanges a horse for another... or they abandon them at
will and without reason.'[77]

Lanfranc's and Anselm's letters portrayed Irish marriage habits as wilful and
lacking in normal principles of order, either legal (contra canonicam prohibi-
tionem), rational (sine omni ratione) or natural (uxores... uxoribus... commu-
tant sicut... equum equo). In fact, under Irish secular law marriage and divorce
were regulated in a strict and complicated way. The accusation of wilfulness
and lawlessness reflects only the inability of Anglo-Norman churchmen to
see order and legality of a kind different from their own. What was outside
canonical rules of law could not be law at all.

Twelfth-century English chroniclers shared this view—one wrote that the
Irish 'had as many wives as they wished and were even accustomed to marry
their cousins'.[78] Gerald, too, saw Irish marriage customs not as a different law,
but as an infringement of law. He described the Irish as 'an adulterous, incestu-
ous people',[79] much given to bestiality.[80] 'They do not contract marriages, they
do not avoid incest... no, rather, a thing which is truly detestable and contrary
not only to the faith but to any kind of decency, brothers in many places
throughout Ireland marry the wives of their dead brothers—or rather seduce
them, since they know them so foully and incestuously.'[81]

Despite the fact that Irish reformers themselves were attempting to eradicate
uncanonical sexual practices,[82] the sexual irregularities of the Irish were used
as an argument for the Anglo-Norman invasion, an invasion which was 'to
widen the boundaries of the church, declare the truth of the Christian faith to
rough, untaught people and root out the plants of vice from the Lord's field'.[83]
When Ralph of Diceto mentioned the revision of Irish marriage customs, he
thought of it as a recognition of English norms.[84]

In 1172 Alexander III wrote to Henry II about Ireland. He catalogued the
many ways in which the Irish had fallen below Christian standards and failed
to be dutiful sons of the Church. He recounted their sexual vices, including
various elaborate forms of incest, and prayed that 'just as these vices are already
beginning to decline through the power of your greatness, so, with God's
help... this people may, through you, submit to the discipline of the Christian
religion'.[85] Papal approval was given to the conquest of Ireland partly because
of the picture which had been created of Irish sexual habits.

Divergences of sexual behaviour are clearly capable of provoking violent
and irrational antipathy. In medieval Wales and Ireland this antipathy was allied

with national hostility, resulting in a deep-seated prejudice on the part of the invaders. This prejudice, in its turn, was reinforced by the highest principles and blessed by the Church, thus creating an ideology able to sanctify the aggressiveness of the Anglo-Norman invaders, reinforce their hatreds, and allay their self-doubts. The metamorphosis of Church reform into an 'ideology of colonization'[86] was complete.

CHAMPION OF ST. DAVID'S

It is clear that there is a political significance to the ideals of 'Church reform' which Gerald expressed. No one has ever claimed that Gerald was a saint, and it is not surprising that the ideals he had absorbed at Paris were pressed into service for the practical, political requirements of his active life. Nor is it surprising that they were sometimes distorted in the process. Gerald's life and writing resound with the clash between principle and expediency. He inveighed against nepotism, but was promoted to the archdeaconry by his uncle and arranged for its transfer to his own nephew. He fulminated against the uncanonical influence that kings exerted over episcopal elections, but he declined nomination to St. David's in 1176 because the King's congé d'élire had not been given. He spent ten years in royal service, but criticized 'curialist' churchmen.

It would be a fatuous exercise to express surprise or indignation at these contradictions. It is important, however, to realize the divergencies between the way Gerald presented himself and his behaviour. Our knowledge of him is drawn almost entirely from his own works, and we must, therefore, be hypersensitive to omissions, self-justifications, and retrospective judgements. Fortunately his writings are so varied and prolific and cover such a long period that the corrective to these distortions can often be found in the works themselves.

Such caution is particularly necessary when considering Gerald as episcopal candidate for St. David's (1198-1203). This episode, which stimulated so much of his writing, was stormy and violent. It culminated in Gerald seeing himself (and subsequently being seen by others) as a champion of the Welsh Church. Clearly it was a crucial experience for him and throws light on both 'Gerald the Welshman' and 'Gerald the ecclesiastic'.

Michael Richter has published a detailed and accurate account of Gerald's attempt to become archbishop of St. David's,[87] and has also written articles which place that attempt in the context of twelfth-century ecclesiastical politics.[88] It will not be necessary, therefore, to go over these events again, except for illustration of particular points. This discussion will centre upon the arguments that Gerald advanced in the case and the various pressures upon him, with especial reference to the questions already posed about his political loyalties and sense of nationality.

In his autobiography, written late in life,[89] Gerald presented a picture of his career in which his election to St. David's in 1199 formed a natural culmination. According to this account it was his 'manifest destiny' to become the champion of St. David's, and his activities throughout his life were consistent with this role. As a young archdeacon, for example, when he thwarted the attempt of Adam, Bishop of the rival diocese of St. Asaph, to consecrate a disputed church, Gerald described himself as acting 'to defend the rights of St. David's'.[90] He mentioned various attempts of the canons of St. David's to assert the metropolitan status of their see[91] and reported his own effort, when Peter de Leia was elected Bishop of St. David's in 1176, to dissuade Peter from taking the oath of obedience to Canterbury, except in general terms—'And above all, on behalf of God and St. David, he [Gerald] was at pains to prevent him from taking an oath carrying with it the abjuration of the rights of his church'[92] (i.e. the claim to be an archbishopric). Writing of the period in the 1180s when he had the administration of the diocese in his hands, Gerald mentioned 'the love and devotion which he showed in such ample measure to his church' and claimed 'he set the peace of the church of St. David's above all things else'.[93] This teleological autobiography had its culmination in his election to St. David's, when the canons urged him to go to the Pope for consecration 'so that by his laudable efforts in Rome he might vindicate the metropolitan rights of his church, fulfilling the unique and special hopes which they had conceived concerning him since his early youth'.[94]

Other events in Gerald's life, and opinions he expressed in other works, give us reason to question this picture. In 1188, for example, he accompanied Baldwin, Archbishop of Canterbury, on a preaching tour of Wales. The Archbishop's purpose was not only to stir up fervour for the imminent crusade. He also seized the opportunity for a symbolic assertion of Canterbury's supremacy by celebrating mass in each of the four cathedral churches of Wales. Some of the canons of St. David's realized this and urged the Lord Rhys to prevent the Archbishop coming to St. David's, claiming that, 'if he made his progress, without a doubt great prejudice and trouble could arise in the future about the recovery of the ancient dignity [of St. David's] and the honour of the metropolitan seat'.[95] Gerald's participation in the preaching tour represented acquiescence in the exercise of the Archbishop's authority in Wales. It indicates that, at this stage, his devotion to the claims of St. David's was less absolute than his later polemical writings would suggest.

An insight into the nature of his ambitions before 1198 is given by a passage included in a late work, the *Invectiones*.[96] Gerald described a dream or vision that he had some time during the 1190s 'when greater hope was held for his promotion'. In the dream he was led past twenty episcopal thrones. These represented the bishoprics of England 'wherein at this time he placed all his hope' and also those of Wales 'which, at that time, he completely rejected from consideration because of the poverty of the land and the wickedness of the people'. In the vision, however, only St. David's was offered to him. When he recounted this experience to his friends they were downcast. Both he and they abandoned the prospect of his promotion to an English bishopric and sadly faced up to the possibility of his becoming Bishop of St. David's 'in the extreme west of the kingdom. They had hoped for better things for him...' Indeed, by his own account, he had already declined Welsh and Irish bishoprics partly because they were 'poor and barbarous'.[97]

If this picture of his early ambitions is credited, then his acceptance of the St. David's nomination in 1199 was not the natural apex of his career that he suggested in his autobiography, but rather the last hope of a man in his mid-fifties, who had turned down lesser prospects in the anticipation of greater, but had been denied the greater. When Gerald complained that his literary efforts had not been rewarded by the generosity of princes,[98] the concrete reward he had in mind seems to have been a rich English bishopric.

However, once Gerald had accepted election to St. David's and undertaken to pursue its metropolitan claims at the highest level, the Roman Curia, he was embarked upon a new and hazardous course. Events were to develop their own momentum and force Gerald's arguments into unexpected paths. This pressure resulted from the intermingling of political and ecclesiastical issues in the affair. The St. David's case could not be decided simply in terms of the respective episcopal claims of St. David's and Canterbury: it also involved the sensitive issue of the relationship between England and Wales.

It was a recurrent (if not persistent) policy of medieval English kings to expand the power of the English crown throughout the whole of the British Isles, and the English Church had an important role in this expansion. From the time of Lanfranc and Anselm, English prelates had tried to extend the authority of the English Church into Wales, Scotland, and Ireland whenever conditions were favourable. During the course of the twelfth century these attempts were frustrated in Scotland and Ireland, largely through the alliance of the Scottish and Irish Churches with the papacy. The Scottish Church entered a special affiliation with the Pope and in Ireland a papal legate organized four metropolitan sees under the primacy of Armagh. Canterbury's efforts to subordinate the Welsh Church, however, were more successful. From the early twelfth century the archbishops of Canterbury consecrated Welsh bishops and received professions of obedience from them.[99]

The reason for this success, compared with the failure in Scotland and Ireland, is clear. The English Church extended its authority under the shelter of the political and military conquest of Wales. Hervey, the first bishop of Bangor to be consecrated by an English archbishop, in 1092, was intruded by force (and very soon driven out by the Welsh).[100] Bishop Bernard of St. David's (1115-48), chaplain to Henry I's queen, was elected by the King's command 'against the will and in despite of all the clergy of the Britons'.[101] The background to this interference was the military occupation of large parts of Wales.

Just as the ecclesiastical subjection of Wales was made possible by the English conquest, so English political power was buttressed by the influence of the English Church. It has been said that 'the Norman church was just as much an instrument of conquest as the Norman knights'.[102] Hubert Walter, Archbishop of Canterbury, explicitly recognized this fact in a letter written to Pope Innocent in 1199:

> If the barbarity of that wild and unbridled nation had not been restrained by the censure of the church, wielded by the archbishop of Canterbury to whom it is known that this race has until now been subject as being within his province, then this people would by continual or frequent rebellion have broken from their allegiance to the king, whereby the whole of England must have suffered disquietude.[103]

Any attack on the authority of the English Church in Wales, then, involved an additional political dimension. The logic of such an attack led inevitably towards criticism of the policies which the English crown was pursuing towards the Welsh. In his attempt to free St. David's from the jurisdiction of Canterbury, Gerald found himself drifting into a position hardly in line with his previous political career. A new note of nationalism entered his arguments.

It was a nationalism first stimulated, very characteristically, by a sense of grievance. Gerald believed that the King and the Archbishop were opposed to his promotion because of his family connections in Wales. He was rejected, he wrote, 'because he was related by blood to the chief men of Wales. It was on account of this that the kings of England always suspected him and secretly hated him.'[104] He would only have accepted the renewed offer of St. David's in 1215 if the King and Archbishop had agreed to it, 'which, in truth, could scarcely happen on account of his lineage, by which he was related to the chief men of Wales'.[105]

Of course, he was related to the 'chief men of Wales' among both the Anglo-Norman Marchers and the native Welsh. The Lord Rhys and the fitzGeralds were both his cousins and either connection might give reason for King John or Hubert Walter to be apprehensive. It has been suggested, in fact, that his Marcher connections were of great importance in arousing suspicions.[106] But clearly a large part was also played by his Welsh blood. Gerald himself claimed that Henry II's opposition to his election in 1176 was due to his kinship with the Lord Rhys[107] and Peter de Leia's insinuations about him were based on the same grounds. Gerald described Archbishop Hubert Walter as implacably hostile to the promotion of any Welshman to a Welsh see. This was the reason for his opposition, not only to Gerald but also to the bishop-elect of Bangor, a Welshman, who temporarily allied with Gerald.[108] Obviously, episcopal elections in Wales represented a delicate political issue. A similar situation in Ireland is illuminated by official records. A royal letter of Henry III's minority reads: 'To the Justiciar of Ireland. We order you, by your fealty to us, not to allow any Irishman to be elected or preferred in any episcopal see in our land of Ireland, since this might disturb our land, which God forbid.'[109]

Gerald's opponents did not tend to draw a sharp line in their arguments between 'the Welsh' and 'those born in Wales' (which would include the Marchers). The Archbishop wanted 'no Welshman or even anyone born in Wales' to be promoted.[110] Gerald, highly conscious of his own dual descent, preserved the distinction more clearly. But even here his own definition of himself was changed by the pressure of the struggle. Although he continued to be proud of his descent from the Marchers and, especially in the early years of the case, referred to their loyal defence against the Welsh, he was also beginning to be more insistent upon his Welsh identity. He described the Welsh as 'our British race'[111] and even referred to himself (once) as Walensis.[112] Opposed because of his 'Welshness', he became 'more Welsh'.

The arguments that Gerald raised in pursuit of his case reflected this new alignment. The frustrations of the St. David's case, working on his harshly critical temperament and on his considerable store of latent hostility to the crown, produced in his invective a new national perspective.

An early element of the debate concerned the political function of the subordination of the Welsh Church. Hubert Walter's letter, already quoted, argued for the political expediency of having Wales dependent upon Canterbury. Gerald reported Henry II as saying, at the time of Gerald's first candidacy in 1176, 'it is not expedient to give strength to the Welsh and increase their pride by the promotion of such a man'.[113] King John, writing to the Pope and Curia, echoed this opinion; if they allowed Gerald to be elected and permitted St. David's to gain metropolitan status, 'they would greatly disturb the peace of his realm on account of that wild, violent, and easily rebellious nation'.[114]

Gerald vigorously attacked this view. He considered that Canterbury had abused her pastoral authority in the pursuit of political aims. Hubert Walter, he said, 'contrives to defend his case by associating with the king, saying that unless the church of Wales is subject to the English Church by provincial law, then that people, falling away from the King of England, will continuously or frequently rebel'. The Archbishop seemed to suggest that the King of England needed the help of the spiritual sword to conquer 'that tiny people'. He also criticized the Archbishop's use of excommunication against the Welsh when they rose in arms. Gerald argued that it was unjust to condemn the Welsh to hell simply 'because they protect their bodies, lands, and liberties against a hostile people, repelling force by force'. In 1198 the Welsh besieged Painscastle (Radnorshire), 'not in England but in Wales, a castle constructed by the English for the purpose of depriving them of their lands'. Hubert Walter was directing operations. He excommunicated every Welshman in arms. The Welsh were defeated, three thousand of them were killed, and the Archbishop ordered bells to be rung and the Te Deum to be sung in celebration, 'like a good pastor giving God thanks that he had sent so many souls of his parishioners to Hell in one day'.[115]

Gerald referred to this abuse of excommunication elsewhere. The intention of the English in promoting only Englishmen to Welsh sees, he argued, was to enable them to excommunicate the Welsh as soon as they took up arms, 'that is, because they fight for their country against a hostile people and strive for liberty'.[116] As these words show, Gerald's criticisms of the abuse of the Church's spiritual weapons for political ends went hand in hand with a sympathetic attitude towards the Welsh struggle against the Anglo-Normans. It is a curious paradox, considering his own family and upbringing. But he had always admired the independence of the Welsh and had an aristocrat's respect for the freedom and spirit of the Welsh tribesman. 'They strive so much after the safety and liberty of their country', he wrote approvingly. 'They fight for their country, they strive after liberty. For these things it seems sweet not only to fight with the sword but even to give up their lives.'[117] There was even an element of idealization of the primitive in his picture, a preference for 'natural man'—'they strive more after nature than elegance'.[118] He praised Welsh warlikeness, nobility, generosity, and boldness of speech, and compared the Welsh favourably with the English in some respects.[119]

Gerald's respect for the Welsh struggle for independence became more explicit during the St. David's case. He saw Welsh self-defence as entirely justified and the activities of English prelates in Wales as a travesty of canonical behaviour. His commitment to the cause of St. David's drew him ever deeper into criticism of the policy of the English crown in Wales. St. David's, he wrote, had been subordinated to Canterbury through the *violentia*, the naked power, of Henry I—'conquering Wales with a strong hand, he ordained that the Welsh Church, which he found free, should be placed under the Church of his own realm, just as he subdued the country to his kingdom'.[120] 'The English plantation of Wales was not introduced naturally or adoptively, but violently.'[121]

Just as Gerald's reforming ideals had a latent political significance in the context of Anglo-Norman colonization, so these same ideals came into play in defence of his pro-Welsh position during the years of the St. David's case. The violent subjection of the Welsh Church and the intrusion of English bishops seemed an outrage to his ideal of pastoral care. The very fact that they were intruded went against the precepts of canonical election. Peter de Leia and Geoffrey of Wenlock (bishops of St. David's 1176-98 and 1203-15) were 'translated more by power than by canonical election'.[122] Gerald observed that foreign bishops were never found among the Irish or Welsh 'unless they are elected through the violence of the public power'.[123] These intruded 'bishops were unhappy in Wales and were always scheming for promotion to a wealthy English bishopric.[124]

> All of the bishops translated from England in our time have been greedy, rapacious, although always simulating great poverty, continually begging through the abbeys of England, forever at the Exchequer seeking greater things through translation or augmentation, and, in order to seize their ambition more effectively, assuming for themselves the role of paid look-out between England and Wales to the neglect of their pastoral duties.[125]

In this passage Gerald's anti-curialism, his ideal of 'the good bishop', and his newly discovered sympathy with the Welsh came together to create a cogent critique of English ecclesiastical policy in Wales.

Gerald argued that Wales would be best off with bishops who came from Wales. This paralleled his belief that the Marchers were the best choice as advisers to the king for Welsh affairs—he believed that attention should be paid to the people who knew the area. The political argument against him was that it was dangerous to have local bishops. He counter-attacked vigorously. The insistence on putting English bishops into Welsh sees is 'as if in the whole area of Wales no one could be found worthy of a bishopric, but good preachers and confessors should be sought among the English less suitable for this position in their own regions, men who are ignorant of both the ways of the country and its language'.[126] Hubert Walter, writing to the Pope, had said that Gerald was 'of the Welsh nation', and Gerald angrily responded 'As if he openly says that since he was born in Wales he should not be a bishop in Wales. Similarly, nor should Englishmen be bishops in England or Frenchmen in France... So let pastors ignorant of the language be mingled together—then you will find good preachers!'[127]

This insistence on appointing bishops in Wales who had a knowledge of the Welsh language sounds strange coming from Gerald's pen. There is little possibility that his Welsh could have improved between the time that his sermons had to be translated for Welsh hearers, in 1188, and his election in 1199. He may have had increasing reason to practice it during the four years of his case, but even before his election he wrote, 'the chapter of St. David's will not consent to a monk or a physician ignorant of the language of our people, who cannot preach or receive confessions except through an interpreter'.[128] Gerald certainly had more knowledge of Welsh than most of the Archbishop's candidates, but it is hard to escape the conclusion that he was implicitly overstating his eligibility on the grounds of knowledge of the Welsh language.

Nevertheless, he gradually built up a case for appointing local men in Wales and thus came to stress the distinctness of Wales. The distance of the country from Canterbury and its distinctness in language, laws, and customs were adduced in support of an independent archbishopric in Wales.[129]

In January 1203 Gerald presented to Pope Innocent III a letter from the Welsh princes (which he had almost certainly drafted himself) specifying the abuses inherent in the subjection of the Welsh Church.[130] It covers all the arguments that Gerald had developed and is a useful summary of them. The subjection of the Welsh Church, effected through the violence of the English kings, involved dangers to souls. The Archbishop appointed Englishmen ignorant of Welsh ways and language, who had to use interpreters. These men were not canonically elected but intruded, and their election took place in the King's chamber and under pressure. These intruded bishops were rapacious; they were non resident; they alienated church land. The archbishops of Canterbury excommunicated the princes by name and the people in general whenever there was war between Welsh and English. The bishops in Wales, whom the archbishops appointed at will, connived at this.

This letter thus summarized Gerald's arguments on the subject of 'Welsh bishops for Wales'. That is not its only significance. The fact that it was sent out by the Welsh princes both indicates and symbolizes the development of Gerald's struggle and the metamorphosis of his national position. By 1203 the Welsh princes were virtually the last of Gerald's important supporters. In the earlier years of his fight he had support from his Marcher relations and from many churchmen in Wales, both Welsh and Anglo-Norman, but as the political pressure built up his non-Welsh support fell away. The power of the English crown was mobilized against him: his supporters were threatened and their property distrained; bribery was employed. The canons of St. David's split into hostile kindred factions, while even Gerald's family had to give up supporting him. In 1203 Gerald was declared an enemy of the realm. In this desperate situation he had recourse to the only powerful figures who possessed a degree of independence from royal pressure—the Welsh princes.

In a sense this sealed the fate of his cause. The financial help he received from Llywelyn of Gwynedd, the letters written on his behalf by virtually all the Welsh princes, and the honourable reception that greeted him in Powys and Gwynedd must have encouraged him, but each of these things ensured that the English crown set its face ever more firmly against compromise or accommodation. The accusation brought against Gerald by his enemies, that he was a fomentor of Welsh rebellion, was given plausibility by such political connections. There was a close link between the support the princes gave to Gerald and their hostility to the English crown. Gwenwynwyn, Prince of Powys Gwenwynwyn, said of Gerald, 'Our Wales often wages great wars against England, but never anything as great and serious as has been done in our time by the bishop-elect of St. David's. He has not ceased to attack and trouble the king, archbishop, and the whole clergy and people of England as well, with long and sustained efforts, for the honour of Wales.'[131] Conversely, when Gwenwynwyn entered an alliance with the English against Gwynedd, he withdrew practical support from Gerald.[132]

In such circumstances it is not surprising that Gerald's sense of his own Welshness should be heightened. As he was pushed out on to a limb and became involved in hectic polemics and litigation, he adopted a temporary, rhetorical identification with the Welsh: 'Our British people (now wrongly called Welsh), defending their liberty against both Normans and Saxons by continual rebellion, have thrown off the yoke of servitude from their necks, even up to today, by strength and arms.'[133]

An interesting parallel can be drawn with Bishop Bernard of St. David's, who had raised the metropolitan claims of the diocese in the 1130s and 1140s. He too had been forced into alliance with the Welsh princes.[134] The following comment was made by the editor of Gerald's Invectiones: 'Hostility to Theobald [archbishop of Canterbury] was the common ground on which Bernard and the Welsh princes met. The new alliance was not due to any access of Welsh patriotism on Bernard's part.'[135] The same point can be made about Gerald. In the light of his behaviour before and after the St. David's case his 'patriotism' of the years 1198-1203 appears, for the most part, as a rhetorical and polemical stance. The pursuit of his ecclesiastical ambitions had led him into unexpected paths.

Consideration of the interplay between the political, national, and ecclesiastical aspects of Gerald's career thus reveals a complex picture in which ambition, principle, and outside pressures all play a part. 'Gerald the Churchman', in a sense, runs the gamut between 'Gerald of Wales' and 'Gerald the Welshman'. As a self-righteous reformer he often appears as an alien intruder, contemptuous of the Celtic societies he encountered and providing ideological support for Anglo-Norman colonization. As candidate for St. David's he can sometimes be seen in the unlikely garb of a Welsh patriot.

Gerald's identification with the Welsh, however, did not survive his defeat in the St. David's affair and its settlement in 1203. Indeed, some of his most deeply disillusioned remarks about the Welsh are to be found in the accounts of the dispute which he produced in the years after the settlement. The period from 1203 to Gerald's death (c.1223) is a bitter, if active, one. Many of his works from this period have an unpleasantly shrill polemical tone. He had quarrelled with the English crown and with the Archbishop of Canterbury. His opinion of the English people had never been high. He was disillusioned with the Welsh. In this bleak situation such hopes as he had were directed towards France. The old man idealized the country of his student youth. The Capetians, at least, were just and generous princes; and, as he praised the

Capetians, so he poured out his spleen upon the Angevins, who had so frustrated his life's ambitions. Gerald's responses to the ruling dynasties of his time form an important element in his political life; these responses are explored in the next chapter.

KINGS

PATRONS, PANEGYRIC, AND CRITICISM

Gerald was eventually to prove one of the harshest and most hostile critics of the Angevin kings. But there was a period of ten to twelve years[1] during which he was in their service. During those years, as might be expected, he sought their favour, by praising them in his writings and dedicating his works to them. The Topographia Hibernica was dedicated to Henry II, the Expugnatio Hibernica to Richard, Count of Poitou, just before he became king. Richard also received a presentation copy of the Topographia Hibernica after his accession, while, during Richard's absence from England, Gerald dedicated his works to the chief royal ministers. Clearly he was seeking patronage, hoping to win the attention of those at the top of the pyramid of power.

It is easy to feel that Gerald made a miscalculation if he thought that admiration for his literary achievements would induce such tough and practical rulers as Henry II and Richard to appoint him to the English bishopric he longed for.[2] Some of the most notable literary figures in England in the late twelfth century, Walter Map, Peter of Blois, and Gerald himself, never rose beyond the rank of archdeacon. Curial appointees tended to have administrative talents rather than literary polish—Hubert Walter is a classic example. The skills of literacy, especially letter-writing, certainly could take a man a long way in the court of king or prelate. But literature itself was not a ladder to positions of power in either royal government or the Church.

Gerald regarded the panegyric of Henry II which concluded the Topographia Hibernica as one of his finest literary creations.[3] The first edition of 1188 included praise of Henry as the first conqueror of Ireland (with the exception of the Vikings). 'For your victories challenge the boundaries of the world', he wrote. 'You, our western Alexander, have extended your hand from the Pyrenees as far as the furthest western limits of the northern ocean.' He exalted Henry's triumphs, lamented the rebellion of 1173-4 that had checked the King's ambitions, and praised him particularly for the mercy he showed in victory—according to Gerald, Seneca's De Clementia was always in his hands.

In the second edition of 1189, Gerald expanded this panegyric and included long accounts of Henry's four sons, which form a standard source for the personalities of the Angevins. He now praised Henry not only for his triumphs and clemency but also for his literary and intellectual talents. 'As a lettered prince,' he wrote, 'suitably learned in moral philosophy, you would have shone forth like a brilliant jewel among the princes of the earth, and, by your endowment and rich vein of intelligence and through wealth of instruction and erudition, you would, in a short while, have equalled the greatest philosophers, if you had not been snatched away so untimely from instruction in letters to worldly duties.'

The ideal of the lettered prince was a recurrent theme in Gerald's works.[4] The lettered prince was one who knew how to compensate literary efforts adequately. In the preface to the second edition of the Topographia, Gerald expressed the causal connection he saw between patronage and high levels of literary achievement. He lamented the contemporary decline in literature:

> It is not literature but lettered princes that are lacking. The honours due to the arts, not the arts themselves, are failing. The best writers would not have stopped today if chosen emperors had not stopped too. Therefore, given Pyrrhus, you will have Homer; given Pompey, you will have Cicero; given Caesar and Augustus, you will have Virgil and Horace.[5]

Despite his eulogy of Henry II, included in this very work, Gerald thought that effective literary patronage had failed in the contemporary world and that he himself had been unduly neglected. This idea was to grow in his mind and his writings throughout his later life.

The high standard of Henry II's education and his independent interest in reading and study were noted by contemporaries,[6] and the particular distinction of the literary figures associated with his court has been discussed by several historians. Gerald was willing to eulogize Henry II's learning—or, at least, his early promise—in the Topographia Hibernica, dedicated to that monarch, but his disappointed ambitions made him increasingly dismissive of the cultural talents of the Angevins. His own picture of the literary culture around him was less favourable than that of modern commentators. It has been said that Henry's court possessed 'the most dazzling group of literary men the Middle Ages had ever known'.[8] Gerald, on the other hand, asked 'Where are the divine poets? Where the noble moralists? Where the moderators of the Latin language?...The honour due to literature, once established to the highest degree and now collapsed in ruin, has sunk so low that men devoted to literary pursuits now not only remain unimitated and unreverenced, but are even hated.'[9]

After the disappointment of his hopes of recognition from Henry II and Richard, Gerald attempted to gain the attention of English bishops through his writing. In the 1190s, both before and after retirement from court, he dedicated or presented works to William Longchamp, Bishop of Ely, Hubert Walter, Archbishop of Canterbury, and St. Hugh, Bishop of Lincoln. His change of tack seems to have brought him no more success and he gave up the practice of dedicating his works at all, until the return of Stephen Langton to England in 1213 raised before him yet again the hope of a powerful and encouraging patron.[10]

Gerald's efforts, and their failure, illustrate two important points about his life. Firstly, although his family connections brought him swift local patronage and a comfortable ecclesiastical position in south-west Wales, he was not well-connected enough to have immediate access to the sources of central patronage. His obvious talent and energy meant that he won appreciation and gained a solid position in the local churches with which he was associated—Hereford and Lincoln—but the royal road to an English bishopric presented obstacles. Secondly, Gerald's elevated sense of the dignity of literature and his insistence upon the life of letters as, virtually, 'a calling', gave him an inflated and unrealistic view of the rewards he could expect for his writing. He expressed his love for writing and saw literary attainment as a way of escaping the transience of life, transcending mortality.[11] Throughout his life, he was one of his own most favourable critics. This high self-evaluation led him to bitter and enduring disappointment.

The praises of Henry II which Gerald included in the Topographia Hibernica and Expugnatio Hibernica thus did not give him a passport to high position. Nevertheless, they do illuminate his situation while in royal service. Court panegyric is not the most immediately attractive literary genre, but Gerald's sycophancy reflected as much upon the nature of court life as upon his personal servility. Among court clerks preferment was unpredictable, patronage essential, and jealousy easily aroused. The mean and bitter hostilities that Gerald's Welsh origin involved him in have been mentioned, and his quarrel with Wibert was a classic case of rivalry between curial clerks.[12] In this world appeal to a patron through eulogy might seem like the first step to high places.

Gerald's dedications and laudations were intended to serve his ambitions, and we should not expect them to reflect his full and private feelings about the great men concerned. He sometimes wrote publicly in the language of panegyric while we know that he was privately pouring out bitter invective against the same figure. His letter to King John of about 1210,[13] for example, was deferential and included high praise of Henry II, while at the same time Gerald was busy writing the De Principis Instructione, which bitterly attacked both father and son—a truly Procopian situation. Moreover, the agile eulogist had to be up to date about the political fortunes of the figures he praised. The original edition of Gerald's Itinerarium Kambriae of 1191 was dedicated to William Longchamp, Bishop of Ely, Chancellor, Justiciar, and papal legate.

After Longchamp's fall in October 1191, however, Gerald hastily suppressed the dedicatory epistle, and his later writings included savage denunciations of Longchamp.[14]

In his old age, writing in the De Principis Instructione, Gerald admitted that his early praises of Henry II had been 'somewhat flattering, as they were written while that King was still reigning', but he argued that 'they were, nevertheless, underpinned in everything by historical truth'.[15] He was aware that he had placed constraints upon completely free expression through fear of royal power, but he prided himself that he had taken a reasonable risk for the sake of truth. His description of Henry II in the Expugnatia Hibernica, he wrote, 'was put out dangerously rather than fruitfully, since the king was then still alive. Like a real historian, following the truth, we did not keep silence about conflicts. Nevertheless, as we criticized, we tempered our statements with excusing phrases.'[16]

In these judgements, Gerald was being reasonably fair to himself. Clearly, the eulogies of the Angevins that he included in the Topographia Hibernica and Expugnatio Hibernica, works dedicated to those princes, tended to be flattering. But Gerald did not refrain from criticism, even in the midst of these praises. It seems unlikely that his habit of pointing out the faults of great men in writings addressed to them can have increased his chances of preferment. In the Topographia Hibernica and Expugnatio Hibernica Gerald criticized Henry II's generosity to outsiders, at the expense of his own people (domestici),[17] his lack of religious devotion, his adultery, his perjury, and his bad treatment of the Church.[18] Such open criticisms support Gerald's own contention that his praises were not lacking in 'historical truth'—that is, he portrayed the bad with the good.[19]

Gerald was also aware of the possible dangers of criticizing kings. It is difficult to judge the true risk involved in such criticism. In some ways criticism of royal government was a less perilous activity in the Middle Ages than in early modern times. The Church had a generally acknowledged role of moral leadership and exhortation, which meant that its criticisms were sanctioned by tradition. It was, in fact, the duty of ecclesiastics to rebuke and encourage laymen, including rulers. Of course, some kings would be unwilling to listen and might even put pressure on ecclesiastics who offended them. Yet it is remarkable how outspoken some ecclesiastics, especially those with an aura of sanctity, could be. The relationship between St. Hugh, Bishop of Lincoln, and Henry II is a good example.[20] In addition, the absence of the printing press made written criticism much less threatening and hence of less concern to rulers. The apparatus of censorship, informers, and treason laws that was developed by the early modern state had no twelfth-century counterpart. The spoken word was more dangerous than the written, and travelling preachers and prophets might be arrested as potential fomentors of public or popular disorder,[21] while cases also exist of kings inflicting punishment on those who composed scurrilous songs about them.[22] Written criticisms, however, were not hunted down and destroyed. This was probably a fair estimate of their importance. Anti-curial chronicles in monastic libraries might stiffen the monks' resolve in conflicts with the crown but were hardly likely to incite any large-scale disturbance.

Nevertheless, Gerald was nervous. On several occasions he delayed publication of parts of his works or published them anonymously explicitly through fear of repercussions. Book III of the Expugnatio Hibernica, which was to have contained 'a new interpretation' of the prophecies of Merlin, broke off with these words:

> But enough. For the publication of the third Book and the new interpreta-
> tion of the prophecies must, by wiser counsel, await its time. For it is better
> that the truth, although most useful and desirable, should nevertheless be
> concealed and suppressed for a while than that it should break forth into
> light and immediately cause dangerous offence to great men.

Book I of the De Principis Instructione ends with similar words and it seems likely that the publication of Books II and III was delayed until after John's death.[24] Gerald's Vita Galfridi was published anonymously, presumably because its current political comments were controversial, and so was a late work, the De Jure et Statu Menevensis Ecclesiae, since 'It is better and safer to lose the uncertain reward of your labour than to incur hatred and certain danger through acknowledging it.'[25]

Gerald's sensitivity to the possible political danger he might encounter because of his writing seems less febrile in the light of an incident that occurred during his dispute with his nephew, Gerald junior, who succeeded him as archdeacon of Brecon. During the course of this quarrel, which centred on the revenues of the archdeaconry, Gerald junior and his ally, William de Capella, made excerpts from Gerald's historical works and jotted down parts of his dinner-table conversation that could be seen as 'insults to great men'.

'They made very careful excerpts in their notes', wrote Gerald, 'so that, if they could not keep peacefully what they stole shortly afterwards, they would immediately try to accuse us from our own books, and, as it were, to attack and wound us with our own weapons, and they would denounce us for treason (maiestas) to the powers temporal and ecclesiastical, as they have often threatened and still do.'[26] Here is a good example of the danger inherent in expressing extreme hostility to established authorities: in the wrong hands such material could be a tool of blackmail. Gerald junior and William de Capella obviously thought that such material gave them a real weapon with which to exert pressure on Gerald senior. They probably had no precise intention of raising charges of treason, but if, for example, King John had come to know the contents of the De Principis Instructione, it seems likely that Gerald would have felt the heavy hand of royal displeasure once again. In normal circumstances such literary attacks remained unknown to the kings and 'great men' who were their targets. Only if manipulated by the writer's enemies did they become truly perilous.

Gerald's criticisms of the Angevins took on a much sharper tone after his retirement from court. The exact political circumstances surrounding this event are obscure and even its dating is not certain.[27] In the early 1190s Gerald's loyalty was apparently the object of suspicion and some 'great men at court' thought he had pro-Welsh sympathies.[28] The Vita Galfridi he wrote in or shortly after 1193 took a strong stand on contemporary political conflicts. The work shows partiality for Geoffrey, Archbishop of York, illegitimate son of Henry II, and extreme hostility to William Longchamp, the man Richard had left as virtual viceroy in England on his departure for the Crusade.[29] Gerald also criticized Hubert Walter, who became Archbishop of Canterbury and Justiciar in 1193, and Hugh de Puiset, Bishop of Durham (d. 1195).[30] The exact political groupings of the early 1190s are extremely obscure, but Gerald's criticisms do seem to have been directed against several of Richard's men. At this time he was *familiaris* of Count John.[31] The fact that Gerald's retirement from court followed shortly after John's unsuccessful rebellion and Richard's return from captivity in 1194 may not be entirely coincidental.

Be that as it may, during the course of his life Gerald built up a number of different grounds for hostility to the Angevin kings. Some were personal. He felt that his exertions in royal service had been unrewarded and his literary offering snubbed. The St. David's case of 1199-1203 involved a prolonged and direct clash with the royal government, and his personal ambition and high sense of justified mission were staked on this abortive effort. In addition, however, some of his criticisms of the Angevins can be placed in a more general context of aristocratic or ecclesiastical opposition.

Gerald's position as a spokesman for the Marchers has already been discussed.[32] He expressed their resentment of the role of the king and royal officials in Ireland and, in general, their hostility to strong royal government. One of his charges against Henry II was that he was an 'oppressor of the nobility',[33] and he saw an unnatural reversal of order in this 'anti-aristocratic' policy. 'Who', he asked, 'behaved more nobly to commoners and more ignobly to the aristocracy? Who raised the lowly higher or depressed the high so low?'[34] This resentment of the elevation of new men through executive power is a recurrent baronial complaint during the Middle Ages.

Writing in the decades before Magna Carta, Gerald advanced criticisms reflecting the climate of opinion from which the demands of 1215 emerged. His castigation of Henry II as 'a delayer of justice and law'[35] calls to mind clause

40 of Magna Carta: 'To no one will we sell, refuse, or delay the operation of right or justice.' Gerald was hostile to the Forest Law.[36] In 1215-17 the barons attempted to formalize such hostility by legislative action in Magna Carta and the Forest Charter. Most striking of all is a set of proposals which, it has been said, 'reads like a summary of the principal provisions of Magna Carta'.[37]

These proposals were delivered to a Lincolnshire knight, Roger of Asterby, by voices who identified themselves as St. Peter and the Archangel Gabriel. They presented him with seven demands to be taken to Henry II. Roger was at first suspicious, but the voices gained his confidence: they showed concern for the poor, they were vouched for by a speaking crucifix, and they recovered Roger's mail-shirt which, significantly, had been pawned to Aaron the Jew, the great Lincoln money lender. Convinced by these demonstrations, Roger took the demands to Henry. They are couched in quite general terms, but enable us to picture the programme they aimed at:

> These are the seven commands: I the three things he swore at his coronation concerning the maintenance of God's Church; II Concerning the observance of the just laws of the kingdom; III That he should not condemn anyone to death without judgement, even if guilty; IV All inheritances to be restored and right done; V Concerning the free rendering of justice without charge; VI Concerning the services to be rendered to his ministers; VII Concerning the Jews, that they should be expelled from the land, keeping a part of their money to enable them to leave and to maintain their family, but that they should not retain any pledges or charters, but everyone should recover his own.[38]

The similarities with Magna Carta are clear. There is a similar stress on accessible and equitable justice; a similar combination of demands for the *libertas ecclesiae*, expressed in general terms,[39] with demands relating to the interests of the lay landholders, expressed in greater detail; a similar concern over the rightful descent of estates.

Indebtedness to the Jews, an issue of evident importance to Roger of Asterby, was also a matter of concern to the barons of 1215. Clauses 10 and 11 of Magna Carta provide some protection for the families of men dying indebted to the Jews. It is not surprising that these provisions do not approach the severity of Roger of Asterby's proposal. The Jews were valuable royal property and the barons had to give some consideration to what the King would accept. The Lincolnshire knight, however, spoke for a far more embattled class, those knightly landowners who were feeling the economic pinch. The Asterby family connection, as Lincolnshire charters reveal, was in considerable financial difficulties in the late twelfth and early thirteenth centuries, and turned to the local monasteries, as well as Jewish money-lenders such as Aaron, to acquire cash.[40] The cancellation of debts to the Jews would have provided important, although probably only temporary, relief.

The articulation of the grievances of the lesser aristocracy is, however, only a subordinate aspect of Gerald's political criticism. He castigated the Angevins far more often and at far greater length for their infringement of the *libertas ecclesie* than for the pressure they put on the lay aristocracy. He attacked Henry II as a usurper of Church property, as 'one who always favoured the laity against the clergy'.[41] He criticized his simoniacal practices and the way he confused the laws of the regnum and the sacerdotium.[42] He attacked Richard, too, for 'raging against the church with harsh exactions',[43] and lamented in general the 'insular tyranny' under which the English Church suffered.[44]

The special targets of his attacks were royal control of elections, the appointment of curial bishops, and royal appropriation of the revenue of vacant sees. All three were ancient customs of the kingdom but had been vigorously attacked by 'high churchmen' throughout the twelfth century. Gerald's comments are typical of this tradition. He was opposed to royal control of episcopal appointments both as an assault on the independence of the Church and for its tendency to produce unworthy bishops. The quality of bishops had declined, he claimed, since canonical election had been replaced by royal mandate.[45] Gerald himself associated good canonical practice with his schools' training and contrasted the principles he had learned from Peter the Chanter and the other Paris masters with those that animated Hubert Walter, Archbishop of Canterbury and (successively) Justiciar and Chancellor, a living embodiment of the marriage of ecclesiastical and secular office. When Gerald was elected to St. David's in 1199, 'in the church and not in the [royal] chamber', he attributed Hubert Walter's opposition to 'a wish to reduce everything to that method of election which he had learned, not in the schools, but in the court, not in philosophical study, but at the Exchequer. Since everything is done at the King's command, this is the school (gymnasium) from which virtually all the English bishops are taken, as the storm of this tyrannical age besets us'.[46] Gerald saw himself as an upholder of vital principles against royal tyrants and curial bishops. The suspicion of royal officials felt by the Marchers in Ireland mingled with Gerald's Paris-trained rigour in the question of ecclesiastical freedom. *Curialis* is a word with negative associations in Gerald's works.

The kingly power not only invaded ecclesiastical freedom of appointment but also robbed the Church of its material substance. Gerald was highly sensitive to lay appropriation of ecclesiastical property, on all levels, and he recorded numerous stories of how plunderers of churches had been struck by miraculous revenge.[47] At the highest level, there are his criticisms of the Angevins for usurpation of Church property: Henry II was attacked for his practice of keeping bishoprics vacant for long periods in order to enjoy their revenue.[48]

Gerald's criticisms of the Angevins form a reasonably coherent, but not surprising, whole. He spoke for the knightly class and lesser aristocracy who had not made their way by royal service but relied upon independent resources or military adventure. He expressed their worries about the pressure of royal government and the inadequacies and political manipulation of the machinery of justice. In the Roger of Asterby story he recorded the responses of a knightly family under economic pressure. In addition, he had absorbed a rigorous ideological position concerning the *libertas ecclesie* while at Paris, and attacked the Angevins as tyrannical intruders into the freedom and property of the Church.

The two elements in his criticism, the lay aristocratic and the ecclesiastical, were frequently found in alliance in the twelfth and thirteenth centuries. The aristocracy was strong in coercive power, but weak in ideology; for the Church the reverse was true. Each could supplement the other. Fears of baronial opposition, for example, were one of the factors which induced John to accept Langton and end his quarrel with the Church, while Langton's influence moulded baronial demands in the period before Magna Carta. Church support provided respectability and theory for the baronial opposition.

DE PRINCIPIS INSTRUCTIONE—FORTUNE AND PROVIDENCE

It would be wrong, however, to discuss Gerald's criticisms as if the most important thing about them was a political programme, a series of points which he hoped to see realized. His individuality, his distance from real political power, above all his vivid imagination, meant that he was a long way away from the men who drafted Magna Carta. The heart of his attack on the Angevins, the work in which he poured out the depths of his hatred, is not a political critique or programme. It is a personal drama—the rise and fall of a tyrant. This work is, of course, the De Principis Instructione.

The history of the composition of the De Principis Instructione is complex. Gerald described it as 'begun almost among my first works, published, however, among my last'.[49] He was engaged in writing it by the time of the first edition of the Itinerarium Kambriae (1191).[50] He wrote the original preface to the work after he had left court in about 1195 and there is some indication that Book I circulated separately.[51] Parts of Books II and III were written early in John's reign, but the work as a whole did not take its final form until shortly after John's death.[52] Book I was reworked and includes material that could only have been written in 1216-17.[53] Clearly, a work whose composition extended from about 1190 to about 1217 will have many different elements. What is striking, in fact, is how unified is the theme presented in Books II and III.

Book I is really quite separate. It is a conventional 'Mirror for Princes' and is largely derivative.[54] Gerald drew a large number of his classical quotations from the Moralium Dogma Philosophorum, a compilation of ethical maxims from Cicero, Horace, Seneca, and other Roman authors.[55] The work discusses general ethical qualities; Gerald took the quotations he found there and reapplied them to the particular ethical qualities required for a king. Hence the chapter headings of the Moralium Dogma Philosophorum read 'Of prudence', 'Of patience', etc., while Gerald's are 'Of the prudence of a prince', 'Of the patience of a prince', etc. He illustrated the moral platitudes he advanced by the use of historical exempla. Here too he was often derivative, taking long passages from Hugh of Fleury's Historia Ecclesiastica of the early twelfth century.[56] Hugh was the chief source for his accounts of the Roman emperors, both pagan and Christian, and the Carolingians. Other passages, of different kinds, were borrowed from Hildebert of Le Mans,[57] the Gemma Animae of Honorius Augustoduniensis,[58] legal texts,[59] and various other sources.

Not all of Book I of the De Principis Instructione consists of borrowings, and there are some important passages of Gerald's own, including his reflections on contemporary affairs, besides less relevant, but no less interesting, sections on subjects such as the origin of the Picts and the Scots and the discovery of Arthur's tomb.[60] Yet, over all, Book I is neither original nor very illuminating as regards Gerald's views on political matters. Distinctions between rex and tyrannus and exhortation of the prince to be just, merciful, and prudent were commonplace. Sometimes there may be a contemporary echo, and when Gerald urges 'A prince should never punish when he is angry'[61] we may be justified in thinking of the notorious Angevin ira and malevolentia.[62]

The real structural role of Book I in the De Principis Instructione as a whole is to emphasize the distinction between tyrants and good princes. The distinction is given weight by being presented in its operation throughout history: Herod and Nero are set against David and Augustus. The hand of God is at work, and tyrants always die bloody and wretched deaths, while 'chosen kings and free and generous princes' end their lives in praiseworthy ways.[63] Books II and III can then be seen, as Gerald intended them, as a sustained example illustrating these maxims. 'Book I', he wrote in the preface, 'contains teaching and precepts concerning the instruction of a prince from the varied testimony of theologians and pagans and moralists. Books II and III teach the rule of government through examples'.[64]

The second and third books are planned to illustrate the rise and fall of Henry II. Book II covers the reign up to 1185. In this period Henry was usually successful in his undertakings, even against the odds. Despite the rebellions of his sons and the enmity of the Capetians 'everything turned out victoriously'.[65] Then Book III describes the last few years of Henry's reign, when everything turned against him. Philip Augustus's successes, Richard's rebellion, and John's defection led directly to Henry's miserable death. Gerald wished, in these last two books, to present a drama of kingly hubris. Henry's fall was not only a vivid example of the mutability of human life, but also a moral tale. His fall was the result of divine judgement. Throughout the successes of his reign Henry had failed to recognize their true author, God, and had obstinately persisted in his evil ways. God had sent troubles to afflict him, to open his eyes, but Henry ignored them. Visions and revelations, divine warnings to him, were likewise ignored. Eventually 'full judgement and complete justice'[66] caught up with him.

Gerald employed two, slightly different, frameworks in presenting this classic drama of the rise and fall of a wicked king. One was God's activity in blessing, chastising, and eventually judging. The other was Fortune's wheel.[67]

The reality of God's government of the world thoroughly imbued Gerald's account of Henry II in the De Principis Instructione. Gerald was not, indeed, the kind of writer who thought that attributing an event to God's will was the beginning and end of what could be said about it. In describing the natural world, for example, he was well aware of material causes. Even when describing such events as the fortunes of nations in war, he presented, alongside providential and moral language, explanations based on practical military factors. He wrote 'you will never find that any race has been conquered unless this has been brought on by their sins', and attempted to describe the complex relationship between the partial English conquest of the Irish and the relative sinfulness of the two peoples, but analysed, at the same time, the initial military advantages of the English and how the Irish, by learning from them, had eventually diminished the momentum of conquest.[68] Explanation in terms of God's judgement on sin did not exclude other factors, but in his portrayal of Henry II's fate Gerald was more insistent on a kind of moral causality. Every event in Henry's reign was interpreted as reflecting God's intention towards the king. His successes were God's means of encouraging him; his adversities were God's chastisements; his fall was God's judgement. The weakness of this framework was that it could, of course, too easily explain anything. It thus solved the problem of how Henry could have continued his successes, in some part, after Becket's death even into his final years. Gerald explained 'The more he removed himself from the Lord by his wicked actions, the more readily the Divine Kindness by turns harassed him with scourges and induced him with benefits, in order that he should come to himself again.'[69] In this way both 'scourges' and 'benefits' were fitted into the schema of God's attempts to turn Henry from his errant ways.

The image of Fortune, in comparison, involved only a minimal moral element. The fall of the great and the rise of the humble had an inevitability quite apart from the dynamics of sin and providence. Moral conclusions could be drawn from the turning of Fortune's wheel—no man should put his trust in transient earthly things—but the motor driving the wheel was a general sense of mutability, not a feeling for the purposiveness of the moral drama of human life. Gerald had discussed the point in the Expugnatio Hibernica:

> A prudent man should also realize that Fortune's favour is fickle and her wheel is always turning. Few young men and virtually no older men avoid experience of this fact. What was it that extinguished the glory of a great man, who had been distinguished in the world by his triumphs and had obtained great pre-eminence in the City [Pompey is meant], unless it was the necessity, brought by age, that a man who had once climbed the highest steps of honour should fall to the bottom; he was not permitted to be raised higher nor to stand on those steps any longer.

The peculiar fame of Caesar and Alexander, Gerald wrote, was due to the fact that when 'placed at the top of the wheel and at the height of victory, a premature death forestalled Fortune's malice and the turn into descent'.[70]

A man's political career was like a series of steps, but it was not possible to rest when you reached the top—you had to go down the other side. The topos of Fortune's wheel provided similar imagery: every moment was either rise or decline, and there was no stable point.

Gerald thus mixed a system of explanation and interpretation based on God's purposes and man's sin and salvation with one based upon a personified Fortune and the inevitable mutability of human affairs. The two systems represent, to some degree, different cultural heritages, the Judaeo-Christian and the classical. Sometimes they sit together easily; sometimes there is a definite sense of strain.

The central problem of a Christian sense of Fortune can be illustrated by a short phrase Gerald used when writing, in the Expugnatio Hibernica, of Henry II's successes: 'Fortune (if, however, anything is fortune) advanced him so happily in so many things...'.[71] The words 'if anything is fortune' indicate that, in the last analysis, there is no place for the concept in the Christian scheme—in any of its senses. Neither the idea of the purely fortuitous, nor that of a man's innate 'luck', nor (emphatically) that of a rival providential deity can really find a place in any rigorously Christian outlook.

However, it is clearly not the case that all elements in the mentality of an educated man in the twelfth century were rigorously Christian, and Gerald employed the concept of Fortune recurrently in the De Principis Instructione, often in conjunction with more explicitly religious terms. The preface to Book II provides a good example:[72]

> According to the various mockeries of Fortune, we see some men oppressed and humiliated for a long time so that they may be exalted subsequently

more thankfully to a higher place; and, on the other hand, others who are raised up on high suddenly and unexpectedly so that they may be ruined by a more grievous fall. Hence, by treating the latter case, Book I of this little work will explain the unexpected elevation and glory of Henry II King of the English, so that no one should despair, and the next Book will deal with his grievous fall and distress, so that prosperity should not raise anyone to pride.

In the opening words, Fortune is thus personified as a power who mocks men and takes a perverse delight in reversing their fates. Man's best response to this helter-skelter element is the adoption of a stoical detachment. Lowly status or failure should not cast him down; success should not puff him up. The next section of the preface immediately changes the tone, however. Henry's early successes, Gerald wrote, particularly the attainment of the English throne against all the odds, were the consequence of God's plan. 'The Divine disposition, which nothing can resist, cleared away all dangers and, while it was favourable, granted every benefit.' When he had become King and shown himself to be a tyrant, 'scourges seemed to be prepared for him by God', but he survived. Then God began the long process of alternately encouraging and chastising him. 'This long delay and postponement of vengeance clearly shows that God's kindly patience seeks the conversion of the wicked more than their downfall.' Eventually, however, the sentence fell. The opening sentence of this preface, with its picture of a mocking Fortune, thus led on to a different picture, portraying a purposive divine providence concerned with human moral qualities. The two pictures are harnessed together, but not harmonized.

In other parts of the De Principis Instructione, however, a stronger connection between sin and Fortune is asserted. An explicit case is the passage which follows Gerald's account of Becket's murder: 'After the daring sacrilege of this detestable crime and wicked villainy, the turning wheel of Fortune began to sink back to the depths more quickly for him and to be raised to the heights more slowly; the royal lot gradually began to be diminished; the strength of the reign began to be weakened day by day.'[73] This sinister picture of the luck and strength of Henry's rule slowly draining away involved a mingling of the two kinds of process, moral causation and the course of Fortune. Fortune's wheel still turns, but it has been affected by Henry's crime. The upward climb is now slow and painful, the downward fall a vertiginous rush. This is no autonomous and inevitable process—Fortune has been integrated, to an extent, into that system of moral causes dependent on divine providence.[74]

Gerald intended to present a drama, the rise and fall of a great but wicked king. He was willing to draw on imagery from various sources. Although 'Fortune's wheel' sometimes seems little more than a turn of phrase,[75] in the work as a whole the image of the turning wheel, which reaches a high point and must then decline, is very significant. The idea of 'a turning point' is crucial to the work. The very arrangement of the De Principis Instructione is determined by the split between Henry's successful years (Book II) and his fall (Book III). However, Gerald had to face certain structural problems when fitting the events of Henry's reign into this pattern.

The desire to see 'a turning-point' in anyone's life is strong. Such a turning-point creates dramatic and dynamic patterns and harmonizes naturally with moral lessons and religious explanations. Henry II's enemies had felt the desire to describe his reign in these terms long before Gerald wrote his De Principis Instructione. Writing in exile in 1166, John of Salisbury saw the turning point of the King's reign as the moment when he imposed heavy and unjust exactions on the Church to pay for the Toulouse campaign of 1159. 'Surely from that day has not his fortune ebbed and have not his abundant successes dried up?'[76] John was writing early in Henry's reign, and therefore the drama of rise and fall had to be compressed into a short span—Henry's star passed its zenith in 1159, only five years after his accession. Gerald was writing with the whole of Henry's reign in his mind, to structure as he would. Even so, there was a tension between the schema he employed and the actual course of the reign.

The most dramatic and most obvious event to take as the beginning of the end for Henry II was the murder of Becket in 1170. However, the events of the 1170s did not exhibit the required decline very convincingly. Henry received the submission of Ireland in 1171, and even the rebellion of 1173-4 was successfully crushed. In the first years of the 1180s Henry's reputation was very high.[77] On the other hand, the last five or six years of Henry's reign saw a series of setbacks culminating in a wretched death. His eldest son, Henry the Young King, rebelled and died in 1183; his son Geoffrey of Britanny rebelled and died in 1186. John's expedition to Ireland in 1185 was a disaster. The Capetians went on the offensive successfully, for the first time in decades, under Philip Augustus in 1187-9. In the last twelve months of his life Henry II faced the rebellion of his son and heir Richard in alliance with Philip Augustus, their successful invasion of the Angevin heartlands, including the burning of his birthplace, Le Mans, and the defection of his youngest and favourite son, John. 'Woe, woe on a vanquished King!', Gerald has Henry say on his deathbed,[78] and the words were a fair reflection of reality. Thus, in presenting the drama of Henry's reign, Gerald stressed the mid-1180s as the turning-point and emphasized particularly Henry's unwillingness to respond personally to the appeal of the Patriarch Heraclius of Jerusalem, who visited England in 1185 in order to seek aid for the Holy Land. This was the true crisis, and Becket's murder had to be fitted in as a secondary, although important, dramatic moment.

Gerald sometimes portrayed the murder as the decisive point in Henry's fortunes in some sense,[79] but did not interpret it as leading directly to Henry's fall. In a similar way William of Newburgh saw Henry's miserable end as a consequence of Becket's murder, but in an indirect way: 'because, as I believe, he had not yet sufficiently repented the severity and unfortunate obstinacy which he had shown towards the venerable archbishop Thomas, the end of this great prince was, in my opinion, so wretched'.[80] Becket's murder was clearly one of the greatest crimes of Henry's reign in the eyes of most ecclesiastical commentators, but it occurred almost nineteen years before Henry's own death, and as much of that period was prosperous for Henry, the martyrdom was not entirely imaginatively satisfactory as the source of the King's nemesis.

Nevertheless Henry's reputation was blackened by his behaviour towards Becket. Gerald regarded the Archbishop as a particular patron[81] and extolled him as a champion of ecclesiastical rights.[82] The king responsible for the death of such a saint, even if the murder had been committed only on his account (propter ipsum) and not by him (per ipsum),[83] was clearly compromised in Gerald's eyes. In the course of time, moreover, he came to attribute to Henry a much more direct part in Becket's murder. In the Vita Sancti Remigii[84] he reported that one of the four murderers had confessed that the King had bound them with an oath to perform the crime.[85] Later in the Vita Gerald described Henry as 'the author' of the murder.[86] This work also claims that things never went right for Henry afterwards. To substantiate this Gerald had to juggle with the facts, presenting an almost continuous picture of rebellion and strife from the time of Henry's visit to Ireland after the murder (1171-2) to the end of the reign: 'By the Providence of Him who mocks the impious and laughs scorners to scorn, rendering them laughable and ridiculous, during this escape and winter delay in Ireland a great rebellion arose against the king among his sons, household familiars, and his barons across the sea. This persecuted him almost continuously until his wretched death.'[87]

This cannot be regarded as an accurate picture for the whole of the 1170s and 1180s and, in general, Gerald preferred to present Becket's murder as the crisis of the reign in only a vague and general sense. The true crisis, as presented in the developed picture of the De Principis Instructione, centred rather on Henry's failure as a crusader.

DE PRINCIPIS INSTRUCTIONE—THE CRUSADE

Although he did not go on the Third Crusade, Gerald was personally involved in the preparations for it. He preached the Crusade in Wales and was himself signed with the Cross in March 1188. He was released from his crusading vows in November or December 1189, but retained a strong emotional commitment to the crusading ideal.[88] Book II of the Expugnatio Hibernica is overshadowed by the imminence of the Crusade,[89] while the fate of the Holy Land, and the responses to it on the part of the rulers of western Europe, formed important themes in the De Principis Instructione.[90]

Even Gerald's dreams were troubled by the Crusade. He gives a long account of a dream that he had in 1189 'at Chinon around first cock-crow on the night of 10th May'.[91] The precision with which he remembered these details indicates the impact the event had on him. In the dream Gerald and a great crowd of others were looking up through a gap in the clouds into the Empyrean where 'the court of heaven' was being attacked and massacred by enemies. As the crowd of onlookers flung themselves on the ground Gerald alone continued looking, to see God in Majesty [92] dragged off his throne and pierced with a lance. A great cry went up, 'Woch, woch, Pater et Filius! Woch, woch, Spiritus Sanctus!' Gerald woke up and sat up in his bed. For half an hour he felt as if he was going out of his mind, but eventually remembered to make the sign of the Cross on forehead and breast. Even so he could not sleep that night. He gradually recovered some degree of equanimity, but could never recall the dream without horror.

Naturally enough, he sought to interpret the dream. The most likely meaning seemed to him to be connected with the Holy Land and the Crusade. The suffering of 'the court of heaven' represented the suffering of the Christians in the Holy Land. The cry 'Woch, woch, Pater et Filius!', half German and half Latin, referred to the fact that only the German and Latin speaking nations and their princes—Barbarossa, Philip Augustus, Henry II, and Richard—had responded to the plight of the Holy Land. However, he already had an ominous feeling that the dream might foreshadow some disaster on the Crusade—a feeling that events were to vindicate.

The vividness of this dream, the strong emotional impact it had on Gerald, and the way it stayed in his memory suggest a close identification, on his part, with the Holy Land and the Crusade. The fall of Jerusalem in 1187 had great symbolic importance and had stirred Latin Christendom deeply. 'The sad rumour of these unfortunate events in the East spread quickly through the world', wrote William of Newburgh,[93] 'and brought shock and horror to the hearts of all Christians'. Gerald internalized these feelings to the extent that they entered his nightmare. The Crusade was, in Gerald's lifetime and long after, a goal whose validity was almost universally recognized. As a military endeavour with a religious aim, it harmonized with both an aristocratic and an ecclesiastical ethos.[94] Hence, both in terms of its personal meaning for Gerald and as a public ideal, the issue of the Crusade was important enough to play the central role it does in Gerald's drama of Henry II. Henry's dilatory attitude to the Crusade, as presented in the De Principis Instructione, was the hinge upon which his fate turned.

Even in his earliest writings about Henry II the issue of the Crusade was a crucial one in Gerald's eyes, although in the Topographia Hibernica of 1188 he seemed to have entertained no doubts about the seriousness of Henry's crusading intentions. He thought, in fact, that it was only the 1173-4 rebellion that had disturbed Henry's plans 'to spread the faith of Christ most notably through victories in the East'.[95] In 1189 he predicted that even the rumour of Henry's coming 'will restrain the raging fury of the pagans both of Asia and of Europe'.[96]

But, even at this stage, he also expressed worries. He thought that the failure of John's Irish expedition of 1185, for example, could be attributed to the fact that he had been sent off on an expedition against Christians, when the Patriarch's appeal had provided the perfect opportunity for him to be sent against pagans.[97] The conflict between Henry and his son Richard, in alliance with Philip Augustus, disturbed him. He saw the Crusade jeopardized by such strife. He also regarded the 'Saladin tithe' of 1188, levied to pay for the Crusade, as extortionate. He summed up his reservations in these words:

> Oh, would that our princes had been worthy to set out on this expedition with the favour of the people and popular applause, with their provisions for the journey acquired justly, not extorted, with an open and generous hand, not a tight fist, and with a pure conscience, perfected by penitence, wholly lacking envy and arrogance. Oh how much I would have preferred them to have started on their glorious, though laborious, journey in this way, with fewer men—but them all the better and more pleasing to God; instead they lacked unity and concord and prided themselves in this struggle on their vast and varied financial resources, gathered in an indiscriminate way, and on their huge multitude of peoples.[98]

Gerald's comments pinpoint the dilemma of Holy War. The Crusade was a religious duty and, as a special kind of war, should be undertaken in a special way. The participants should cleanse themselves spiritually and place their trust in God, not in numbers. The normal preparations for warfare could thus be condemned as a sign of inadequate faith. 'You will always find it is not abundance of men or forces, not human power but virtue and divine grace that brings victory',[99] Gerald wrote. Thus ecclesiastical writers might simultaneously urge the rulers of western Europe to embark on Crusade and criticize them bitterly for their preparations to do so.[100]

The De Principis Instructione presents a much more developed picture of Henry's failure as a defender of the Holy Land and points to the direct relationship between this failure and his fall. Throughout the work Gerald expressed complete scepticism about Henry's crusading intentions. Henry 'always delayed, always postponed in time' his arrangement to go on Crusade with Louis VII.[101] One of the terms of his reconciliation with the Church in 1172, after Becket's murder, had been a commitment to go to Jerusalem, but he made an agreement that he should found three monasteries instead. Then, to compound his evasiveness, the King did not found new monasteries but simply transferred existing houses from one order to another.[102] Gerald saw this transaction as a typical trick of a wily king anxious to avoid his crusading duty. His picture of Henry at this time is of a man, delighted with his own guile, who cannot see that by ignoring broader and more central values he is heading for disaster. The chapter dealing with Henry's promise to found the monasteries culminates in the chilling picture of God the logician. 'God is the best dialectician', Gerald wrote. 'This logician does not fatigue himself with a long disputation. For he closes and concludes everything with one syllogism: the Law is his major premiss; Sin his minor premiss; Damnation his conclusion.'[103]

The climax of Book II of the De Principis Instructione is the account of the Patriarch Heraclius's visit to England, his rebuff by Henry II, and his prophetic warnings to the King.[104] Gerald set the scene by describing the dangers that faced the Holy Land at the time—the threat from Saladin, the extinction of the line of the kings of Jerusalem, internecine strife among the barons of Outremer.[105] He emphasized the dire situation in Palestine by quoting a letter of appeal from Pope Lucius III.[106] The Pope recalled to King Henry the traditional involvement of the Angevins with Palestine[107] and concluded 'show care and zeal in this matter, so that your conscience may not accuse you in the Terrible Judgement and the interrogation of the strict Judge, who is not deceived, may not condemn you.'[108] The Church had a large reservoir of such ultimate appeals in its vocabulary, appeals that could be used in dealings with secular rulers.

Sometimes, however, secular rulers kicked back with a robust anticlericalism. Gerald recounts a fascinating conversation that took place between himself and the king while hunting at Clarendon which illustrates this point.[109] It highlights the difference between the idealistic, outspoken, and somewhat pompous ecclesiastic, in his late 30s, and the experienced, perhaps rather cynical, monarch, who had been on the throne for thirty years, a man given to impatience and irascibility, especially with what he sensed as posturing or cant. Gerald mentioned to Henry what an honour it was that the Patriarch should have come to him. 'The coming of the Patriarch', he had said, 'is the greatest honour, not only to you but to the whole kingdom. For this great man has come here from a very distant region and has brought his great and honourable message, not to any emperor or the king of any other land, but to you and your land.' The King, 'mockingly and taking these words neither well nor kindly', replied tartly, 'If the Patriarch or anyone else comes to us, they are seeking their own advantage here, not ours.' Gerald persisted: 'You ought to regard it as the greatest honour and advantage, O King, that you alone of the kings of the earth have deserved to be chosen for such great service to Christ.' Henry's reply was full of the resentment and scorn that active military aristocrats could feel for the clergy. 'These clerks', he said, 'can incite us boldly to arms and danger, since they themselves will receive no blows in the struggle, nor will they undertake any burdens which they can avoid.'

Henry's remarks indicate the hostility that could arise between those who did the fighting and those who urged them on. On the one hand there was the lay world of war and the raising of families, with its largely unarticulated ideology. On the other, the ecclesiastical world, consisting of men who had vowed neither to wield the sword nor to raise up children, yet who were able to justify themselves and, indeed, explain the whole world, by a complex and articulate ideology. King Henry's response to Gerald's effusiveness sprang not only from a hard-headed king's irritation at the difficulty of drawing money from the clergy, but also from a dislike, bordering on contempt, felt by fighters towards non-combatants, especially militant non-combatants.

There seems no reason to doubt the essential truthfulness of Gerald's account of this conversation. On the other hand, Henry's response did not necessarily mean that he had no intention of giving help to the Holy Land. W.L. Warren points out that 'Gerald, with his customary insensitivity and predisposition to think the worst of the Angevins, assumed from this dismissive remark that Henry had no intention of rendering help to the Holy Land', but, he argues, Henry's crusading intentions were quite serious—1185 was not a good time for Henry himself to take up the crown of the kingdom of Jerusalem, but the Crusade had always been one of his eventual goals.[110] The picture of Henry II that Gerald built up in the De Principis Instructione had no room for such genuine crusading aims. At a council held in London in March 1185, Henry II, at the advice of his magnates, declined the Patriarch's offer, and also refused to send his son John to the Holy Land. He offered financial aid, but the Patriarch replied 'We are looking for a leader, not for money'. Gerald's rhetoric booms out against Henry's wickedness: 'O stiff-necked and incorrigible man! O mind obstinate and inflexibly stubborn in evil!... surely you have struck a pact with death, you miserable man, and have made an agreement with Hell?'[111]

Twin themes are developed. One is that of the symmetry of the relations between God and man: Henry abandoned God and deserved to be abandoned by him. Later in the De Principis Instructione this idea was invoked even more explicitly.[112] The other theme is the terrible commonplace of Judgement: 'Do you not consider that you should fear and tremble at the thought of that day of fearful judgement, on which even the angels will be afraid, when you will be presented before the tribunal of the Judge, to whom everything is naked and open, with these words, "Behold the man and his works with him!"'[113]

Following this passage, Book II of the De Principis Instructione comes to a crescendo with the Patriarch's prophetic warnings to Henry.[114] As we shall see, Gerald used prophecy, visions, dreams, and strange foreshadowings to give his story of Henry II a deeper, more ominous tone. We are not only in the world of mundane time, skipping along the surface of events. These dark warnings send down deep roots into a world whose patterns transcend time. The Patriarch's prophetic words sound the knell of Henry's doom:

> Until now, O King, you have ruled gloriously among the princes of the world, through incomparable grace, and up to now your honour has grown more and more, up to the height of the heavenly kingdom. But without a doubt you have been reserved for this test—which you fail. Because of this, abandoned by the Lord whom you abandon, and completely devoid of grace, your glory will be turned to disaster, your honour to ignominy, until your last gasp.

Here is the moment upon which the drama turns. As this point is reached, the earlier crisis of Henry's reign, Becket's murder, is recalled. At crucial moments in the movement towards Henry's death the figure of Becket reappears. In the crescendo of his interview with Henry at Dover, the Patriarch takes on the person of Becket.

This interview, as described by Gerald, although utterly implausible, does have a central dramatic significance. The Patriarch is supposed to have listed the many blessings God had bestowed upon Henry, especially the acquisition of the English crown. He then went over Henry's acts of wickedness, including his disloyalty to 'his lord King Louis' and the murder of Becket, 'which he had perpetrated as if by his own hands, through sending executioners to do it'. Finally, the Patriarch rebuked Henry for refusing the command God had given him to help the Holy Land. In short, the Patriarch recapitulated Gerald's own picture of the reign. In response, as one might well imagine, Henry grew very angry. The Patriarch offered him his head and neck: 'Do to me what you did to the blessed Thomas! I would as well have my head cut off by you in England than in Palestine by the Saracens; without a doubt you are worse than any Saracen.'[115]

The Patriarch's gesture served to bring Henry's greatest crime to the foreground again at this crucial moment. From then on everything went wrong for Henry. 'He ruled for thirty-five years' wrote Gerald, 'Thirty years were given to him for worldly glory, for toleration of his behaviour, for the testing of his devotion. In the last five, like an ungrateful servant, like an abject reprobate, he faced vengeance, disaster, and ignominy.'[116]

DE PRINCIPIS INSTRUCTIONE—THE FALL OF HENRY II

Book III of the De Principis Instructione, which describes this 'vengeance, disaster, and ignominy', interweaves three strands. The first is the narrative of Henry's last years, with particular emphasis on the dealings between Henry, Richard, and Philip Augustus in the years 1187-9. As a story it is well told, has a striking momentum, and some memorable incidents and quotations. It is, however, designed as part of the overall pattern or schema within which Gerald was presenting the reign, and must be understood in the light of that schema. It does not present a historical account in the sense that Howden or William of Newburgh do. W.L. Warren has written 'Gerald's account of the last years of Henry II's reign, though heavily drawn upon by many historians, is so blinkered and wildly partisan that it is worthless for the purpose of interpreting events'[117] and this judgement, if overstated, is basically true. The intention here, however, is not to pick a path through Gerald's bias to the truth beyond, but to explore the pattern of his bias.

The second main subject of Book III is the recurrent one of the Crusade. It is interwoven with the former theme, since Henry, Richard, and Philip Augustus all took the Cross, and some of their dealings with each other are only comprehensible within the context of the Crusade. The passages on the Crusade also have a structural purpose. The narrative which focuses on Henry II breaks off at Chapter 14, with the King very ill as various dreams are recorded concerning his death. Then the story shifts to Barbarossa's Crusade. Chapters 15-18 are entirely concerned with the Crusade[118] before the narrative again takes up the story of Henry's last days and death. Not only does the long section on the Crusade lend suspense, but it provides an image of what Henry might have been doing—what, in fact, he should have been doing—rather than being involved in dynastic squabbles in France. The two parallel narratives complement each other. It was 'the discord and envy of our princes'[119] that was fatal to the Crusade, and the switching between the struggle of Angevins and Capetians in the Loire valley and Barbarossa's army slogging through Anatolia emphasizes the point.

The third element in Book III is not a narrative. It is the elaboration of a general framework that is historical, political, and prophetic. The sharp contrast between Angevins and Capetians is developed through extension in time, backwards to the pious Louis VII and the tyrannical Norman kings, forward, through visions and premonitions, to the eventual triumph of the Capetians and the fresh promise of Philip's heir, Louis. The viciousness of the Angevins is presented not only as a personal quality of Henry II and his sons, but as a result of tainted stock, while Capetian France is praised and exalted. The De Principis Instructione contains, in fact, a general interpretation of the history of England and France from the eleventh century down to Gerald's own day.

In his account of Henry's last years in Book III Gerald continued to stress the King's remissness as a crusader. Saladin had been encouraged by the Patriarch's failure, and the loss of Jerusalem and most of the Holy Land was attributed largely to 'the empty promises of the king of the English'. 'Woe to the man whose lack of boldness gave the Holy Land over into perdition!' Gerald wrote.[120] In 1189 Gerald had described how even the rumour of Henry's arrival would restrain 'the fury of the pagans'. Writing years later, in the De Principis Instructione, he recorded how Saladin had indeed been prompted to seek a truce through fear that the European rulers, especially Henry, might send help to the Holy Land. The rumour of the King's coming was, however, 'a false fabrication'.[121] The impressive reputation of 1189 had been revealed as a hollow lie.

Not only did Gerald lay responsibility for the disasters of 1187 largely on Henry's shoulders, he also blamed him for the difficulties encountered in getting the Third Crusade under way. He claimed that Henry was jealous of Richard, who had taken the Cross first and wanted to start out for the Holy Land straightaway, and that, to prevent this, Henry had secretly stirred up the Aquitanian magnates and the Count of Toulouse against him.[122] Henry envied Richard; but his own crusading intentions were not genuine. He regarded his crusading vows as a political ploy, felt he could buy a papal dispensation easily enough, and was delighted that he had 'tricked' Philip Augustus into taking the Cross.[123] Gerald depicts Henry as a petty schemer, unable to rise above selfishness and guile even when confronted with the ultimate appeal—the salvation of the Holy Land.

The theme of God's abandonment of Henry as a reaction to Henry's abandonment of God has already been mentioned. In Book III this motif took a new turn. Henry's alienation from God was depicted not as simply remissness but as a conscious unashamed defiance (diffidatio). His misfortunes prompted him to blasphemy. 'Why should I venerate Christ?' Gerald has him say. 'Why should I deign to honour him, who deprives me of my honour in the world and allows me to be confounded so shamefully by this boy [the king of France]?'[124] Henry's idea of the relationship between God and man was a simple one based on mutual benefits. God would obtain the honour and reverence he desired if he granted men the honour and power they desired. The experience of misfortune would prompt men to harm God, to pay tit for tat. This is the idea behind Henry's violent speech when, in flight from Richard and Philip Augustus, he looked back on the city of Le Mans in flames: 'Today, O God, to pile up confusion and increase my shame, you have so foully taken from me the city I loved most in the world, where I was born and raised, where my father lies buried and St. Julian's body is interred. So I will repay you for such a deed as far as I can, by taking away from you that which you love most in me.'[125] This conscious turning-away of the soul from God is the climax of Henry's evil. His response to misfortune, which Gerald contrasted with the patience of Job and Tobias,[126] was an insane and self-destructive defiance.

Becket is once again introduced into the picture. The fall of Châteauroux to the French in June 1188 was prefigured by a dream of one of the King's chaplains in which Becket appeared with a flaming sword whose blows were to smite the King.[127] A year later, when Henry came to his final negotiations with Philip Augustus and Richard, Gerald observed significant parallelisms with the Becket case. Henry wanted to submit himself to Philip's mercy 'saving his honour and the crown and dignity of the kingdom', but the French King would not accept these reservations. In the same way Henry had refused to make peace with Becket when the Archbishop had agreed to submit 'saving the honour of God, the dignity of his order, and the liberty of the Church.'[128] Again, just as Henry had persecuted his spiritual father, the Archbishop, so 'through the careful justice of divine vengeance' Henry's sons persecuted their physical father.[129]

Such parallelisms sprang from a sense of poetic justice, a feeling which is only a more specific form of the general idea of moral causality already discussed. A man's moral fate took precise forms, which emphasized the interconnections between his deeds and his eventual fortune. One wicked deed could have distant repercussions that would destroy the perpetrator. So, for example, because of the shameless way in which Henry had taken Eleanor of Aquitaine from her husband, Louis VII, the offspring of his marriage to Eleanor were destined to be his bane. 'He merited punishment', Gerald wrote, 'at the hands of his own offspring, whose origin was less licit and legitimate than is fitting...'[130] Gerald was in no way idiosyncratic in this interpretation. William of Newburgh also thought that Eleanor's marriage to Henry was of dubious legality and saw in it a source of Henry's misfortunes. 'So it came to pass by God's careful deliberation', he wrote,

> that he raised up from her distinguished offspring to his ruin. It was also just that he, who through his inordinate love for his sons is acknowledged to have injured many others as he exerted himself unduly for their advancement, should have been punished by their wicked rebellion and premature deaths. All this, however, manifestly occurred by the admirable dispensation of the heavenly Judge.[131]

The urge to see a man's misfortunes as appropriate and fitting results of his misdeeds was strong, and the notorious family feuds of the Angevins were thus traced back to Henry and Eleanor's wicked union.[132]

This kind of poetic justice recurred throughout Gerald's portrayal of Henry, especially in his picture of the last weeks of the King's life. Indeed, these last few weeks were pictured as full of spiritual and prophetic meaning. The machinery of divine justice reached a new pitch—peace talks failed 'by the divine command accelerating vengeance'.[133] Henry's past sins, his shameful union with Eleanor, his persecution of Becket, were all recalled. Philip Augustus stood revealed as the man of the future, whose glory had been adumbrated by prophecy and omen.[134]

But at the heart of this prophetic and providential complex lay the sad and simple story of a great king hounded to death by his enemies and his rebel-

lious sons. The ignominy of Henry II's death, it has been truly said, 'was the
ignominy of an ailing lion savaged by jackals'.[135] After his flight from Le Mans
and the fall of Tours, Henry, stricken with a mortal fever, had to submit himself
entirely to Philip's mercy. He learned that his favourite son, John, 'his heart',
had taken up arms against him, and he turned his face to the wall, saying 'Now
let everything go as it will, I care no more for myself or the world.'[136] On 6
July 1189 he died at Chinon.

> He laboured in his death throes, repeatedly groaning these words, which the
> vehemence of the disease, and of his sorrow and indignation too, extorted
> from the rest of his thoughts, since 'the mouth speaks from an abundant
> heart': 'Shame, shame, on a conquered king!' At last, among words of this
> kind, full of suffering, the herald of his own confusion, he breathed his last
> and died, overwhelmed and crushed rather than dying a natural death.[137]

Gerald was nothing if not a vindictive and malicious enemy, and there is
something decidedly unattractive about the only partially suppressed gloating
which hovers around his narrative. However, the bleak misery of Henry's death
has a moral and literary point in the De Principis Instructione, besides the
personal gratification it afforded Gerald. It is the fulfilment of the trajectory
of rise and fall; it is the King's 'come-uppance'; it is the point to which all the
previous momentum of the work has been leading. Gerald's description of the
plundering of the King's corpse and of the poor trappings at his funeral is not
to be trusted, but makes a dramatic finale to the reign.[138]

As has already been pointed out, the drama of Henry II's rise and fall was
not only a series of mundane events set in the world of usual, unilinear time.
It was also prophetic and visionary, transcending everyday temporal sequence.
Henry's fate was foreseen and prefigured, even to small details. When his naked
corpse was covered, by a servant boy, with a short cloak, this was the 'fulfilment' of his nickname 'Curtmantel'.[139] His death was announced in dream and
revelation.[140] Such prophecies gave an air of awesome inevitability to events,
and suggested a world whose operations went far beyond mundane experience.
They heighten the dramatic quality of Gerald's history: we are moved by a
sense of inexorable tragedy.

Many of the dream-visions which Gerald records concerning Henry's fate
had a vivid and violent flavour to them. Images of filth and of convulsive,
violent action predominate. In one dream Henry's corpse, lying on a bier in
church, suddenly sits up and demands to be taken outside.[141] In another, he
falls into a muddy ford and, when his black and muddy body is pulled out,
it is headless; when the head is found, it proves impossible to rejoin it to the
body.[142] Images of defilement occur: Henry and his sons spread their excrement
and urine on an altar.[143] There are sudden disappearances[144] and bizarre shifts of

size, as when Henry diminishes into a dwarf-like form.[145] After these disturbing and fragmented images, the dream in which Henry's sons are represented as four mallards on a river bank, with a falcon (Philip Augustus) hovering above them, has an almost pastoral quality to its menace.[146]

Gerald ascribed the dreams he recounted to different sources. Some were anonymous, some credited only to 'a monk', others were ascribed to famous and saintly figures—Becket, Archbishop Baldwin, Godric of Finchale. But perhaps the most vivid of all is the one which Gerald dreamed himself, and it maybe worth giving it a slightly more extensive treatment.

'I saw', he wrote,

> the King's dead body brought by night into the left aisle of a certain church. Suddenly a flock of rooks, crows, and jackdaws, frightened by the number of lights, left their perches and took to flight, knocking to the floor the torches which were hanging above, and suddenly extinguishing and breaking them. The birds also knocked over the two tapers which stood at his feet, and these went out. The two tapers at his head, before those around could steady them, fell, of their own accord, out of the candle-holders and on to the ground, breaking as they did so. Thus all the lights were extinguished and we, who seemed to be assisting at this night funeral, immediately dashed out, not in an orderly way but in hurried and fearful flight. Because of our fear and horror we left the corpse there alone, completely devoid of all human solace, as if it were haunted by unclean things.[147]

The imagery of this dream is rich and dark. It is night-time; the body is brought into the left aisle of the church, the traditionally unlucky side. The sudden plunge into darkness is a common motif in narratives of horror, and the horror is accentuated by the flocks of black birds. They exhibit the jerky disorder and dislocation already noticed in the other dreams. Dark, flitting masses of birds seem to strike the human mind as peculiarly anarchic and threatening. In the Middle Ages they would also tend to suggest carrion images. Moreover, flocks of birds could be seen as demons. Caesarius of Heisterbach, for example, told the story of an apostate novice and described how 'when he died so great a wind blew up around the house and so vast a flock of rooks gathered on the roof that, except for one old woman, everyone in the house was terrified and ran away, abandoning the dying man…That blast of wind and flock of croaking rooks were plain signs of the presence of demons', concluded the Cistercian.[148] In the same way Gerald's dream companions were struck by horror and fled, sensing that 'unclean things' were haunting the place.

The dream has more literal implications, too. The four tapers, two of which are knocked over by the birds, two of which fell of their own accord, presumably symbolize Henry's four sons, two of whom died in his lifetime, two of

whom reigned after him and (it could be said) brought down their own ruin
on their head. The images are multivalent. The tapers falling to the ground of
their own accord stir up deep anxieties about inanimate objects coming to life
while representing, simultaneously, a political symbol of the Angevins. Henry's
corpse, alone—unless beset by demons—and abandoned, stirs the human fear
of the dead as well as indicating Henry's actual miserable death and the deser-
tion of his own men.

By employing prophecies and dark dream images of this kind, Gerald made
the De Principis Instructione something much more than a straightforward
criticism of Henry's reign. If it is not useful as a guide to interpretation of the
political events of the 1180s, it is, nevertheless, a powerful dramatic construction.

ANGEVINS AND CAPETIANS

The drama of the De Principis Instructione is not, however, simply the rise and
fall of Henry II. It also has a wider canvas—the destinies of the royal dynasties
of England and France. In Book III Gerald developed and emphasized the
contrast he had already established in the earlier books between the divinely
favoured 'natural princes' of France and the tyrannical kings of England. Gerald
generalized his point beyond the single example of Henry II to assert that the
whole line of Norman and Angevin kings who had ruled England since 1066
were rapacious tyrants, whereas the Capetians, Louis VII, Philip Augustus, and
his son and heir, Louis, were presented as mild and pious rulers.

Gerald regarded Henry II's stock as tainted, and related the famous story of
Angevin descent from a 'demon countess'.[149] This legend was well known in the
twelfth century, and Gerald recorded that St. Bernard, the Patriarch Heraclius,
and Richard I himself referred to it.[150] 'Since the root was so completely corrupt,' Gerald asked, 'how can fruitful or virtuous offspring come from it?'[151]
The fratricidal and patricidal fury of the Angevins was their inheritance and
their nature.[152] Geoffrey of Anjou, Henry II's father, had been guilty of sexual
crimes, and had persecuted Gerard, Bishop of Séez, in a way that paralleled
Henry's persecution of Becket;[153] Henry's mother, Matilda, had been guilty of
bigamy.[154] The Angevin poison was made even stronger by admixture with the
venomous blood of the house of Aquitaine. Eleanor, herself descended from an
immoral union, had scandalous sexual relations with Geoffrey of Anjou while
she was still married to Louis VII, and then proceeded to leave her husband
for Geoffrey's son Henry.[155]

Gerald couched these accusations in terms of family. In the twelfth century,
when consciousness of family was powerful and universal, attacks upon dynasties, as well as expressions of dynastic pride, used the language of blood and
descent. It was convincing to explain the wicked behaviour of individuals in

terms of their tainted blood, the innate viciousness of family stock. Gerald
advanced such explanations on other occasions, too, such as when involved
in his bitter quarrel with his nephew, Gerald junior, son of his brother Philip,
when he explained his nephew's perverse and wicked behaviour by attributing
it to his maternal family, the Baskervilles. He talked of the 'perverse Baskerville
nature',[156] *diabolicum genus illud*,[157] and had a simple explanatory model for trac-
ing behaviour to blood: 'Your perverse cousin is sarcastic and scornful. Why?
Because he is a Baskerville.'[158]

If wicked behaviour was seen in terms of family, it was reasonable to see
the punishment of such behaviour in similar terms. Dissension among the
Angevins, as already mentioned, was seen as a consequence of flaws in their
ancestry. More serious, childlessness (the worst disaster which could strike a
family, in Gerald's view) could be visited as a punishment upon those who
broke God's laws. Gerald wrote of Eleanor of Aquitaine's sons, 'Great hope was
placed in them in the flower, but they withered before the fruit.'[159] Two of her
daughters had unhappy ends, one dying childless. In fact, the Angevin family
tree does not show any striking demographic aberrations; Gerald's comments
illustrate, rather, the tendency to expect family disaster in a *diabolicum genus*.
Gerald thought, for example, that the childlessness of many of the first Norman
invaders of Ireland must have been a consequence of divine displeasure.[160]

The flaws in the ruling house of England and the disasters which flowed from
them went back to the Norman Conquest. Gerald was proud of his Norman
descent and despised the native English,[161] but his hostility to the ruling dynasty
led him to decry the Conquest and idolize the last of the Saxon rulers.[162] 'It
is well known', he wrote,

> how the Norman tyrants ruled in the island, not naturally or legitimately,
> but through an inversion of order (quasi per hysteron proteron). Because
> of this few or any of them died a praiseworthy death. The brothers of both
> Henry I and Henry II died miserably before they had lived out half their
> days... None of the Norman kings, six or seven of whom have passed up to
> our time, have ended their lives with a praiseworthy death.[163]

The king whom Gerald selected to epitomize this Norman tyranny at its
worst was William Rufus. Rufus's hard policy towards the Church had left
its mark on the chronicle record, and the historical tradition was invariably
hostile to him. Gerald introduced the figure of Rufus in the last few chapters
of the De Principis Instructione as a dramatic figure who adumbrated many
of the features of Henry II and his son, showing that their tyranny was in the
tradition of kings of England. Rufus foreshadowed Richard I in his vainglori-
ous boasting[164] and in his death, shot down by an arrow.[165] Like Henry II, he
had forced into exile an archbishop of Canterbury who desired to protect

ecclesiastical freedom.[166] His brutal extensions of the Royal Forest[167] were similar to those of the Angevins which the Charter of the Forest tried to curb. Rufus was an enemy of God's Church and had tried to convert monastic lands into military fiefs.[168]

The parallel to the arrow in the New Forest was the cross-bow bolt at Châlus which killed King Richard, but the visions and dreams surrounding Rufus's last days remind us more of those that prophesied Henry II's end. The King's dream of wanting to hack up and eat a naked man spread on the altar of a desolate church[169] has the same sinister, violent tone noticed in the dreams about Henry II. The visionary warning Rufus received and the way he ignored it[170] are reminiscent of the many similar warnings sent to Henry II. The very same words were used of both Rufus and Henry when talking of God's mercy in sending them warnings: 'He desires the conversion of a sinner, not his downfall.'[171]

In every direction the antecedents of the Angevin kings were inauspicious. The house of Anjou itself, the Aquitanian dynasty which produced Eleanor, and the Norman kings who had preceded the Angevins on the throne were stained with violence, oppression, sexual crime, and bad blood. In this hideous, blood-stained world, Gerald looked for hope to 'the milder and gentler kings'[172] of France.

His elevation of the Capetians was the counterpart to his denunciation of the Angevins. His loathing for the 'insular tyranny' of the English kings contrasted with a vigorous Francophilia. He compared French laws favourably with English ones,[173] admired 'the good practices of the French Church'[174] and exhorted the young King of Scots to 'behave towards God's ministers and ecclesiastical rights in conformity with the practice of the natural and praiseworthy kings' of France.[175]

Gerald was not alone among twelfth-century English writers in his Francophilia.[176] John of Salisbury wrote a memorable description of the joy and relief he felt on arrival in Paris,[177] and Walter Map recorded stories that presented the Capetians in a favourable light.[178] This attitude had many sources. Gerald, John, and Walter Map were all students in Paris, and these formative experiences seem to have left a warm memory. At this time Paris was clearly more exciting as a place of learning than anywhere in England, and Gerald had wished to return there to study after his retirement from court (although circumstances prevented him).[179] For men who placed a high value on letters and learning Paris had a natural magnetism.

In addition to the intellectual pre-eminence of Paris, ecclesiastics, especially those of a 'high clerical' bent, saw the Capetian domain as both a model and a refuge. It was a model since the Capetians maintained good relations both with the papacy and with their own prelates, having a lightness of touch in their ecclesiastical dealings that the Angevins could not match. They were

favoured sons of the Church, who also provided a very convenient refuge for
ecclesiastical opponents of the Angevins. Becket was the most famous example,
but many other ecclesiastics, in the 1160s and at other times, sought refuge in
France. It suited the Capetians very well to give aid to the opponents of the
Angevins at the same time as winning a favourable reputation as defenders
of the Church.

In the later twelfth century France was a centre of wealth, art, and learning,
where chivalry was cultivated and ecclesiastical status was high, where royal
rule was just and blessed. Gerald's version of the theory of 'transfer of empire'
(translatio imperii) and 'transfer of learning' (translatio studii) saw military
and cultural prowess moving together from east to west and culminating in
Capetian France: 'It is noteworthy that the study of philosophy and the study of
arms always accompany one another, as in Greece under Alexander, in Rome
under the Caesars and now, for a long time, in France under the Carolingians
and their royal descendants up to the present.'[180] The Capetians, enhanced by
their Carolingian connections, were the Alexanders and Caesars of Gerald's
own time. Gerald praised them extravagantly both for their personal virtue
and piety and for their abilities as good rulers. Unlike the English kings, they
were sexually virtuous, avoided blasphemous oaths, and showed, generally, a
mild and simple manner.[181] Their court ceremonial was straightforward, they
were accessible to their subjects, and dealt out prompt and free justice.[182] While
the line of the kings of England was constantly broken and twisted by violent
deaths and usurpations, the Capetian succession was a peaceable one, passing
from father to son.[183] They were 'natural princes':

> They always acquire the royal patrimony through hereditary succession
> and natural right. They zealously preserve moderation, modesty, and mercy
> towards their subjects and avoid any atrocity or cruelty in the rule. As a
> result their reigns are long, prosperous, and tranquil, by command of God,
> who often rewards merit even on earth. Their honour increases day by day
> and, at last, as they end their life below, they die a blessed death and receive
> eternal reward in heaven for such just and pious rule, leaving their realm
> happily to their sons and heirs.[184]

This idyllic picture was reinforced at every point by contrast with the Angevins.
While the Capetians commanded willing subjects, the Angevins could inspire
no loyalty or love.[185] In fact, the essence of the contrast was that the French
were free and the English were not. The fall of Normandy, for example, was
due to the fact that the once proud Norman nobles had been oppressed by
the tyranny of the English kings. 'How could the necks of the nobility, pressed
under the cruel heel of tyranny, arise to resist the free arms and fierce spirits of
the French?'[186] Just as in the case of the Welsh,[187] it is the joyfulness of liberty

(libertatis hilaritas) which makes a people free, admirable, and strong. But the Angevin realm was characterized by its opposite, the oppressiveness of servitude (servitutis oppressio).

Gerald's animosity towards the Angevins and idealization of the French royalty eventually reached its natural climax, the desire to see England under French rule. In 1216-17, the years immediately preceding the completion of the De Principis Instructione, such an event seemed very likely. In 1216 the rebel barons invited Prince Louis of France to come to England to help them in their war against John, and the Capetian heir occupied London and made war throughout the kingdom, until defeats at Lincoln (May 1217) and Sandwich (August 1217) led to his withdrawal from England (Treaty of Lambeth, September 1217). During this period Gerald was very hopeful, and placed himself firmly in Louis's camp.

In his eyes Louis's expedition of 1216-17 was the climax of the Capetian destiny. The rapid rise of the dynasty during Gerald's lifetime showed that it had been specially favoured by God. Just as visions and prophecies cast a dark shadow over Henry II's downfall and death, so visions, prophetic utterances, and good omens foretold Philip Augustus's glory.[188] Inspired by divine grace, Philip had brought his kingdom to a peak of honour and expanded its boundaries to an extent that had not been paralleled from the time of Charlemagne.[189]

Gerald clearly hoped that the triumphs of the Capetians would continue until England, or even the whole of the British Isles, was under their rule. In this respect he was not acting as a mouthpiece for the Marchers, the feudal grouping with whom one would naturally associate him, for they were almost entirely loyal to John in 1214-16. Gerald was responding to the political situation in a way that could have been predicted from his bitterness towards the Angevins and his admiration for the French and their kings. He probably had few important political connections and little influence at this time, and his comments are not so much representative of the rebel barons as illustrative, in a general way, of the hostility which the Angevins could generate and which, in certain circumstances, could lead to armed resistance.

A political poem Gerald wrote at this time survives and reinforces the impression gathered from the De Principis Instructione.[190] The poem is a celebration of Louis's arrival in England, a eulogy of France, and a political statement, animated by a strong concern about the estrangement between the papacy and the Capetians which Louis's expedition had precipitated. It was probably composed in the second half of 1216, about the time the De Principis Instructione was taking its final shape.

'It has rained the whole night', it begins. 'In the morning sights return. The pleasant day knows no cloud or mists.'[191] This theme of stormy times and the return of good weather, as symbols for political troubles and deliverance, is also

found in the De Principis Instructione.[192] The Angevin tyranny had been a time
of threatening clouds and stormy weather; Louis's arrival was a *dies serenus*,[193]
a *lux nova*.[194] The poem celebrates deliverance: 'The madness of slavery now
ends; times of liberty are granted; English necks are freed from the yoke.'[195]
It praises the Capetians and even compares Prince Louis to St. Augustine of
Canterbury. Both had landed at Thanet when arriving in England: 'From this
place freedom was given to bodies and to souls... Happy the place on whose
shore both bringers of such great good first landed. One frees souls, the other
bodies. Let the English, free from both yokes, be grateful to both of them.'[196]
Nor, of course, did Gerald omit to mention that Thanet had been Becket's
landing-place in 1170. The identification of the internal clerical opposition and
the external dynastic opposition, so assiduously cultivated by the Capetians,
was complete.

The poem is also a eulogy of 'France, flower of the world'.[197] Gerald
recounted the triumphs of French arms, and envisaged further victories against
the Saracens. He painted his familiar warm picture of France: 'Here the people
rejoice, the clergy rejoice in honour. Here the arts of war and learning flourish.
Here are just laws and a prince who rules piously, scarcely wishing to punish,
and grieving to be cruel.'[198] The justice of French laws, the mildness of the
Capetians, and the symbiosis of martial and cultural achievement are all recurrent themes of the De Principis Instructione.

Yet the poem is not simply a complacent celebration. It is also written as
an appeal to the papacy not to discountenance Louis's enterprise. After John's
reconciliation with the papacy and his surrender of England as a papal fief
in 1213, Innocent III had been a consistent supporter of the King. He had
condemned Magna Carta and suspended Langton for his lukewarmness in
excommunicating the rebels. In May 1216 the papal legate Gualo had excommunicated Prince Louis and his followers. Gerald was aghast at this disturbing
and, to his mind, perverse alliance: 'Rome strives for this goal: that the bride
of Christ should serve tyrants and that slaves should press down free necks. But
the French engage their arms and hands to drive away the tears of the clergy
and the sorrows of the people with their weapons.'[199] It seemed particularly
distressing to him since he conceived of the relationship between the French
and the papacy as a 'natural alliance'. The French had supported and restored
the papacy when it was expelled from Rome and despoiled; now let the Pope
show his gratitude by dealing gently with Louis. 'It will be through the French
that Peter's boat will rise again and pristine joys return to Mount Zion.'[200]

This vision of the French as the 'chosen people'[201] disturbed as it was by
Innocent III's opposition to Louis's expedition, sustained Gerald in the last
few years of John's reign. He hoped for a union of France and the British Isles
under the Capetians.[202] The union would have served 'to increase the Worship
of God'.[203] (The argument here is a curious inversion of that which justified

the Anglo-Norman invasion of Ireland.) John, the worst tyrant of all,[204] might be replaced by just princes.

The De Principis Instructione was probably completed while Louis was in England. Gerald said that, if the work were to be dedicated to anyone, it would be dedicated to him.[205] He praised Louis's conduct in England,[206] and there are many glimpses of the hopes which inspired him at this time. But these hopes were clearly fading. There are passages in the work which acknowledge Louis's failure and must date from after the defeats of Lincoln and Sandwich, if not from after the Prince's withdrawal from England.[207] Yet the civil war was still in progress when Gerald finished the book.[208] The failure of Louis's attempt on the crown was evident, but the ultimate course of events was not clear.

Gerald, naturally, had a supply of reasons to assign and blame to apportion when discussing Louis's failure. The baronage had not resisted John during the Interdict when they would have had papal support, but had waited until afterwards, when the King was strengthened by his good relations with Innocent.[209] The French had plundered churches and offended God.[210] But he did not intend the De Principis Instructione to be a chronicle of John's reign. He recorded these events because they were going on all around him at the time he was writing [211] and, more importantly, because they seemed to be the climax of the long drama of Angevin tyranny and Capetian justice. The crisis of 1216-17 seemed, to him as to modern historians,[212] a product and a commentary on 'Angevin kingship'.

The closing pages of the De Principis Instructione tell of failed hopes. The Capetians, that 'happy line of fortunate and natural kings', had triumphed over 'the tyrannical whelp', King John. A new dawn had appeared to be breaking after the 'cloudy times' of tyranny: 'it was hoped and anticipated that these western regions, oppressed for so long under insular tyranny and the insufferable yoke of servitude, would see at last complete liberation and liberty', but, because of God's wrath at the plundering of churches, 'the hope could not be fulfilled'.[213]

Spes ad effectum provenire non potuit. This phrase could stand as the motto of Gerald's life. Throughout his career, his political and ecclesiastical ambitions were frustrated. As a spokesman for the Marchers he had to record, along with their triumphs, their frustration by royal policy. As a champion of St. David's and claimant to an archbishopric he had to face the defeat of his cause and disillusion with the Welsh. As a critic of the Angevins who placed his hope in Capetian rule he witnessed the defeat of Louis's invasion and ended his days in the reign of John's son, placed firmly on the English throne under papal protection. Disappointment was Gerald's constant companion.

Gerald's last recourse, amid the failure, frustration, and bitterness of his active life, was to turn to posterity. Even if his political and ecclesiastical hopes had remained unfulfilled, he had the compensation of his literary labours. He had produced a large and impressive corpus of writings, which future generations would know how to appreciate:

> Care for posterity drove me to choose literary activity. Because this present life is momentary and transitory, it delights to live in future memory at least and to be honoured by the distinction of praise and perpetual tokens of fame. It is an indication of a distinguished mind to strive to produce work which, although it brings envy in this life, brings glory after death. What authors aspire to is something everlasting...[214]

This hope, at least, did not go entirely unfulfilled.

PART II

THE NATURAL
AND THE
SUPERNATURAL

INTRODUCTION

Gerald completed the first version of his Topographia Hibernica in 1187 or 1188. Shortly afterwards he gave a public recitation of it at Oxford. The brief introduction which he composed for that occasion included a description of the arrangement of the work. It was in three parts: the first contained an account of the site of Ireland, the various properties of the land, its fish, birds, and beasts; the second described the marvels and miracles of Ireland; the third comprised the history of the Irish people and a description of their customs and ways of life.[1]

The first two categories that Gerald mentioned, natural history and marvels and miracles, must be taken together, since the first category represented the works of nature, while the second category comprised things that were, in a sense, *contra naturam* (contrary to nature). The natural and marvels and miracles were defined and identified in relation to each other.

Many scholars have seen the twelfth century as a period when 'a new naturalism' came into being, as a time of 'the discovery of nature'. Historians of science and of art, historians of theology, historians, too, describing institutions and law, have been willing to talk of twelfth-century 'naturalism'.[2] It is in the context of this 'naturalism' that Gerald's observations on the natural, the marvellous and the miraculous will be discussed.

MIRACLES AND MARVELS

'THINGS CONTRARY TO NATURE'

It is perhaps useful to approach Gerald's views of the natural indirectly, from the vantage-point of his views on those things that were contra naturam. This phrase covered both miracles and marvels.

A very large part of Gerald's work consists of stories of the miraculous. The latter half of Book II of the Topographia Hibernica is a collection of miracle stories. The Gemma Ecclesiastica is a mosaic of miraculous exempla. Every work of his gives some instance of miracles, omens, the activities of demons, warning dreams, or malevolent magic. For Gerald, these things were part of the texture of the world. They were a special part, it is true, but not a surprising one. The matter-of-fact quality of his accounts of conversations with demons[1] or of some vindictive miracle[2] suggests the literalness with which he accepted such events as real, non-problematical phenomena. The miraculous represented not a rare occurrence but an almost daily incursion into the world of men.

Of course, Gerald was in no way extraordinary in this attitude. Whereas different writers of the time might place different stress upon the miraculous, none rejected the possibility of direct divine or demonic irruption. There was, moreover, a deep predisposition to accept miracles, a wish, even, to believe in them. Walter Map has an interesting story of how a crowd brought a demoniac to the saintly Peter, Archbishop of Tarentaise, to be cured. At the head of the crowd was John, Bishop of Poitiers. He explained to Map, 'On several occasions I have seen fancies or pretences where they proclaim they have witnessed a miracle and I have always perceived the illusion; nor have I ever seen a true miracle.' When Peter cured the man, the Bishop was overjoyed.[3] The fact that he had seen through false miracles did not make him sceptical; it rather increased his desire to witness a true miracle.

There was virtually no scepticism about the miraculous as such, although particular miracles might be discounted on partisan grounds. Gerald told the story of a Jew who mocked the miracles of St. Frideswide at Oxford, whose recent translation had provoked a spate of miraculous cures. The Jew tied his arm to his side or bound up his legs with a length of rope and then, bursting out of his bonds, cried, 'A miracle! A miracle!' He had mocked the credulity of those who came to be cured: 'Behold the kind of miracle St. Frideswide works!'⁴ This, of course, is the special case of non-Christian scepticism. As Gerald adds, divine retribution was not far behind as, driven by God, the Jew straightaway went and hanged himself with the same length of rope he had used in his mockeries.⁵ Map's anti-Cistercian feelings led him to cast doubts on St. Bernard's miraculous powers,⁶ but this satire occurs in a book of credited miracle tales. As in the case of wartime atrocity stories, one could defend or attack the validity of particular accounts from a partisan position without putting into question the basic framework.

It was also generally thought that the natural world had a tendency to produce striking novelties and anomalies. Despite the development in the twelfth century of a stronger sense of nature's order, it remained an order shot through with curious and inexplicable exceptions—marvels.

While explaining the structure of his Topographia Hibernica, in his introduction to that work, Gerald drew a distinction between marvels and miracles. 'Part II', he wrote, 'describes the prodigious works of playful nature… It also praises the saints, glorious with exceptional powers and declared in extraordinary miracles.'⁷ This distinction was repeated at the beginning of Part II itself:

> Now let us turn our pen to things which occur contrary to the course of nature and are worthy of wonder. I have not thought it irrelevant to narrate some things which are wonderful in themselves and striking in their novelty, and which nature has placed in these ends of the earth; and also some things done in an extraordinary way and truly miraculously, through the merits of the saints.⁸

Gerald maintained this distinction in the actual contents of Part II. The first twenty-seven chapters deal with such subjects as irregularities of the tides, the strange properties of certain islands, petrifying wells, wood which does not float, huge fish, and the strange lands of the Far North. Then our attention is drawn to the transition to his next category: 'Now let us turn to miracles.'⁹

The crucial distinction in Gerald's mind between a marvel and a miracle was that the miracle was produced by divine power, usually, though not exclusively, working through a saintly man or woman, while the marvel, however remarkable it might be, was a work of nature.

The ascription of miracles to the divine power, through the instrumentality of the saints, is clear from the language Gerald employed. When, for example, St. Nannan freed a village in Connaught from a plague of fleas, it was 'the divine power' which 'cleansed that place, through the merit of the saint'.¹⁰ The protection accorded to wild animals in certain sanctified places showed 'the wonderful power of God, through the merits of the saints'.¹¹ The component elements which went to make up a miracle are well exemplified in a story from Gerald's Itinerarium Kambriae.¹² The Cistercian abbey of Margam in

South Wales was renowned for its charity to the poor and to pilgrims. One year, when famine was pressing and large crowds of the poor gathered at the abbey door, the monks sent a ship to Bristol to fetch grain. However, it was delayed by contrary winds, and it seemed that both paupers and monks would have to go hungry. They were saved by a miracle.

> It happened that a field near the monastery was suddenly found, to the amazement of many, to be ripe, a month and more before the common time of ripening and before any crop in the country ripened. Thus the Divine Mercy provided sufficient food until autumn for both the brothers and the crowds of the poor. Therefore, by this and other powerful signs, the abbey came to be loved and revered by all as a place acceptable to God.

We can distinguish in this account four elements which went to make up the miracle. Firstly, something objectively extraordinary had occurred. It can be called 'objectively extraordinary' since it was measured against the normal course of events, against demonstrable regularities. The field ripened 'before any crop in the country ripened' and 'before the common time of ripening'. Secondly, intimately bound up with this first point, was the subjective element, 'the amazement of many'. A third element was the direct dependence of the event upon God: it was 'the Divine Mercy' which 'provided sufficient food'. This distinguished true miracles from magical or demonic wonders. Lastly, the miracle was a sign, pointing to the special acceptability of the monks of Margam. It revealed their merits as much as it provided relief for the hungry.[13]

Some of the characteristics of miracles can also be seen in marvels. Clearly, the subjective element was common to both. The extraordinary, whatever its nature, was *mirum*, that is, it excited wonder in human onlookers by its rareness and unexpectedness. In a sense, too, marvels were exceptions to demonstrable regularities; they were objectively extraordinary—but in a rather different way. Their origin, their cause, was different. This is strikingly illustrated by the words Gerald used to describe the leaping of salmon, which he had probably witnessed himself in Irish and Welsh rivers. Their ability to leap up waterfalls amazed him. 'They are carried up', he wrote, 'by a marvellous leap, which would be miraculous if it were not that the property of the fish requires it. For this kind of fish strives to leap from nature.'[14] He clearly believed that what followed from the 'property' (proprietas) of the fish, however amazing, could not be miraculous. The marvellous belonged, in fact, to the world of creatures following their own nature. Although marvels were natural, however, they were extraordinary in so far as they were exceptions to the usual course of nature. The sub-group 'salmon' had a different proprietas from the group 'fish', in which it was included.

The same point can be illustrated very explicitly from Gerald's account of a forest in France, where half the trees produced wood that did not float, while the other trees had normal wood. The heavy wood, he wrote, 'sinks to the bottom of the river like a stone and with the weight of a stone, through a certain hidden, but innate heaviness, quite alien to the nature of wood'. The other trees 'preserve the common nature of woody lightness'. Gerald held up for admiration 'such an unnatural heaviness of light things' and 'such great variety in a little space'.[15] Here again the wonder consisted of the fact that the property or nature[16] of the sub-group differed from the property or nature of the group in which it was included. Yet, again, the property is natural; it is called 'innate'.

Although Gerald did make this explicit distinction between marvels and miracles, there are times when the qualities which the two kinds of event had in common seem more important than the differences. The qualities usually proper to miracles might be ascribed to marvels, suggesting that a nebulous category existed in Gerald's mind, prior to the theoretical distinction between divine and natural.

For instance, both marvels and miracles might have the function of signs. In the twelfth century (as in earlier centuries) many occurrences in the natural world were read as signs. They were not seen simply as the automatic consequences of autonomous natural processes; they had significance. Thus an extraordinary event would be read for its message. Consequently, the role of 'accident' was relatively small, comparable, in some ways, to that found by anthropologists in the thought-systems of some primitive peoples, for whom all misfortunes indicate malevolent will and nothing 'just happens'. For the medieval thinker the physical world was suffused with meaning—moral, symbolic, or predictive. The distinction between a social, human realm, in which meaning, motive, and intention are relevant categories, and a physical world, in which they are not, was not sharply drawn.

Sometimes the very lack of precision with which prodigies were interpreted reveals a predisposition to interpret the natural world as a bearer of messages. Gerald, for example, after telling how a knight in Breconshire had vented a calf, added: 'this manifested a portent of some new and unusual future event or, rather, angry vengeance for an abominable crime'.[17] Although uncertain as to whether the event was an omen or a punishment, Gerald saw it as having a meaning. He sought to explain it in terms of its significance, not in terms of antecedent causation.

An even more striking example of the cloudy twilight from which both miracles and marvels emerged is provided by a story in the Itinerarium Kambriae. Gerald told how Einon ap Rhys, a Welsh chieftain, had gone out hunting, and one of his archers had shot a doe. Apparently,

The doe, contrary to the nature of her sex, was found to have twelve-branched antlers and, moreover, in her tail and elsewhere she was fatter than a stag. Because of the novelty of such a great prodigy, the monster's head and horns were sent to Henry, King of the English. Something else also occurred worthy of great wonder. The man who shot the beast, by what fate or misfortune it is not known, was struck by a sudden disease and immediately lost the sight in his right eye. In the same hour he was afflicted by paralysis, and he remained weak and incapable until his death.[18]

This reads strangely like an account of a vindictive miracle from any number of contemporary miracle collections. Blindness and paralysis were punishments commonly inflicted on those who committed sacrilege or mocked the saints. Gerald himself had just told how the Lord of Radnor went blind after kennelling his dogs in a church.[19]

This horned doe was not, of course, a sacrosanct animal. It was not connected with the protective power of any saint. It was simply extraordinary, and the story seems to indicate that the extraordinary possessed unknown powers which it was dangerous to meddle with. An aura of numinousness surrounded whatever was unusual. Prior to the distinction between saintly miracles and natural marvels, there existed the category of the odd, the uncanny, the perilous.

GERALD, AUGUSTINE, AND THE MIRACULOUS

There are two passages in Gerald's Irish works which contain general statements about the miraculous and marvellous. These are the introduction to Book II of the Topographia Hibernica[20] and the preface to the Expugnatio Hibernica.[21] The former passage, as has already been mentioned, explained that the subject of Book II—'things which occur contrary to the course of nature and are worthy of wonder'—could be divided into two categories, miracles and marvels. It then went on to advance a justification against the charge that many people would regard these wonders as 'impossibilities':

It is not surprising if marvellous things should be discovered, reported and written about the works of him who made all things as he wished; for him nothing is impossible; being lord of nature, he changes nature however he wishes and, as it were, makes nature from non-nature. Besides, how can it truly be said that anything happens against the first, true nature, which is God, when it is agreed that it is accomplished with him as its author. 'Contrary to nature' is therefore a customary rather than an exact expression to describe that which occurs contrary, not to nature's power, but to her frequency.[22]

The passage from the Expugnatio Hibernica, like this one from the Topographia Hibernica, is concerned to defend the truth of the wonder-stories in the earlier work. The Bible and the Fathers, Gerald wrote, describe many marvels—would his critics wish to condemn them too?[23] He appealed again to God's omnipotence to argue that nature's regularities were not absolutely binding: 'In nothing can nature prevail against the lord of nature.'[24] Augustine's discussion of wonders in Book XXI of the Civitas Dei was heavily mined for supporting quotations:

> How can an event be contrary to nature when it happens by the will of God, since the will of the great creator assuredly is the nature of every created thing? A portent, therefore, does not occur contrary to nature, but contrary to what is known of nature.[25]

> So, just as it was not impossible for God to set in being natures according to his will, so it is afterwards not impossible for him to change those natures which he has set in being, in any way he chooses.[26]

Gerald's deployment of extensive quotation from St. Augustine is simply the most visible part of his debt. Augustine's thinking and language about miracles, marvels, and nature deeply influenced Gerald's position on these subjects. This is clear if the passages from the Irish works quoted above are compared with Book XXI of the Civitas Dei. Of course, Augustine's purpose was much broader. He was attempting to defend the miracles of biblical and Christian tradition against the scepticism of pagans trained in ancient physical theory. Gerald's brief was the slighter one of vindicating his own improbable tales. Yet both men were led to arguments of a formally similar kind. Both asserted that the observation of natural regularities in the world did not disprove the possibility of other phenomena, which might appear to be exceptions to those regularities: the world contained much that was outside the usual patterns noticed by men.

Neither Augustine nor Gerald refused to admit the existence of natural regularities. Their strong assertion of God's omnipotence and the limits of human knowledge did not lead them to dissolve the very idea of 'the natural'. This extreme position was not unknown: Tertullian, for example, stressed God's power and his freedom to suspend the regularities of the created universe[27] and, in the eleventh century, Manegold of Lautenbach attacked the desire to seek regularities in nature on the grounds that God's repeated interventions meant that virtually no regular natural order existed. 'Nature's custom', he wrote, 'has been overcome so often that she can now have little confidence in herself.'[28] The consequence of this view was that every event was directly dependent on God's will in an unmediated way, and so there was no philosophical distinction to be drawn between miraculous and non-miraculous occurrences. In a sense, every event was a miracle; hence Manegold's position has been called 'miraculist'.[29]

This extreme position was not common, for it conflicted with the concept of natural regularity which was part of the intellectual equipment of most educated men, in medieval as in ancient times. Even at a banal level, the concept *natura* 'explained' why bean seeds produced beans and grain seeds grain.[30] A man committed only to achieving spiritual perfection, who saw the world and its learning as irrelevant or worse, might dispense with the concept of nature, but most writers and thinkers tried to integrate it into a religious framework rather than dismiss it. In this they were encouraged by the biblical vision of orderliness in the universe—'By measure and number and weight didst thou order all things' (Wisdom 11:20) was a favourite quotation of Augustine's.

When thinkers like Augustine in the fifth century or Gerald in the twelfth committed themselves to the defence both of the idea of a regular nature and of marvellous or miraculous anomalies, they encountered problems. One difficulty was God's apparent inconsistency in breaking his own order.[31] Here the pervasive parallelism between medieval social theory and medieval physical theory had some influence. Nature had her own 'custom' (consuetudo) and if God, the 'lord of nature' (dominus naturae), infringed this custom, he would be perpetrating 'an injustice against nature' (iniuria naturae). The experience of custom, protecting inferiors against the arbitrariness of lords, thus charged the terms of the debate on the constitution of the natural world.

Marvels and miracles could both be described as, in a sense, *contra naturam*, 'contrary to nature'. Here too were pitfalls. Few Christian writers were willing to describe any of God's actions as *contra naturam*. The impulse to avoid the phrase was as much emotive as intellectual. Nature was a normative concept, not simply descriptive. The natural state was a healthy or desirable state, so what was 'contrary to nature' was monstrous or immoral. The Vulgate, for example, described sodomy as *contra naturam* (Romans 1:26). The extremely negative connotations of the phrase thus created difficulties for Christian writers dealing with the subject of miracles.

Origen provides a good example:

The proposition that God does not will anything contrary to nature has to be broken down. If the phrase refers to wickedness, we deny that God wills anything contrary to nature, evil things, things contrary to reason; but if, however, whatever is done by God's counsel and will is necessarily said to be not contrary to nature, then whatever God does, however incredible or however incredible it may seem to some, is, nevertheless, not contrary to nature.[32]

It seems here as if Origen, by rejecting with outrage the idea that any of God's actions might be contrary to nature, has lost the distinction between the natural, on the one hand, and special divine provisions and interventions on the other. He retrieved this useful distinction, however, by introducing a new phrase: 'If we may strain our terms, we may say that certain things which God can do are above nature.' Origen's distinction between things contrary to nature, which are disorderly or wicked, and things above nature, representing God's grace and special interventions, was maintained by the Fathers and marked an important step in the development of the concept of the 'supernatural'.[33]

Augustine showed a similar unease in using the phrase *contra naturam* of God's actions. He wrote, 'God, the creator and founder of all natures, does nothing contrary to nature; what will be natural to each thing is what he made; every mode, number, and order of nature is from him.'[34] This insistence that all God's actions are natural since he is the source of nature could be put even more strongly: 'God does nothing in any way against the highest law of nature... any more than he does anything against himself.'[35] The tradition of apotheosizing nature by equating it with God's will had Stoic and neo-platonic roots. In this sense nothing was contrary to nature. Arguments of this kind recurred in the writings of many medieval thinkers. John of Salisbury, discussing portents, wrote that 'If we follow Plato, who asserts that nature is the will of God, none of these things actually happens contrary to nature, since he made what ever he wanted... and, indeed, God's wisdom and goodness, which is the cause of the origin of everything, is termed "nature" most justly; nothing occurs contrary to this.'[36] When Gerald equated God with 'the first, true nature' and wrote that 'being lord of nature, he changes nature however he wishes', he was firmly in this tradition.

However, the argument that God does nothing contrary to nature, since, in some sense, he is nature, has unsatisfactory consequences. While it meant that his actions were now free of the negatively charged term *contra naturam*, this was achieved only at the cost of a certain vacuousness; To say that everything happens because God wills or allows it to happen, while it stresses God's power and points out the flimsiness of human conceptions of natural order, also breaks down any useful distinction between the natural and the miraculous. For the purposes of philosophical differentiation, the idea is fruitless.[37]

A more constructive approach to the problem of reconciling natural order and divine intervention was to redefine nature as 'the usual course of nature'. In this way, at least the idea of a realm of natural regularities could be established; events which occurred *contra naturam* happened outside this realm. Gerald was in line with this in describing marvels as 'contrary not to nature's power but to her frequency'. In this way the patterns and order of nature could be acknowledged without excluding the possibility of the marvellous.

Here, too, Gerald was influenced by Augustine. But it is important to notice the specific kind of contribution which Augustine made to his thought. At the time there were as many 'Augustinianisms' as there were 'Platonisms' and, even in the restricted field of theories of miracle and nature, developments of Augustine's thought were taking place which Gerald would have found quite alien. These involved the scholastic refinement of an objective theory of miracle.

An objective and a subjective theory of miracle are distinguished by the status they accord the regularities of nature. For the objective view, they are laws or innate propensities of matter, whereas for the subjective view they are simply generalizations from human experience, and have no higher claim to predict the behaviour of the universe. Augustine has often been interpreted as having a subjective theory of miracle, and some of his writings bear this out: 'It is human practice to call something contrary to nature which is contrary to nature's usage as known to man... what is called contrary to nature is contrary to the custom of nature which human knowledge comprehends... for we term 'nature' the accustomed course of nature known to us; what God does contrary to this we call wonders or marvels.'[38] However, the alternative theory of miracle, which sought the objective characteristics of miraculous events, normally in a peculiarity in their causation, can also be found in Augustine. His use of the concept of seminales rationes demonstrates this.

The idea of the seminalis ratio was of Stoic ancestry. Seminales rationes explained the regularities of nature, for the seed inside each thing determined the direction in which it would develop. Besides resolving an exegetical dilemma of Augustine's,[39] the seminales rationes also played a role in demarcating the natural and the miraculous. Nature had her determining laws: her regularities stemmed from the seminales rationes implanted in things. Yet there were miracles distinct from this regular course. Augustine's explanation of the way miracles were differentiated with regard to their seminales rationes has been interpreted in two different ways. It is possible that he was making a contrast between a natural world whose development was governed by seminales rationes, and the transcendent power of God to intervene to change that nature.[40] Alternatively, it might be argued that he thought both natural and miraculous events arose from seminales rationes, but rationes of different kinds.[41]

In either case, the theory of seminales rationes makes an objective analysis of miracle possible too. If miracles are distinguished either as being produced by a particular kind of seminalis ratio or as not being produced by these rationes at all, then a miraculous event will be distinguished by the fact that it has a special kind of cause. This is the distinction that was elaborated by the scholastic thinkers of the twelfth and thirteenth centuries.

Peter Lombard, for example, distinguished the miraculous and the natural by distinguishing different kinds of cause. The Augustinian influence on him is clear from his language. Natural events arose from a 'seminal cause'; miracles had their cause in God alone.[42] Clarembald of Arras, writing at about the same time, used the same terms,[43] and in the following century Albertus Magnus elaborated the idea of the seminales rationes with great subtlety.[44] Augustine had thus provided the foundations for such scholastic developments. In the De Genesi ad Litteram he had written: 'This whole usual course of nature has its natural laws... the creature has determinate passions... the physical elements their definite power and quality.'[45] This idea of nature regulated by law-bound causal chains was the basic premiss of Aquinas's discussion of miracle. He asserted a distinction between 'an order of things depending on the First Cause' and 'an order of things depending on any secondary cause' (the natural world). In order to produce a miracle God can 'produce the effects of secondary causes without them or produce certain effects to which secondary causes do not extend'.[46] This picture of a natural world composed of causal chains, with miracles representing divine interventions in these chains, became a standard one.

It should be clear that Gerald's dependence on Augustine was very different from that of contemporary scholastics. They were attempting to draw out, to harmonize, and to refine the elements of an objective, causal theory of miracle which were to be found in Augustine's works. Gerald relied on Augustine's general religious reflections on miracle, not on his philosophical attempts to delineate the natural and the miraculous. He was faithful to the Augustinian tradition, but did not try to give it greater rigour or precision as scholastic writers did.[47]

The kind of Augustinian influence which Gerald's writing exhibits is demonstrated by several passages in the Topographia Hibernica. After describing the spontaneous generation of the barnacle goose from rotting wood, Gerald used this fact as an argument for the credibility of the Virgin Birth: 'Nature daily begets and produces new animals without any male or female as a demonstration of our faith, for our instruction'.[48] 'In order to instruct and strengthen us', Gerald wrote elsewhere, 'the Creator supports and confirms the more improbable articles of the approved faith by familiar examples from natural things.'[49] The appeal to natural marvels to support belief in miracles is very Augustinian. 'Why should not God have the power to make the bodies of the dead rise again,' we read in the Civitas Dei, 'and the bodies of the damned suffer torment in the everlasting fire, since he made the world so full of innumerable marvels...?'[50]

Both Gerald and Augustine regarded the source of wonder as rarity, but asserted that the world as a whole, in its normal courses, was really more wonderful than any individual marvel. 'Human nature is so composed', wrote Gerald, that it considers nothing valuable or wonderful except that which is unusual and happens rarely. There is nothing in the world more beautiful or more deserving of wonder than the rising and setting of the sun, but because we see it every day we pass it over without admiration. But the whole world is stunned by an eclipse of the sun because it happens so rarely.[51]

This is a truly Augustinian stress on the wonder of the world, epitomized in the following statement from the Civitas Dei: 'The world is beyond doubt a marvel greater and more wonderful than all the wonders with which it is filled.'[52] Such a position is more religious or contemplative than philosophical. It springs from admiration for God's creation, rather than an attempt to analyse intellectually the processes of the natural world and the characteristics of exceptions to those processes. To say that the world is wonderful is not to attempt a serious classification of it as a miracle. It is wonderful in another sense. It transcends and encompasses us; it is beautiful, infinitely complex, and beyond explanation. This emphasis on the marvellousness of all creation was linked to an awareness of the blinding effect of the habitual. For Augustine, novelty produced wonder, 'but things which come before our eyes in everyday experience are little reckoned of, not because they are less remarkable in nature but simply because of their continual occurrence'. Gerald incorporated these very words.[53]

The conception of nature which permeates Gerald's writing is not based on law-bound causal chains; nor is it the purely subjective one of observed regularities. Nature is, on the contrary, a vital force, a personification, with powers and whims. He wrote, 'For nature always and, as it were, intentionally, adorns her serious activity with certain novelties. In this way she clearly teaches and declares that, although her usual works can be considered by the human intellect, her potential effect cannot be grasped.'[54] Nature was 'playful nature'.[55] Talking of Irish marvels, Gerald wrote, 'Whenever nature, as if tired of her serious and true activity, gradually withdraws and retires, she amuses herself in these remote parts with, as it were, shameful and secret excesses.'[56] Gerald's 'nature' is the powerful personified force one finds in Bernard Silvester or Alanus ab Insulis, not John of Salisbury's 'sequence of causes'[57] or even Augustine's 'usual course of things as known to men'.

Gerald did not have a theory of nature and miracle in the sense that the scholastic thinkers did, but he did have a set of related concepts by which he categorized the events he encountered. God had created nature, and nature was a powerful force whose potentia and frequentia could be distinguished. Her frequentia represented the usual course of things, natural regularities. Yet she could also draw upon the reservoir of her potentia, or potentiality, to produce natural marvels. God, her creator, could also intervene directly in her workings to produce miracles.

MIRACLES AT WORK IN THE WORLD

In his scattered general observations, as in his actual accounts of miracles and marvels, Gerald was simultaneously more traditional than many of his contemporaries, because of his allegiance to the less technical side of Augustinianism, and yet, in his 'naturalism', his sense of the energy and fecundity of nature, completely a product of the twelfth century.

It would be one-sided, however, to discuss miracles as if they represented only a theoretical anomaly in the natural order. Gerald not only discussed the nature of the miraculous, but also showed miracles in their concrete physical and social setting. Miracles were not disembodied phenomena; they had as their matrix a cult object, and they left physical signs. The clearest example was the tomb of the saint, the holy man whose relics worked wonders. Gerald wrote saints' lives that describe posthumous miracles at the tomb, probably drawing upon records kept by custodians of the shrine.[58] But there were other embodiments of the miraculous too. In Ireland, Scotland, and Wales cult objects tended to be quasi-totemic, highly wrought artefacts which served as channels of supernatural power to the community. 'The people and clergy of Ireland, Scotland, and Wales', Gerald wrote, 'greatly reverence the hand-bells of the saints and their curving staffs which are covered with gold, silver, or bronze.'[59] He recorded various stories of the miraculous powers of these bells and staffs.[60] He also frequently ended his account of a miracle with a statement that the signs which are its witness 'are visible even today'. A Jew threw a stone at a crucifix in the Lateran; it bled healing blood; the wound and the dried blood could still be seen in the church.[61] A boy stealing from Llanfaes church stuck to a stone and when he was released the imprint of his fingers remained on it; the stone 'is preserved even today as if it were a relic'.[62] Blood-stains could still be seen on Quenred's Psalter where Queen Quenred's eyes fell as a punishment for perjury and murder.[63]

The signs that miracles were reported to have left are important as an illustration of the need for a visible focus for devotion, for a physical object which encapsulated both the past event and the present power. There was a complex nexus of supernatural events, the written record of them and the still supernaturally powerful objects which survived. The world was thus full of physical objects which acted as transmitters or witnesses of the miraculous.

Human social relations, too, were to some extent governed by prevalent beliefs about the supernatural, and the supernatural was often 'used' to regulate social behaviour. Miracles had economic importance, for example. As a general rule, they were associated with a particular saint and a particular church and the prestige thus accruing to the church and the income from pilgrims and devotees were obviously desirable for local clergy. St. Curig's crozier, for example, was thought to be able to cure tumours on payment of a penny and was thus, presumably, a useful source of income to St. Harmon's Church, Radnorshire, which possessed it.[64] Sometimes income from miracles was the subject of quarrels between churches. In Arras a host underwent a miraculous transformation: half of it appeared to be real flesh, the other half remaining bread, and the words of the sacrament could be read on it. This host was preserved in a parish church belonging to one of the cathedral canons, but 'as miracles multiplied there and offerings from the devotion of the faithful increased', the Bishop of Arras transferred it to his cathedral. The canon protested, and the case was eventually referred to the Pope, Alexander III, who appointed two bishops as judges-delegate to hear the case.[65] Clearly, the profit from miracles was not only spiritual.

The miraculous also played an important part in apologetics. Just as miracles demonstrated the sanctity of those through whom or for whom they were performed, so they could be used polemically against Jews, heretics, and unbelievers. As the Miracula Sanctae Frideswidae, composed in Oxford a few years before Gerald wrote his Topographia Hibernica, puts it, 'When the saints leave behind all human affairs and depart blessedly for the regions above, signs and prodigies testify that they are alive in heaven. While infidelity is stirred to belief by miracles, by this too faith is strengthened. In a wonderful way, miracles encourage the believer and confound the unbeliever.'[66]

Apart from cases in which repentance was secured by the visitation of divine vengeance or the sight of the miraculous punishment of others, Gerald recounted several stories of how doctrinal truths could be vindicated by miracle. In these stories there was a particular emphasis on the Real Presence, a doctrine with which not only Jews and heretics, but also Christian ecclesiastics, had some trouble.[67] The miraculous transformation of the Eucharist into the appearance of human flesh was a traditional motif of religious anecdote,[68] but the development of the doctrine of transubstantiation in the sacramental theology of the twelfth century gave a new significance to such miracles.

The threat from heresy also stimulated these accounts. Gerald described how the miraculous transformation of the host in Arras had led to the conversion of many of the heretical Patari or Catari in that town:

> When the news spread, a great crowd gathered together, not only from the town but also from the surrounding towns and villages. These were people who had been uncertain or had even completely turned aside from the article of faith concerning Christ's body. Observing with their own eyes and touching with their hands, seeing also the many miracles and wonders which God deigned to work there at that time, they returned to the certainty of the faith and the true path, which they had abandoned.[69]

A similar miracle converted many Paterini in Ferrara.[70]

In these ways, Gerald's accounts of miracles reveal their importance as a source of ecclesiastical revenue and their function in polemics. The most striking feature of his miracle stories, however, is that so many of them, especially those which he witnessed himself or heard about rather than drew from written sources, concerned divine punishment. The main purpose of God's interventions, according to Gerald, seemed to be to inflict sudden divine vengeance. It was sacrilege in particular which provoked punishment. The boy trying to steal baby pigeons from a nest in St. David's Church, Llanfaes, for example, stuck to a stone in the church 'through the miraculous vengeance of that saint, procuring the safety of the birds of his church'.[71] Rape in a church,[72] abuse of holy days,[73] and thefts of cult objects[74] were among the sacrilegious sins that provoked divine and saintly wrath. Gerald told many stories of how the Norman invaders of Ireland were punished for looting churches.[75] The justification for such punishments was simple: God never punishes anyone as much as they deserve; he knows who is damned and hence sometimes cuts them off by a terrible judgement as a warning to the rest.[76]

Gerald was extremely explicit about the practical deterrent purpose of these punishments. The preservation of some form of social order in general, and the protection of ecclesiastical persons and property in particular, required miraculous sanctions, since the instruments for their physical enforcement were never more than partially effective. When discussing the particular vindictiveness of the Irish saints, he advanced a reason for it which has a strangely functionalist ring:

> No other reason has occurred to me than this, that the Irish people lack castles but are infested with brigands, and they are accustomed to protect themselves and their possessions in the refuge provided by the churches rather than in the defences of castles. This is especially true of ecclesiastics. Hence, through God's providence and tenderness, it was needful that frequent and heavy punishment should fall on enemies of the church so that the wickedness of the impious should be kept well away from the peace of the church, and that a due, even if servile, reverence should be shown to those churches by the irreverent people.[77]

Clearly Gerald did not believe that tales of miraculous punishment had been consciously invented in order to clothe the nakedness of Irish ecclesiastics: he thought their physical vulnerability had prompted divine aid. But he was aware of the important dissuasive function that such stories could have. The problem of perjury was a case in point, and in the Gemma Ecclesiastica he recounted several incidents involving its punishment. He directed his own Welsh clergy, to whom the work was addressed, in the following words: 'My advice is that, at Sunday prayers and when you preach sermons, you should reproach your parishioners, who are too prone to perjury, about these things, by propounding these and other exempla.'[78] Elsewhere, Gerald pointed out that the Welsh, Scots, and Irish feared to perjure themselves on the holy bells or staffs of the saints since their retributive power was well known, 'from a certain hidden vengeful force, planted in them, as it were, by divine providence (quasi divinitus insita)'. [79]

An interesting example of the effectiveness of this fear was related in the Topographia Hibernica. After the theft of some armour in his household, Raymond le Gros, one of the leaders of the Norman invasion of Ireland, called all his men to him. He made the entire household swear to their innocence on a particularly sacred cross in Holy Trinity Church, Dublin. The young man who had stolen the armour, and thus perjured himself, later returned to England. Yet he felt persecuted by the crucifix; it seemed to be hanging around his neck like a great weight; he could neither rest nor sleep. Eventually he felt forced to return to Ireland and confess his crime. It would be hard to find a better example of how religious sanctions, enshrined in a shared system of symbols, could enforce and internalize codes of social behaviour.

Thus, for Gerald, miracles often represented a retributive justice, descending from above, which protected the weak and enforced otherwise non-enforceable standards. Irish ecclesiastics were vulnerable; the young man who stole the armour evaded his lord's justice. But, beyond mere human protection and law-enforcement, there existed dangerous, miraculous provisions for enforcing obedience.

NATURAL SCIENCE

Discussion of the place of marvels and miracles in Gerald's work has shown how, in his view, the texture of the natural world might be disrupted by bubbles of strangely wonderful material or punched through by the sudden fist of divine punishment. It is now time to turn to the natural world itself; to investigate the sources of Gerald's knowledge of it, and the kinds of explanation he brought to bear on it. In so doing his place in the history of natural science should emerge.

The expansion of the Latin west which began in the eleventh century not only widened economic and political horizons, but led also to a fundamental reorientation of Western thought, particularly in the field of science. The Greeks and their Arab commentators had created a large body of scientific works, distinguished by close observation, a systematic approach, and some experimentation. In 1100 virtually none of this work was accessible to Latin scholars,[1] but by 1280 only a few treatises remained to be translated. The entire scientific knowledge of two cultures had become available through the translation movement.

Before the translators began their work or, more important, before the translations were generally received, the science of western Europe presented a rather scrappy picture. Classical scientific knowledge had been transmitted to the men of north-west Europe not by the writings of Aristotle and the other original scientists themselves, but in the form of the diffuse, unsystematic, and undiscriminating encyclopaedias of Pliny, Solinus, and Isidore. They had inherited a rag-bag of observation, fable, and speculation which was without method and offered no pointers to further scientific development. However, the encyclopaedists did at least ensure the availability of a large deposit of facts (and fictions). Also, in so far as they aspired to comprehensiveness, they presented a model of universal knowledge and inquiry.

More concrete scientific developments were under way, however, stimulated largely by practical requirements. Since the time of the Babylonians, at least, exact observations of the stars had been important for calendrical and liturgical purposes, and the Christian Church, with its complex liturgical year and its chief feast dependent on the lunar cycle, required a certain degree of astronomical investigation. Calendrical anomalies and the variant methods of computing the date of Easter provided a stimulus for astronomical thought and writing. Bede had written on these subjects, and the computists of the eleventh and twelfth centuries produced many treatises on them. Even after the reception of Aristotle's thought, calendrical problems remained an important area of scientific activity to which men of such stature as Grosseteste and Roger Bacon devoted time.

Astrological prediction also necessitated good observations of the stars and planets, and stimulated simple mathematics. The practice of astrology received a great impetus from the influence of the Arabs. The introduction of the astrolabe to Europe in the eleventh century, for example, was one of the first major innovations in the field of observational instruments. Astrological study was closely associated with medicine, which itself provided another great practical stimulus to science. Use of herbal drugs required botanical knowledge, and the herbals of the period contain accurate and detailed illustrations of various plants. Some knowledge of minerals and animal secretions was also involved in medicine. From early in the eleventh century Salerno was the centre of medical study.

Apart from the practical concerns of astrology and medicine, however, the main purpose of scientific inquiry up to and after the twelfth century was an ancillary one, as an aid to biblical exegesis or moral homily. Alexander Nequam's De Naturis Rerum (c. 1197-1204), which contained much scientific material, including early quotations from Aristotle and the Salernitan masters, took the form of a preface to his commentary on Ecclesiastes and was avowedly written as moral and religious instruction. 'In this little work', he wrote,

> we invite the reader towards the works of light, so that, putting aside the works of darkness, he may at length enjoy light eternal. I have decided to use my small talents to commend in writing the natures of certain things, in order that the mind of the reader should run back from their known properties to their origin, namely the creator of things, so that, marvelling at him both in himself and in his creatures, the reader should kiss spiritually the two feet of the creator, justice and mercy.[2]

Nequam called the De Naturis Rerum 'a moral tract'.[3] The animal and plant kingdoms were treated as a great reservoir of sacramental meaning and moral symbol.[4] Curiosity about nature for its own sake was rare. This situation changed radically during the twelfth century, encouraged by two crucial developments. One was the growth of logic, which both prompted an extension of the range of rational inquiry and suggested a method of orderly procedure. The dialecticians made their first and controversial impact in the field of theology in the eleventh century. By the later twelfth century the classic systematizing work of Peter Lombard and Gratian had shown what could be achieved in the structuring of large areas of diffuse material. The system lay ready to hand for application to other areas of study.

The other major development of the twelfth century was the transmission of Greco-Arabic science. Sicily and Spain were regions of cultural and linguistic overlap which became important centres of translation work.[5] Men of different cultural origins, Arabic, Jewish, Latin, and, in Sicily, Greek, could co-operate in this difficult and novel task. It is hard to overstate the very high degree of motivation and enthusiasm that sustained some of the western scholars. Gerard of Cremona, the major figure in the movement, travelled from Italy to Spain in search of a copy of Ptolemy's Almagest.[6] Daniel of Morley travelled from England to Paris and then on to Spain in search of scientific knowledge.[7] Adelard of Bath claimed to have journeyed as far afield as Syria and Cilicia.[8]

English scholars played a prominent part in the translation movement. Throughout the twelfth century men like Adelard, Robert of Chester, Daniel of Morley, and Alfred of Sareshel travelled from England to Spain or Sicily. English scholars were already accustomed to having to go abroad to pursue higher studies, since the cathedral schools of England were so inferior to those of France, especially Paris. Hence nearly all the major English theologians of the twelfth century spent their active scholarly lives in France. Gerald himself spent at least ten years in Paris at the schools. Those whose main interests were not theological were prepared to travel even further afield to find the kind of teaching and knowledge they desired.

Daniel of Morley[9] travelled to Paris at some time around the middle of the twelfth century, but was disappointed at the teaching available. He called the jurists bestiales and infantissimi. He wrote, however, that 'in those days the teaching of the Arabs, which consisted almost entirely of the quadrivium, had achieved great fame at Toledo so I hastened there with all speed to hear the world's wiser philosophers'. This is a good illustration of the magnetic appeal of Toledo, and Arabic science in general, for those who were dissatisfied with the predominantly legal or theological learning that the schools of north-west Europe offered.

Daniel later returned to England 'with a valuable load of books'. Here he met John, Bishop of Norwich (1175-1200), whom he had presumably known before his departure overseas. John was very eager to hear about Toledan teaching: 'At length, as his curiosity led him to inquire about the movements of the heavenly bodies, he turned the conversation to astronomy, among other things those sublunary events which seem to serve the higher bodies by a kind of necessary obedience.' This is typical: a very practical desire to know the future from the stars was a great impetus to scientific inquiry. Bernard Silvester, whose Cosmographia presented a sophisticated scientific and philosophical cosmology, also wrote treatises on astrology[10] and geomantic divination.[11] Daniel's

Liber de Naturis Inferiorum et Superiorum, written at the Bishop's request, was a cosmology which mixed traditional Latin viewpoints with some new ideas and vocabulary taken from the Arab astrologers.[12]

The interest of English scholars in scientific questions, Arab science, and the translation of Aristotle was continued in the last quarter of the twelfth century and the first part of the thirteenth by three figures in particular, Alexander Nequam (1157-1217), Alfred of Sareshel, and Roger of Hereford (fl. 1178-95). Alfred's translation of the pseudo-Aristotelian De Vegetabilibus was dedicated to Roger, and his De Motu Cordis to Nequam, so presumably there was some contact between the three of them. Alfred studied in Spain and was one of the first commentators on Aristotle's scientific works. His scholarship represented a new stage in the deeper reception of Arabic and Aristotelian science.[13]

THE COSMOGRAPHIA

Gerald was not a scientific writer in the same sense as his English contemporaries, Daniel of Morley and Alfred of Sareshel. He wrote no works which attempted detailed and systematic description and explanation of some area or aspect of natural science. He was unreceptive to the new Aristotle, and, of the seven liberal arts, rhetoric and grammar (in its wider and more humane sense) were his chosen fields. Neither medicine nor astronomy are prominent in his writings. But it is erroneous to see him as a purely 'literary' figure, having no place in the history of medieval science. Gerald's works were not scientific treatises, but any account of them must consider his responses to the natural world and his scientific ideas.

Unfortunately, some of his early, more purely scientific works have been lost. He tells us that, when young, he had written both a Cronographia and a Cosmographia in verse, which 'in many places reflected the teachings of the philosophers rather than of the theologians'.[14] Some, perhaps all, of the Cosmographia is preserved as the first poem in Part II of the Symbolum Electorum, an anthology of Gerald's works.[15] The index to Part II is headed 'Tituli in Cosmographia, etc.' The poem itself, of 260 lines, is entitled 'De Mundi creatione et contentis ejusdem'. The Cronographia does not survive. It is probable that both the Cosmographia and the Cronographia were written about 1166-76.[16] This would correspond with Gerald's period of study in the arts at Paris (c.1165-72) and the poems would make sense as a student's exercise in both verse composition and cosmology. Another metrical, scientific work, De Philosophicis Flosculis, included explanations of the tides and the influence of the moon. Gerald mentioned this work once only;[17] it may have been a separate work now lost. It was written before the Topographia Hibernica of 1187-8. These early metrical works are thus represented now only by the Cosmographia.

   A first glance at Gerald's Cosmographia immediately suggests affinities with an earlier and weightier twelfth-century verse cosmology, that
of Bernard Silvester. Bernard wrote his Cosmographia or De Mundi
Universitate before 1147, and it was a popular text.[18] Although he quoted the
Cosmographia only once, and probably indirectly, there is every possibility
that Gerald encountered it as a student in Paris in the 1160s.[19] There are
both structural and verbal parallels between the two works. Like Bernard's,
Gerald's Cosmographia is a description of the creation of the world and man.
There is a basic similarity in the order of the two works. Both have a description of primordial chaos, followed by an account of how the divine generosity created a superior ordering of the world; an account of the separation
of the four elements; and descriptions of the stars, seven planets, four winds,
and the creatures of the world, culminating in microcosmus homo, with a
final eulogy of man's dignity and intellectual power. There are also verbal
similarities:

> Quinque paralellis medium circumligat orbem:
> Hinc extrema rigent, hinc mediata calent.
> Temperat ergo duas algoribus extremarum
> Et medii solis collaterante via.
> Dividit in quadras celum cingente coluro...
>
> (Bernard[20])

> Quinque parallelis medius distinguitur orbis,
> Ultimus hinc illinc extat uterque polus.
> Nix tenet extremos, medios calor, inter utrosque
> Temperiem reddit hic calor, inde rigor...
> In quadras orbem scindunt cinguntque coluri...
>
> (Gerald[21])

> Ut sua sint elementa volo: sibi ferveat ignis,
> Sol niteat, tellus germinet, unda fluat.
> Terra sibi fruges, pisces sibi nutriat unda,
> Et sibi mons pecudes et sibi silva feras.
>
> (Bernard[22])

> Perfecto plus quam nihil est perfectius orbe,
> Herba viret, tellus germinat, unda fluit,
> Mons pecudes et silva feras et sidera coelum,
> Aer quod volitat, quod natat unda tenet.
>
> (Gerald[23])

Affinities of this kind suggest the influence of Bernard Silvester on the young Gerald.

In his poem, Bernard gave poetic treatment to those cosmological themes that also interested his (probably slightly older) contemporaries, William of Conches and Thierry of Chartres. They had drawn upon a series of sources, mainly Neoplatonist in inspiration—the Chalcidian Timaeus, Boethius, Macrobius—in order to develop a coherent account of the physical universe. They were interested in the problem of creation. William of Conches glossed the Timaeus[24] and Thierry, in his De Sex Dierum Operibus,[25] had constructed a plausible physical interpretation of the Genesis story. Bernard used the same sources and much of the same material as these writers.

Despite its parallels with Bernard Silvester, however, Gerald's Cosmographia does not reveal him as a Platonist cosmographer in the same sense as William, Thierry, or Bernard. It is true that there are hints of Platonic terms and ideas in the poem. Gerald described creation, for example, in a way that suggests that the universe was ordered in accordance with pre-existent archetypes in the mind of God:

> Naturae genitor generum concepit ydeas
> Et sic disposuit singula, sicut habent...
> Incultis cultum, formas informis addens,
> In varias species particulavit ylen.[26]

At another point Gerald seems to echo Boethius' O qui perpetua, ascribing the creation of the universe to God's bounty, his freedom from envy:

> Sed tandem pietas mota est pietate, nec ultra
> Res tantas et opes pertulit esse rudes.
> Nec sibi thesauros recludere censuit uni,
> Sed dare cuncta suis, sed retinere sua.
> Cuncta sibi sed cuncta suis livore remoto
> In se largiri, gaudia cuncta suis.[27]

Boethius has:

> Quem non externae pepulerunt fingere causae
> Materiae fluitantis opus, verum insita summi
> Forma boni livore carens, tu cuncta superno
> Ducis ab exemplo, pulchrum pulcherrimus ipse
> Mundum mente gerens similique in imagine formans
> Perfectasque iubens perfectum absolvere partes.[28]

The ultimate source of this is the Timaeus.[29] The existence of 'the concepts of species' in the mind of God is clearly a 'Platonic' notion in some sense. Yet it is worth asking whether such a concept had not been assimilated within Christian thought for such a long period that it is, in fact, misleading to describe it as 'Platonic' at all. The Christianization of Plato's 'ideas', by the insistence that 'they are contained within the divine intelligence' had been effected by St. Augustine.[30] To characterize the concept of generum ideas in God's mind as Augustinian makes more sense in a twelfth-century context than to label it 'Platonic'. In other areas, too, it is difficult to isolate what is essentially Platonic and what is simply part of a common Christian tradition.

There are two places in Gerald's Cosmographia which might be adduced as more direct evidence of a truly Neoplatonic element in the poem. Unfortunately the passages are obscure. The description of the ordering of the universe begins:

> Prodiit imprimis coelum, coelique minister
> Angelus, hoc ignis, spiritus ille sacer.
> Purius hoc auro est, aura subtilior ille,
> Stellatum hoc solium, nuncius ille Dei.[31]

This 'angelic minister' plays no further part and it would be rash to equate it with Bernard's Nous, 'a metaphysical intermediary between God and the world'.[32] It is the only hint in Gerald's poem of anything like the allegorical figures, Nous, Natura, Physis, and so on, who play an indispensable part in Bernard's Cosmographia. But it is not impossible that this 'coeli minister angelus... spiritus sacer... nuncius Dei' echoes either, in general terms, the Neoplatonic emphasis upon the intermediaries through whom God works or, more specifically, the idea of the anima mundi.[33] A more precise identification is not possible, given the briefness and allusiveness of Gerald's description.

An even more fleeting reference is Gerald's description of the primordial universe as the 'ancient globe' (vetus globus): 'Non veteris fuit ulla globi divisio...'.[34] This can be compared to Bernard's '...cum silva teneret/Sub veteri confusa globo primordia rerum.'[35] The existence of 'the chaotic primal elements of the universe' in the vetus globus raises the issue of the creation of matter. The teaching of the Timaeus and of Genesis on this subject are contradictory. In Plato's cosmology matter is eternal and the activities of the Deus opifex represent an 'ordering' rather than a creation of the universe. Genesis is, of course, the Christian authority for ex nihilo creation. It has been suggested that Bernard Silvester and Thierry were toying with a Platonic interpretation of creation; certainly, there is twelfth-century polemic against such beliefs in the eternity of matter.[36] If Gerald's use of the phrase vetus globus is significant, then it may indicate sympathy with the concept. It is more likely, however, that his presentation of a pre-existent material chaos is a poetical topos. Ovid's influence is strong throughout Gerald's poem,[37] and the first book of the Metamorphoses presents a picture of the primordial 'aspect of nature' (vultus naturae):

> Ante mare et terras et quod tegit omnia caelum
> Unus erat toto naturae vultus in orbe,
> Quem dixere chaos: rudis indigestaque moles
> Nec quicquam nisi pondus iners congestaque eodem
> Non bene iunctarum discordia semina rerum.[38]

Other features in Gerald's poem also reflect contemporary commonplaces rather than Platonic influence. The correlation between the seasons, ages of man, elements, and humours, went back to Bede.[39] The characterization of the seven planets is similarly traditional.

Gerald was not, therefore, 'Platonist' in the sense that Bernard Silvester was. Moreover, Bernard, William of Conches, and Thierry of Chartres were 'Platonists' only in the sense that they used Plato as a tool. Their primary intention was to create a novel synthesis of natural philosophy and the traditional biblical and religious studies and, in doing so, to erect a structured scientific world-picture. All these major twelfth-century masters died around the middle of the century; none lived long enough to benefit from the new Aristotle.[40] Those translations which they did possess, for example Constantine the African's, or, in Bernard's case, Hermann of Carinthia's translation of Abu Ma'shar,[41] they used eagerly. It was not a peculiar sympathy for Platonism that they shared—an investigation of their different responses to and developments of Plato will bear this out—but an interest in building a naturalistic picture of the universe which led them inevitably to the only available model for such an ambition.

Thus Gerald's Cosmographia is not so much in a tradition of platonizing authors but in that of a school of writers who were attempting a scientific synthesis on the basis of the meagre available resources. However, even if the poem cannot be characterized as Platonic, it does give us a glimpse of Gerald's interests when an arts student at Paris. Like the early twelfth-century masters, he was interested in cosmology and creation. Like them, he relied for his main outlines on traditional sources. Like Bernard Silvester, he was concerned to give his material attractive and elegant literary form. His education at Paris in the 1160s reflected the continuing influence of the teaching of these masters.

These affinities, however, remained undeveloped. Gerald was to write detailed accounts of the natural world, but of a very different kind from this youthful poetic cosmology. After completing his studies in the arts, Gerald returned to South Wales and received ecclesiastical preferment. In the late 1170s he spent a further three years at Paris, studying civil and canon law, before returning to an active ecclesiastical life in the diocese of St. David's. It was after this that he entered royal service, and the period of ten years he spent as a royal clerk (c.1184-94) saw the production of his most famous works, the two on Ireland and the two on Wales.

NATURALIS HISTORIAE DILIGENS PERSCRUTATOR

These works, distinguished by Gerald's detailed personal acquaintance with his subject, are a curious mixture of geography, topography, and ethnography, of history and natural history, of anecdote, fable, and moralization. It is clear that there had been much development in his approach to the natural world since the Cosmographia. The grand overview of nature, as much poetic as scientific, had been replaced by a detailed, individualized observation, alive to the natural world as a motley multitude of particulars rather than a cosmic pattern.

Even when giving systematic sketches, Gerald filled out the features with scientific detail. The passage, for example, in which he surveyed 'the ladder of being',[42] although rivalling the Cosmographia in scope, showed quite a different approach. Gerald distinguished rocks, stones, and inanimate matter, which have no intrinsic motion and 'tend towards the centre'; trees and plants which possess a 'quasi-vital force' and 'vegetable life', enabling them to move and grow, although without sensation; and animals, which can move from place to place, possess sensation, and, by a 'certain imaginative power' (vi quadam imaginaria), recognize their regular haunts and remember past events. Finally (on an earthly level), there is microcosmus homo, who excels them all, possessing reason, speech, and upright stance. It was not original to distinguish these levels and qualities, but it is interesting to see how Gerald's 'cosmological sense', his awareness of the hierarchy of nature, had been articulated by an increasingly scientific precision. His analysis depended on motion and psychological capacities, which are empirical categories.

This tendency is even more apparent in the actual observations and descriptions in the Irish and Welsh works. Gerald's genius was not truly theoretical, and he tended to be interested in the particular, vivid, and immediate. His unusual qualities as an observer of the natural world have been generally recognized. He was interested in birds, fish, and animals, the movements of the tides, climatic phenomena, and the structure of the land. He tried his hand at cartography, and drew a map of Wales showing 'the tough mountains, bristling forests, lakes, rivers and high-raised castles; also the cathedral churches and many monasteries'.[43] His Irish and Welsh works show an alert and curious mind at work.

The accuracy of Gerald's observations is often very high. He has been called 'a realistic observer',[44] and a scholar who has studied Gerald's natural history concluded, 'The information on Irish fauna alone contained in the Topographia Hibernica is indicative of his superior talents as an observer... he shows exceptional curiosity and fondness for observation... equal to Albert the Great at his best.'[45] Gerald earned the title naturalis historiae diligens perscrutator which he gave himself.[46]

In discussing the wetness of Ireland, he gave a clear if simple description of the processes of evaporation: 'The mildness of the place means that the water collected and massed in clouds is neither consumed by the heat of the etherial fire, nor bound in the grip of aerial cold and solidified in the form of ice and snow, but is more easily resolved into rain.' Hilly places, he added, are more rainy because they are cold; fogs, clouds, rain, and snow are all the same thing called by different names.[47] This may seem very uncontroversial and, perhaps, uninteresting. But these kinds of atmospheric phenomena were being discussed at the time, different explanations being advanced with a curiosity about the origins of everyday phenomena which is fundamental to science. Gervase of Tilbury, a contemporary of Gerald, describing the nourishment of the trees of Paradise, wrote: 'They say the dew descends from a vaporous mist, "the waters above the heavens", as appears in summer. There are also those who say that the summer dew rises up from a lower vaporization of the earth, which they prove by the fact that a cloth spread on the grass will be wet underneath but quite dry above.'[48]

The tides and lunar influence, too, are described in the Topographia Hibernica.[49] Gerald noted spring and neap tides and the different times of high tide at different places, as also the powers of the moon: 'Phoebe is the fount and stimulus of all liquids, so that not only the waves of the sea but also the bone marrow of living creatures, brains in the head, and the sap of trees and plants are directed and influenced according to her waxing and waning.' In suggesting reasons why the tides in the Atlantic are greater than those in the Mediterranean, Gerald revealed how he saw Ireland as the very edge of the World. The land mass of Europe, Asia, and Africa was viewed as a whole, around which the ocean circled:

> From the four opposite and most remote parts of the ocean there is a certain violent dragging, gulping, and bubbling (attractio, absorptio vicissim et ebullitio) of the sea... the ocean has a freer and less impeded course of ebb and flow around the extremities; within land masses, however, it is restricted on every side and, rather like a lake, is forced by these obstacles to be placid. Hence it cannot wander freely.

Gerald's sense of the vastness and wildness of the ocean beyond the edge of the world is expressed, vividly and poetically, in his second preface to the Topographia Hibernica: 'Beyond the bounds of these regions no land exists, nor is there any dwelling-place for man or beast; but across every horizon, going on for ever, the ocean alone circles and wanders in unreachable and hidden paths.'[50] Yet, coupled with this imaginative response, Gerald always displayed a searching after causes. His purpose was 'mundi causas... mente percurrere'.[51] He had been reading philosophers who argued that tides and winds were caused by four great whirlpools at the four ends of the earth.[52] This kind of large-scale question, approached naturalistically and causally, is a typical interest of Gerald's.

Another example is the way he dealt with the problem of the origin of islands.[53] He believed that islands must have been created not violently and suddenly but gradually, by inundation. The evidence he brought to support this argument was that, since many distant islands had poisonous snakes and other harmful animals, these must have been cut off on these islands since the time of the Flood, for 'no one in his right mind would have brought them over voluntarily'. Since at the time of the Flood all animals were shut up inside the Ark, they must have diffused from one point since that time. The interest of this argument lies in the way it attempted to connect the distribution of species with the history of the earth's land-forms. Gerald here used empirical data, psychological generalization, and biblical evidence to produce a complex explanation of a problem in natural science.

Gerald brought his observation to bear intelligently, and sometimes used it to decide the issue between alternative explanations of natural phenomena. For example, while describing the different kinds of hawk in Ireland, he mentioned that individual sparrowhawks had different coloured markings. 'Therefore', he wrote, 'many people conjecture that these variations arise from the natures of the trees in which they were born. But, since you will often see this diversity in offspring from the same tree and in the same nest, a surer opinion holds that this discoloration comes rather from the parents naturally.'[54] Here direct observation, critically applied, had proved adequate to the task of distinguishing two hypotheses. However, there are other accounts in the Topographia Hibernica which suggest the limitations of simple observation. The most famous, perhaps, is the story of the barnacle goose. This is a particularly telling example, since it was put to the test in a more rigorous way only a few decades after Gerald's death, and thus serves to highlight the contrast between his simple or passive observation and more controlled and exacting forms of observation which could be attempted.

Gerald described the birds in the following way:

There are many birds here called barnacles (bernacae). Nature produces them in a marvellous way... For they are born at first in gum-like form from fir-wood adrift in the sea. Then they cling by their beaks, like seaweed sticking to wood, enclosed in shell-fish shells for freer development. Thus, in the process of time, dressed in a firm clothing of feathers, they either fall into the waters or fly off into the freedom of the air. They receive both food and increase from a woody and watery juice... On many occasions I have seen with my own eyes more than a thousand of these birds' tiny little bodies, hanging from one piece of wood on the sea shore, enclosed in their shells and already formed. Eggs are not produced from the copulation of these birds, as is usual; no bird ever incubates an egg for their procreation; in no corner of the earth have they been seen to give themselves up to lust or to build nests.[55]

The confusion about this bird was understandable. The goose in question nests only in very remote spots, the cliffs of the Arctic. The first nest was not seen, in fact, until 1907. Hence they had never been seen to breed or nest by medieval observers. In addition to this, the shellfish called the barnacle, which attaches itself to ships' timbers, etc., has many cirri, long feathery extensions for taking in food. These were mistaken for the birds' feathers. Indeed, one variety of barnacle has a long extension for suspending itself from rock or wood, which could be mistaken for the goose's neck.[56] Although Gerald is the earliest written source for the story, he was probably not its originator. He interpreted the evidence of his own eyes according to his expectations. Observation is obviously never mere perception.

In many ways the connection between the bird and the shellfish was not implausible. There in the sea were feathery shellfish; in the same waters were geese who appeared never to nest or lay eggs. Spontaneous generation was universally accepted as a rare, but possible, form of procreation. The explanation was, in some ways, elegant and economical. It posited 'a marvellous mode' of procreation, but the marvellous is not the impossible.

Gerald's account of the barnacle has a wonderful counterpoint in the passage on the bird written by Frederick II in his De Arte Venandi cum Avibus of the 1240s.[57] Frederick had heard the story and, in order to test its truth, sent out messengers who brought back floating timbers from the northern seas. 'In them', he wrote,

we saw a kind of shellfish clinging to the wood. In none of their parts did these shellfish exhibit any form of a bird and, because of this, we do not believe this opinion [i.e. the development of the bird from shellfish] unless we have a more convincing demonstration of it. It seems to us that this opinion arose because barnacle geese are born in such remote places that men are ignorant of where they nest...

Frederick was presumably unimpressed by feathery cirri.

The crucial difference between Gerald's and Frederick's response to the barnacle story is that while Gerald heard the story and then interpreted his perceptions in the light of his expectations, Frederick regarded it as a problem to be tested—he checked the story, sent men out, pursued the truth. Clearly he was helped by his superior resources. Few scientists apart from the Emperor could have men scouring the northern oceans for their specimens. But, more important, Frederick had a rigorous, sceptical, and aggressive attitude to evidence. We cannot say he performed experiments to check the truth of the barnacle story; but he did set up the conditions for controlled observation. Gerald's observation was acute but passive. It took him a long way, but sometimes led him astray. When it did so, he had no method to act as a corrective.

The story of the barnacle goose not only throws light on the limits of twelfth-century observational natural history; it also exemplifies how we can deduce the norms and premisses of Gerald's picture of nature from the natural marvels he described. When he wrote that 'nature produces them in a marvellous way, contrary to nature', he implied that sexual generation was the norm and spontaneous generation an extraordinary exception.

A similar example is provided by his stories of what would now be called the inheritance of acquired characteristics. 'We saw in Anglesey', he wrote, 'a dog which was lacking a tail, not by nature but by accident alone; its offspring suffered a similar lack naturally. It is amazing that the parent's accident alone could cause the offspring to be similar, as if by nature.'[58] Gerald's surprise indicated that his norm of generation did not involve transmission of acquired characteristics. In fact, in further anecdotes of this kind he referred to such transmission as 'a miracle of nature'.[59] While twelfth- and thirteenth-century thinkers accepted the hereditary transmission of some diseases, they specifically denied that mutilation or damage to a limb could be passed on in this way.[60] Gerald shared this assumption, although he accepted that there might be exceptions to it. As in the case of the barnacle goose, it is not that his premisses were strange or incomprehensible, rather that his assumptions about the way the natural world behaved did not take the form of rigid laws.

More systematic and rigorous ideas of the natural world were available in the twelfth century. John of Salisbury, in his Entheticus, used the phrase 'law of nature' to refer to the causal chains of the physical universe,[61] very much as a nineteenth-century physicist might have used it. Some writers attempted explanations of the sensible world solely on the basis of the four elements.[62] Thierry had written his account of the creation secundum physicam, using only the viewpoint of natural science. Gerald's enterprise was not so rigorous, nor did it show such materialist tendencies. He did not undertake to explain the world by a systematic theory based on natural principles. Yet, even so, there were occasions when he advanced explicitly naturalistic explanations, even in opposition to the miraculous explanations of hagiography. A classic example is his discussion of the absence of venomous reptiles from Ireland:

Some people, by an agreeable enough fiction, conjecture that St. Patrick and the other saints of the land cleansed the island of all poisonous creatures. But a more likely account asserts that, from earliest times and long before the establishment of the faith, the island has been devoid of these creatures, just as it has been of certain other things, by a kind of natural lack.[63]

The lack was a natural lack; and this was rendered all the more likely by the fact that other creatures were lacking in Ireland too. 'It does not seem marvellous to me', he wrote, 'that there is a natural lack of these reptiles in the land, just as there is of certain fish, birds and beasts.' Gerald ascribed a physical cause to this 'natural lack': 'It is certain, therefore, that thanks to the Bountiful Mercy, no poisonous animal can survive here, on account of a novel and unknown hidden power, which is hostile to poisons, and is either in the air or the land itself.'[64] This 'novel and unknown hidden power' is hardly precise. But the point here is the kind of explanation being advanced, not the precision with which it was expressed. In this instance, Gerald preferred an explanation based on the physical, although unknown, properties of air or land to one based on miraculous power.

Gerald did not distrust the St. Patrick story on the grounds of its intrinsic improbability. He included in the Topographia Hibernica two stories of how Irish saints expelled pests: St. Nannan had cleansed a village in Connaught of fleas and St. Yvor had driven rats from Fernegenal, near Wexford.[65] Both places had remained free of these pests. Gerald did not, therefore, disbelieve the ability of Irish saints to expel harmful creatures. Nor was he particularly hostile to St. Patrick.[66]

There seem to be two reasons why Gerald preferred a naturalistic explanation in this instance but accepted hagiographic traditions in other cases. The first is the unauthoritative nature of the hagiographic tradition. The story of St. Patrick's expulsion of the snakes from Ireland did not receive written form until Jocelyn of Furness wrote his Life in the late twelfth century.[67] It is probable that Gerald had not encountered the story in writing before he wrote the Topographia Hibernica. He called it a vulgaris opinio.[68] He may even have had some knowledge of the earlier lives of St. Patrick which did not mention the story. Thus his rejection of the legend reflects his suspicion of purely oral traditions and respect for written authority. Gerald was not greedy for hagiographic material. Although quite prepared to believe and record 'the ancient writings of the saints of the land', he did not credit every passing tale that came his way.

Another reason for Gerald's position on this subject is his strong sense of the plausibility of naturalistic explanation. In the absence of an authoritative tradition, he had a predisposition to attribute Ireland's freedom from snakes to an ancient, natural quality of the country. This conviction would be strengthened by Gerald's reading of Bede, who regarded this characteristic of Ireland in much the same way.[69] Gerald was in no sense an aggressive rationalist, eager to contradict or explain away hagiographic tradition, but he was prepared to complement or supplement such traditions with naturalistic explanation.

Gerald was also prepared to entertain both naturalistic and miraculous explanations in the same breath. He attributed the unusual healthiness of Bardsey Island, for example, to 'either the healthiness of the air, which comes from the region of Ireland, or rather to some miracle and the merits of the saints'.[70] On other occasions he did attempt precise physical explanations of phenomena which had been described to him as miracles. The strange groaning of a frozen lake near Brecon was called 'miraculous' by the local inhabitants. 'But perhaps', Gerald commented, 'this is caused by the sudden and violent eruption of the air, trapped by the icy shell above, which gradually exhales through hidden openings.'[71] It is explanations like this which form the backbone of much twelfth-century scientific speculation. They represent a stage in the demystification of nature. But, while Gerald did attempt to puzzle out strange phenomena in terms of physical qualities, he did not do so systematically. His nature remained a 'playful nature' (natura ludens).

Gerald's alert observational powers occasionally led him into criticism of his traditional authorities in natural history, the Latin encyclopaedists. In his account of Ireland he wrote that Solinus and Isidore were wrong to say that there were no bees in Ireland, while Bede was mistaken when he claimed that vines grew there.[72] Yet, while refusing to deny the evidence of his own eyes in deference to these authorities, Gerald was eager to preserve their credibility. 'It is highly likely', he wrote, 'that perhaps there were some vines in the island in Bede's time and that bees were introduced into Ireland by St. Dominic of Ossory, as they say, long after Solinus' day.'[73] Thus Gerald's historical sense saved both the phenomena and the reputation of his authorities. Gerald here observed the maxim: 'Let the times be differentiated and the writings will agree.'[74]

Yet he was also prepared flatly to contradict these writers when it seemed necessary. The story that the soil of Ireland, scattered amongst beehives in other countries, would cause the bees to desert their hives, seemed 'inexcusable'. On this point Isidore and Solinus were simply wrong.[75] Yet even here Gerald was not unappreciative of the difficulties Isidore and others had faced.

> But it is not amazing that they occasionally wandered from the path of truth, since they did not acquire their knowledge through the evidence of their own eyes, but from informants and at a distance. For the surest guide to truth is an eyewitness record. They are, therefore, not unworthy of proper praise for investigation of very distant facts. Since nothing human is altogether perfect and to have knowledge of all things and to make mistakes in nothing is divine

rather than human, their errors, if they have by chance crept in anywhere, are to be forgiven on account of both our imperfect condition and the very distance of the places involved.[76]

One example which illustrates the problems inherent in mingling information based upon observation and that drawn from books is the long account of the beaver in the Itinerarium Kambriae.[77]

After mentioning that the river Teivi, in Cardiganshire, was the only river in England or Wales to have beavers, Gerald went on to give a detailed description of the beavers' behaviour and how they were hunted. Much of this is highly accurate and reflects Gerald's lively interest and observation. He described their method of transporting logs; the sturdy construction of the beavers' lodges from interwoven willow twigs; the many internal chambers with interconnecting passages, above the water line to avoid flooding; the burrows they excavated in river-banks near the lodge; and their tails, broad, not very long, as thick as a man's palm, flat, and completely hairless.

He was not always so accurate. He believed, for example, that beavers, like toads, breathed under water and were able to stay under as long as they liked. This is not observational laziness on Gerald's part, but marks rather the division that always exists between the plausible guesses of an interested observer and the meticulous, relentless inquiries of a professional scientist or experimenter. Gerald had no stop-watch and, even if he had, would probably not have cared to sit patiently for hours on the banks of the Teivi observing the movements of the beaver. He was clearly intrigued by the animals, but was not undertaking 'pure research' into natural history in the way that Frederick II or Albertus Magnus did in the next century. Beavers can stay under water for up to fifteen minutes, and it therefore seemed plausible to Gerald that they could breathe there. He had neither the intellectual outlook nor the scientific equipment which would have enabled him to achieve rigorous proof or disproof of this theory. Again, when he wrote that beavers have only four, broad, sharp teeth, two above and two below, he was noting obvious appearances, although he was not in fact accurate. The beaver's four front teeth are easily the most prominent and Gerald does not seem to have sought a closer inspection of, for example, a dead beaver. He was an interested observer, but not a specimen hunter.

One part of Gerald's account of the beaver was clearly not based on observation. In eastern countries, he wrote, they were hunted for the medicinal properties of their testicles. When cornered, they castrated themselves and flung their testicles in front of the hunter. If, later, they were hunted again, they went up on to a hill and, lifting up their legs, 'showed the hunter that the part he was seeking had been cut off'.

Perhaps the chief point which strikes a modern reader about this story is its extreme improbability. This sense of improbability is based on our strong, although debatable, idea of what is and what is not appropriate to animal behaviour. We cannot credit beavers, not so much with purposive activity per se, but with such awareness of why men are hunting them. It argues a kind of reasoning power which we are anxious to reserve to man. Gerald's concept of animal behaviour, too, was unable to accommodate such a story with ease. He made several uncomfortable reservations. The beaver's protective self-castration was inspired, he wrote, 'by a marvellous—I won't say intelligence—but a certain innate power which is quasi-discriminating (mirabili, ne dicam ingenio, vi quadam ingenita et quasi discretiva)'.[78] He did not dismiss the story as 'a ridiculous opinion of the vulgar', as did his contemporary Alexander Nequam,[79] but was concerned to qualify his statements about what actually inspired the beaver's action; it was a capacity that was 'innate' and only 'quasi-discriminatory'. One feels that the location of these self-castrating beavers 'in eastern countries' also eased his sense of the plausible.[80]

The story of such beavers is an ancient one. It had found its way into Pliny's Natural History[81] and into the Physiologus.[82] It was a standard feature of twelfth-century bestiaries, where it was illustrated vividly and suitably moralized: 'All who wish to follow God's commandments and live cleanly should cut away from themselves all vices and shameful acts and throw them in the face of the devil. Then he will see that they have nothing of his and will retire in confusion'.[83]

Gerald had read bestiaries,[84] but also had access to more learned materials. When reworking the Itinerarium Kambriae, for example, he added quotations about the beaver from Cicero and Juvenal: 'They ransom themselves with that part of the body for which they are greatly sought.'[85] 'They make themselves eunuchs, eager to escape with the loss of a testicle.'[86] Gerald's source for these two quotations was Isidore, and he had clearly been browsing through the Etymologies,[87] alert for quotations to adorn his works. The addition of quotations from authorities was a regular feature in Gerald's later recensions of his work.[88] Isidore himself had derived the quotations from the fourth-century grammarian Servius, who had included them in his commentary on the Georgics. Servius was responsible, too, for the plausible etymology, 'Castores [i.e. beavers]... a castrando dicti sunt'.[89]

This very typical literary transmission involved phrases from Roman rhetors and poets being picked up by a late antique grammarian, who added his own etymology, and passed on through the encyclopaedia of a seventh-century Spanish bishop to the authors of the twelfth century. This tradition was very important for Gerald, but within its framework he was remarkably creative. He incorporated almost the whole of it—the etymology, the quotations, the fabulous story—but added to it observation and criticism which marked a wholly different approach to the natural world.

THE RETREAT FROM NATURALISM

After the completion of his Irish and Welsh works, however, Gerald drew away from this new naturalism. His earlier interest in cosmology, the moon and tides, geography and natural history, was not developed. After his retirement from court (c.1195) his works were of a completely different kind. His literary output from the later 1190s consisted entirely of hagiography, religious works such as the Gemma Ecclesiastica, a blend of sacramental doctrine and pastoral advice, and polemics. After his dispute over St. David's (1199-1203) he produced mainly invectives, either of a kind directly connected with the dispute (e.g. De Invectionibus, De Jure et Statu Menevensis Ecclesiae) or of a more general nature (e.g. De Principis Instructione, Speculum Ecclesiae). The scientific and naturalistic interests of his earlier works disappeared completely.

Moreover, as he reworked his earlier writings, their naturalistic qualities were diluted. The first edition of the Topographia Hibernica, for example, had been relatively free of symbolic interpretation of the birds and beasts it described, in comparison, say, with a work like Alexander Nequam's De Naturis Rerum. There are occasional allegorizations: the eagle's ability to look straight into the sun was compared to the contemplative's direct intuition of the divine nature;[90] the bodies of kingfishers remained uncorrupted after death, like those of saintly men.[91] But the larger part of Book I of the Topographia Hibernica is a record of which creatures are found in Ireland, with an account of their appearance and habits. By the time Gerald completed the fourth edition, however, the work was twice its original length and additional material of an allegorical kind had swamped the natural history. This transformation represents the drift of Gerald's thinking in the 1190s and early thirteenth century. His interests had undergone a change of emphasis.

This very striking shift from topography and history to hagiography and polemic requires some explanation, however tentative. Some of the reasons must be sought in Gerald's wounded vanity. He felt strongly that his ten years in royal service had been rewarded in a very miserly way. This disappointment was exacerbated to the point of obsession by the wearying litigation of the St. David's case. His exceptional talents were redirected to the protection of his exceptional self-esteem. The embarrassingly strident tone of some of these later works reached a sad apogee in the defensiveness of the Speculum Duorum.

But these personal considerations were not decisive. Gerald's shift in the late 1190s from natural history to traditional religious writing was prompted, at least in part, by the pressures and expectations of those around him. A good example is provided by the way Archbishop Baldwin responded to the Topographia Hibernica. It was 'the theological moralizations and allegories' which earned most praise from him. He asked if Gerald had borrowed any of these from the commentators and, when told that he had not, remarked, 'The same spirit certainly inspired both you and the commentators!'[92] A response such as this must have encouraged Gerald in his perpetual expansion of the allegorical elements in the Topographia Hibernica.

Besides positive encouragement to develop his talents as a religious allegorist, Gerald encountered much hostile criticism of his secular literary activities. The ecclesiastical norm of the time saw training in the arts, including the sciences, as a ladder to the study of theology. 'The liberal arts should only be saluted in passing', as Alanus ab Insulis and other late twelfth-century theologians put it.[93] Dallying too long with the natural world was suspect.

Some ecclesiastics were suspicious of secular literature as such. Gerald was under pressure to employ his talents in theology, not in describing the birds and beasts of Ireland. 'Some people', he wrote, 'say that grace conferred from above should not be expended on humble things... what flows from above should be applied to things above and everything should be turned to the glory of him from whose plenitude we receive it.'[94] William de Montibus, a friend of Gerald's from his student days at Paris and his master at Lincoln, criticized the Irish works and thought that Gerald should be writing theology.[95]

Gerald reacted to these criticisms in different ways. Sometimes he was positive, almost defiant, about the independent value of his secular writings. Replying to William de Montibus, he wrote:

> Historians do not hold the lowest rank among authors and writers... Neither Origen... nor our Jerome, nor Augustine, nor Hilary would have been such strong pillars of the church with their theological books... if they had not had such a sound basis and firm grounding in literature and the arts... It is also our desire that you should know that the above works of ours... in time to come... will survive for a very long time. For there is already a superabundance of theological works... in fact these modern booklets are not truly genuine, for they are patched together from the earlier original works of others... We on the other hand took pains in our youth to distill the histories of Ireland and Wales, our own home grounds, from hitherto untouched material, and managed to extract the hidden pearls from the hardest shells...[96]

Here not only did Gerald extol the novelty of his Welsh and Irish works, but counter-attacked by criticizing the redundancy and plagiarism of many contemporary theological writers.[97] Yet he vacillated. In the same letter he also sought to meet criticism by claiming that his works did have moral and spiritual applications: 'In our volume on Ireland the diligent reader will be able to find both theological morals and allegories.' He pointed also to the religious nature of his Gemma Ecclesiastica and Vita Sancti Remigii.[98] He felt defensive, or at least sensitive, when attacked for putting his talents to non-religious uses.

This is even more clearly revealed in his comments on the relative position of theology and the arts. Writing of his Irish and Welsh works in about 1194, he said, 'We have tasted these things first, as prefaces or preludes to the glorious treasures of the science of sciences, which alone knows how to know, how to give men knowledge, how to rule and instruct man; the other branches of study are like attendants following far behind the queen and worshipping her footsteps.'[99] This description of theology is quite traditional.[100] These are youthful works, Gerald was saying; he had reserved his later life for theological study. It was clearly not easy to persist in the study of the natural world. The assumptions and values of Gerald's ecclesiastical milieu led naturally to a high evaluation of theology and a low evaluation of secular writings.

Gerald adopted and internalized these values to such an extent that we find him writing to Walter Map, criticizing Map for his flippancy and urging him to engage in theological studies and adopt a more serious tone. Gerald described literature as purely instrumental to theology: 'You have placed a solid and unshakeable foundation of letters. With great labour you have made an ivory ladder... by which you may scale the high tower of divine scripture... But what use is a foundation, however excellent, unless you construct the building? What use is a ladder, even if raised aloft, unless you climb it?'[101] He urged, 'Make your mouth, which has been witty and eloquent in order to charm human ears, full and fruitful with divine praises. For the rest of your time let your voice delight the divine ears; your mouth was once unrestrained in a host of idle things, for human applause; now open it continually in holy celebration as a saving remedy, for God alone.'[102] 'The books of the pagans', 'the sayings of the poets and philosophers', and 'metres and poems' should be left behind or used only as adornments to religious writing.[103] This letter to Map thus shows Gerald himself advancing the same arguments in favour of going on from secular writing to theology that others had advanced against him.

It is ironical, in the light of the considerable pressure that Gerald felt to move away from history, natural history, and topography, that his Irish and Welsh works were by far the most popular and successful of all his writings. Most of his religious and polemical works survive in only one manuscript; a few are extant in two. In contrast, there are dozens of medieval manuscripts of the Irish and Welsh works. Thus, although the progression to theology was recognized, both by Gerald and his ecclesiastical contemporaries, as the ideal, it seems clear that, in the judgement of medieval as well as modern readers, Gerald was moving away from his true field.

It can be argued that Gerald's shift away from natural history is also a reflection of his divergence from the path which European science was treading at the time. Considered as a naturalist, Gerald fell chronologically between two groups of writers. The first consisted of those earlier twelfth-century thinkers interested in science and cosmology who attempted systematic accounts of the physical world. Adelard of Bath, William of Conches, and Thierry of Chartres are the famous names. The second group, working in the later twelfth and early thirteenth centuries, was composed of those who either sought out Arabic or Aristotelian science by travelling abroad or who readily absorbed it when it became available. Gerald cannot be placed happily in either group.

Adelard, William, and Thierry were distinguished by their emphasis on secondary causes, their search after explanation in terms of the physical elements.[104] They believed that this world of secondary causes was intrinsically comprehensible, that it exhibited ratio and was graspable through ratio. Their enterprise was to seek out 'the causes of things' and, in Adelard's words, 'the causes of things square with reason'.[105] 'Reason is to be sought in all things', echoed William of Conches.[106] As their primary interest was in the rational courses of the physical universe, they tended to play down God's arbitrary interventions. They did not deny his omnipotence—indeed, they argued that his power was all the greater for working through nature[107]—but concentrated on the regular and natural. While claiming not 'to derogate from God',[108] they asserted that it was feeble and stupid simply to attribute things to God's will. God's will was not arbitrary; ratio could always be found.[109]

Such a position prompted fierce attacks from more traditional ecclesiastics. Adelard found himself called 'insane';[110] William of Conches wrote of 'those who are ignorant of the forces of nature... they want us to believe like peasants and not to seek reasons... if they know that someone is making investigations, they shout out that he is a heretic'.[111] Writers like William of St. Thierry and Walter of St.Victor criticized William of Conches and others for their tendency towards materialism. 'He describes the creation of the first man philosophically or, rather, physically', wrote William of St. Thierry of William of Conches, 'saying that his body was not made by God but by nature... in this he seems to follow the opinion of certain stupid philosophers who say that nothing exists except bodies and corporeal entities and that God is none other in the world than the concourse of elements and the proportion of nature.'[112] Walter of St. Victor attacked William of Conches for his reliance on the Timaeus and for his atomic theory: 'We condemn and anathematize their atoms and rules of philosophy, their "something", "anything", and other nonsense of this kind.'[113]

Gerald was not attacked on such grounds, although he himself, in later life, regarded his Cosmographia as an example of philosophical rather than theological doctrine.[114] His picture of the natural world was not as systematic as that of these earlier twelfth-century scientists; nor did he possess their strong preference for physical explanation. As we have seen,[115] he was willing to advance both naturalistic and religious explanations, and the nature he investigated was full of marvels and miraculous interventions.

Nor can Gerald be placed comfortably in the context of contemporary Aristotelianism. During the period of the composition of his Welsh and Irish works and in the immediately subsequent decades many English naturalists became acquainted with Arabic and Aristotelian science. Astronomical and medical material from these sources can be found in the works of Daniel of Morley and Alexander Nequam. The Avicennan De Anima was used by Nequam and John Blund. Blund and John of London were lecturing on the Aristotelian libri naturales in the early years of the thirteenth century. Alfred of Sareshel translated the pseudo-Aristotelian De Vegetabilibus (before 1195) and was familiar with the libri naturales.[116]

Despite the interest in natural history which Gerald had shown, he seems to have had no interest in assimilating this new material. A comparison between his descriptions of animals and those to be found in the Aristotelian encyclo-paedists of the thirteenth century, Bartolomaeus Anglicus for example, reveals an enormous difference. Bartolomaeus Anglicus was not an original thinker, but he had an orderly system, based on an Aristotelian natural teleology and employing the theory of the elements and humours in a consistent way.[117] Gerald, in contrast, was discursive and unsystematic. His achievements in natu-ral history resulted not from a consistently applied system but from the enli-vening effect that a new emphasis on observation had upon the conservative Latin encyclopaedist tradition. He showed, in a sense, what the twelfth century could achieve without Aristotle.

In fact, Gerald saw some aspects of Aristotelianism as dangerous, and, in the preface to his Speculum Ecclesiae (c.1220), he praised the recent con-demnations of Aristotle at Paris and hoped that, because of them, many people, 'abandoning their vain and erroneous teaching, might, through God's inspiration, turn to saner, solider, and healthier doctrines'. The danger of the Aristotelian teaching seemed to him to rest in its 'subtle discussions and philosophical enquiries into the nature of things'.[118] It was the extension of scientific or philosophical method into areas which he regarded as the preserve of religion that really angered Gerald. On the model of Aristotle's De Anima, Christian writers had begun to discuss the soul in an analytical manner.[119] But psychology received no warmer a welcome around 1200 than it did, in new garb, around 1900. Just as Freudian psychoanalysis was seen as an assault on the freedom of man, so in the thirteenth century it was suspected that the attempt to describe and explain the senses and responses of human beings was an intrusion into the mystery of God. Gerald quoted with disapproval the Toledan translator's preface to Avicenna's De Anima: 'It is unworthy that man does not know the very thing by which he knows and cannot grasp by reason that by which he is reasonable.'[120] He counter-attacked with a battery of biblical quotation. 'It was in order to deter him from studies of this kind', he wrote, 'which are more subtle than they are useful and tend to lead to error, that Solomon said to his son, "Seek not the things that are too high for you and search not out things above your strength, but think always on what God has commanded and do not be curious concerning many of his works.'"[121]

This caution, this retreat from the boundaries of knowledge and fear of man's presumptuous curiosity were not merely a result of temper or age. The tension between the confident assertion of the value of natural curiosity and a fear of probing too far had always been present in Gerald. His Cosmographia had given a confident and idyllic picture of man's powers but, even as early as 1188-9, in the midst of his attempt 'mundi causas mente percurrere', we find a warning note. Gerald's chapter on the eagle in the Topographia Hibernica, which was greatly enlarged in the recension of 1189, moralized upon the high flight of the bird:

> Commonly they strive with such lofty flight that their wings are burned by
> the sun's hot fires. So too those who attempt to investigate the high and hidden
> secrets of heaven in the Bible beyond the set limits, which ought not to be
> and cannot be exceeded, are forced to return to themselves and halt, since the
> wings of presumptuous intelligence, which carry them, are burnt.[122]

This adaptation prompted Gerald into a long passage, replete with biblical quotations, in which he thundered home God's incomprehensibility and the deficiencies of man's reason: 'Say then, you fragile pot, how dare you to give reasons for all things on earth and in heaven, even those which are above all reason, presuming against reason and faith. For what is more irrational than to attempt by reason to go beyond reason itself?'[123] He attacked pride in reason in the same way as a moralist would attack pride of any other form. This was the 'rashness of presumptuous inquiry' (temeritas presumptuose inquisitionis) which drew Nequam's criticism.[124]

Conversely, humility was commended. Gerald approvingly quoted the passage from Ecclesiasticus he was to use again in the Speculum Ecclesiae: 'Seek not the things that are too high for you...'[125] Man's reason was partial and limited: 'We have been granted partial knowledge but not fullness of understanding or inquiry.' Gerald told the story, from Augustine, of the man who asked what God had been doing before he made the world. 'He prepared Hell for foolish questioners', came the reply.[126]

The tone of this passage seems quite out of keeping with Gerald's vast natural inquisitiveness and pride in pursuing the secreta naturae. But he made a strong distinction in his own mind between 'things natural' and 'things divine', and was reticent on the deeper mysteries of the faith. 'When discussing what actually happened during transubstantiation, for example, he decided,

> It is safer not to split hairs on this completely miraculous subject, but to
> leave it to the Holy Spirit. We know for certain from our authorities that

the substance of bread and wine is turned into the substance of the Lord's body and blood, so let us not be ashamed of being ignorant of the exact method of the change. As Augustine says, 'Ignorance which believes is better than audacious knowledge.'[127]

Gerald refused to extend his curiosity into the central regions of the Christian faith. He did glory in his own ability to seek out natural causes, but this was absolutely distinct from any ultimate confidence in human reason. This compromise, a strict demarcation of faith and reason, served him well enough, but when there was an attempt to extend reason into the realm of faith, as seen, for example, in the works of some Aristotelians, he entrenched himself in traditional, defensive rhetoric. His shift from secular to scholarly life, pressure from ecclesiastical colleagues, his hostility to the new learning, and his growing sense of the limitations of human understanding led him a long way from his youthful Cosmographia with its eulogy of 'rational man, who sees the secrets of nature and ponders the conditions of things and their causes'.[128]

Gerald is not a major figure in the history of the development of science. That development was to be secured by the growth of a systematic approach, experimental method and, eventually, the application of mathematics to the natural world. Gerald contributed nothing in these fields. Yet his contributions to natural observation and explanation remains interesting. He was most vivid when dealing with material particulars, rather than theory, although he also had a strong tendency to attempt an explanation of those particulars. He would have made, perhaps, a good zoologist but a bad physicist. He gives us an important glimpse of what could be achieved in the field of natural observation before the swamping effect of Aristotle's libri naturales was felt. The curiosity and intelligent imagination he showed at his best were the product of twelfth-century developments, as yet unaffected by Greek and Arabic science. The tensions Gerald felt between naturalistic and theological explanation, between the incomprehensibility of the divine and the strivings of human intellect, between faith and reason, are symptomatic of the most productive hiatus in western culture, felt at this time more acutely than ever before.

PART III

ETHNOGRAPHY

INTRODUCTION

In the following discussion of Gerald's ethnographic writing, as contained in the Irish and Welsh works of around 1188-94, two perspectives have been adopted. The first approach attempts to describe the world that Gerald saw and to explain why his picture of Welsh and Irish society takes the form it does. This explanation involves discussion both of the actual nature of those societies and of the reasons why they might appear in a certain way to an observer from an Anglo-Norman and French background. Parallels can be drawn between Gerald's comments on the Celtic peoples, other Anglo-Norman and French writers on the same subject, and German descriptions of the Slavs and Scandinavians, and in this way a more or less coherent image of the barbarian emerges. Gerald's writings can also, however, be analysed in terms of their intellectual achievement—their scope, coherence, and detail—and in terms of the explicit and implicit concepts that he employed. From this perspective, they appear as part of a tradition of ethnographic writing.

Despite the overlap between the two perspectives, different questions are raised. Both attempt to explain why Gerald's Irish and Welsh works have the characteristics they do, but one does so by pointing to the nature of twelfth-century societies, the other by focusing upon Gerald as an ethnographer.

THE FACE OF THE BARBARIAN

The later eleventh and twelfth centuries have long been recognized as a period of expansion in western Europe. The hesitancies and weaknesses of post-Carolingian society were replaced by a confident expansionism, which eventually produced the imposing edifice of thirteenth-century Latin Christendom. Expansion, of course, presupposes borders, and this leads one to ask what the western Europeans saw when they looked out across their borders. In the Mediterranean regions they confronted highly developed Muslim and Greek civilizations; but when the Anglo-Normans looked westward to Wales and Ireland, when the Germans turned their view north to the Scandinavians or east to the Slavs and Magyars, they saw societies which they conceptualized in much the same way—they called them 'barbarian'.

The writers who give us access to this picture were all, of course, ecclesiastics. The most interesting are those who lived close to the peoples they describe, and two of them are especially useful to compare with Gerald: Adam of Bremen, who wrote an account of the Scandinavians, with some references to the Slavs, in the 1070s,[1] and Helmold of Bosau, who wrote his Chronicle of the Slavs in the 1170s.[2] These writers can be supplemented with ethnographic material drawn from other chroniclers and writers. French accounts of the Bretons form a particularly interesting parallel.

The first crucial distinction the chroniclers and ethnographers saw between the western European societies in which they lived and those societies on their western, northern, and eastern borders was economic. Adam of Bremen described Jutland in these terms: 'except in the neighbourhood of the rivers, it seems to be almost entirely deserted, a land of salt and of vast emptiness... there are scarcely any cultivated areas or places fit for human habitation...'[3] Otto of Freising praised the beauty of Hungary but commented that it was 'not greatly adorned with buildings or houses because of the ways of its barbarous people'.[4] The Welsh and the Irish, according to Gerald, did not engage in trade or manufacture, and the Welsh had no towns or castles.[5] Helmold mentioned the predominance of barter among Baltic peoples.[6] Clearly, the heart of western Europe was more developed economically than its peripheral regions. Even setting aside the Mediterranean world, it was obvious that the plains of northern France and southern England, Flanders, the Rhineland, and other parts of Germany were more densely populated, more intensively exploited, more productive, and more highly urbanized than the Celtic, Scandinavian, or Slav lands.

The eyes that the Germans and Anglo-Normans cast over these undeveloped parts of Europe were greedy eyes. We can catch a hint of this in Otto of Freising's comment on Hungary: 'Fortune is rightly to be blamed or, rather, the divine patience is to be wondered at, which exposed a land as delectable as this to such, not men, but human monsters.'[7] It struck Otto as a waste of good land to see it in the hands of such a backward people. Anglo-Norman writers were particularly concerned about the way that the Irish had neglected the natural potential of their country. William of Newburgh wrote, 'the soil of Ireland would be fertile, if it did not lack the industry of a good husbandman; but the people are rough and barbarous in their ways... and lazy in agriculture'.[8] William of Malmesbury contrasted the thriving urban settlements of the English and French with the poverty-stricken Irish countryside: 'The soil of Ireland produces nothing good, because of the poverty or, rather, the ignorance of the cultivators, but engenders a rural, dirty crowd of Irishmen outside the cities; the English and French, on the other hand, inhabit commercial cities and have a more civilized way of life.'[9] Gerald, too, attacked Irish laziness. 'Cultivated fields are indeed few in number', he wrote, 'through the neglect of the cultivators; nevertheless, the land is naturally fertile and fruitful.'[10] The economically undeveloped regions of Europe seemed, to such observers, ripe for new management.

The contrast they painted, however, was not simply one of greater and lesser economic development. Western European writers emphasized the different basis for economic life in the peripheral regions, in particular pastoralism. One twelfth-century Anglo-Norman writer described Wales as 'a land of wood and pasture... rich in deer and fish, in milk and herds', and Scotland as 'a region... of fertile woods, abundant with milk and herds'.[11] Gerald particularly emphasized Welsh and Irish pastoralism. In Wales, he wrote, arable agriculture was not extensive and the diet of the people consisted mainly of oats and dairy products, with more meat than bread. Even when they did plough, their agriculture was less intensive than the English kind—they ploughed only in spring, not three times a year.[12] The Irish 'despise agricultural labour', he said, and lived 'a pastoral life'.[13] The pastoralism of the Bretons, too, had been noted in the previous century by Raoul Glaber, who derisively described their wealth as consisting in their 'freedom from taxes and abundance of milk'.[14] The uplands of north-western Europe and the lush and grassy pastures of Ireland are natural dairying and stock-raising country. The same is true of parts of Scandinavia, and Adam of Bremen noted the preponderance of pastoralism in Norway, Sweden, and Iceland.[15] Gunther of Pairis, author of the Ligurinus, a poem in praise of Barbarossa, noted other kinds of non-arable activity:

> The people who dwell in the islands of the Baltic
> Do not plough the land, which is sterile with perpetual cold,
> Nor turn the stiff fields with the hard mattock,
> Nor tie the vine to the elm-stake,
> Nor gather fruits from the trees, those gifts of autumn;
> By hunting alone and by frequent plundering raids
> Do they acquire food.[16]

References to pastoralism among the Slavs and Magyars were not so common. Despite the fact that stock-raising and hunting played a larger part in the eastern European economy than in that of western Europe in the twelfth century, the Poles and Magyars did engage in a great deal of cereal cultivation. By the end of the Middle Ages, in fact, this part of Europe was a grain-exporting region. Although this development had not occurred by the twelfth century, clearly the arable component of their economy was so noticeable to German observers that they did not characterize the Slavs in quite the same way as the Anglo-Normans described the Celts. They felt that the Slav lands were economically undeveloped, but did not ascribe this to the pastoral mode.

For it was a 'mode' that pastoralism represented. Both Gerald of Wales and Adam of Bremen saw pastoralism as a way of life, not as an extraneous and unconnected fact about the people they were describing. Adam made this point by bringing in comparative references. 'Norway', he wrote, 'is the most infertile of regions, on account of the wildness of its mountains and the extreme cold, and is fit only for livestock. The Norwegians pasture their herds in far-off empty spaces, just as the Arabs do. They get their living from them, using milk as their food, wool as their clothing.'[17] Later he commented, 'In many parts of Norway and Sweden pastoralists are the most noble of men, living in the manner of the patriarchs by the labour of their hands.'[18] Adam grouped contemporary Scandinavians, the Arabs, and the biblical patriarchs together, because their way of life, their economic and social organization, could be categorized as pastoralism, despite differences of time and place. Gerald was even more explicit on this point and developed a theory of social evolution around it.[19]

In some ways pastoralism became a cultural yardstick, and the dichotomy between bread and milk or meat assumed immense symbolic importance. William of Poitiers wrote that the Bretons 'do not engage in the cultivation of fields or of good morals. They have great quantities of milk, but very little bread.'[20] Here the arable-pastoral polarity was given a moral colouring.

Gerald varied the theme. He described how an English ship, seeking refuge from a storm off the coast of Connaught, encountered two Connaughtmen in a coracle. They were naked except for animal skins and covered in long hair. When invited on to the ship they were amazed at the sight of bread and cheese, never having seen them. Moreover, they had never heard of Lent or even of Christ himself. Here Gerald mixed cultural and religious norms to create an image of the Irish savage. In this permutation of the raw and the cooked, Gerald placed himself—and his readers—on the side of bread, cheese, and Christ, and rendered the Connaughtmen alien and outrageous by placing them on the other side.[21] Agricultural societies had always characterized their non-agricultural rivals or neighbours in a similar way. An ancient Akkadian text described the barbarians as 'the people who knew not grain'.[22]

It seems fairly certain, at least in the case of the Welsh and the Irish, that these twelfth-century writers overestimated the preponderance of pastoralism. Both archaeological and documentary evidence suggest, for example, that the Welsh economy had a far more substantial sedentary and arable element than Gerald's accounts would have us believe.[23] But it would be naïve to expect absolute objectivity in these accounts. They constitute a description of one people, seen from the viewpoint of another, and that description will tell us, implicitly, about the differences between those peoples. Gerald stressed the pastoral and nomadic (i.e. transhumant) aspect of Welsh life because this struck him as contrasting most sharply with the world he knew. He had spent his early life in the arable lowland society of South Wales and in southern England and northern France. The open fields, the rural year grouped around sowing and harvesting—the arable year—and the manorialized village were in the back of his mind when he tried to delineate, by contrast, the chief characteristics of Welsh society.

Similarities between Anglo-Norman comments on the Celts and German comments on their northern and eastern neighbours are by no means exhausted at this, rather basic, economic level. The Celts, Slavs, and Scandinavians were seen as economically backward; they were also seen as possessing certain political features, or, rather, certain political flaws in common. There was a continual insistence in the Anglo-Norman and German writers on the political fragmentation which the barbarians displayed and the fierce internecine strife to which they were prone. Adam criticized the Vikings' habit of enslaving and selling their own people,[24] and Helmold constantly referred to the civil wars among the Danes: 'they are powerful only in civil wars', he wrote.[25] Similar internal dissension was prevalent among the Welsh. Gerald described the quarrels over land, the fratricides, burnings, and blood-feuds of the Welsh.[26] In fact, he and other Anglo-Norman writers thought that this Welsh tendency towards internal strife was the best ally of the English crown in its military efforts. The author of the Gesta Stephani recorded the fruitless military expeditions organized against the Welsh by Stephen, and wrote that eventually the King decided to sit out the trouble, 'since, when warfare ceased, universal discord would divide the Welsh and they would either be struck by famine or, turning against each other, would be annihilated in mutual slaughter'.[27]

At the highest political level, this disunity was exhibited in the relatively small size of political units and the refusal or inability of these peoples to unite under one ruler. Gerald thought that one of the things that would prove fatal to the Welsh was that 'they obstinately and proudly refuse to submit to one ruler and the judgement of one king in the manner of other peoples who live quite happily'.[28] Adam of Bremen noted that the Prussians 'wish to suffer no master among themselves'[29] and that the Swedish kings, war leaders drawn from ancient royal kindreds, had virtually no coercive or executive power in peacetime.[30] William of Newburgh attributed the conquest of Ireland by the English to Irish political disunity: 'Ireland, divided into many kingdoms in the manner of early England and accustomed to have many kings, was dismembered by their disputes. The Irish were inexperienced in foreign wars, but, rushing in mutual slaughter upon their fellow countrymen, they, as it were, disembowelled themselves most wretchedly.'[31]

It may seem odd to describe twelfth-century France or Germany as centralized political units, but on the level of the provincial principality, and even on that of the kingdom, French and German rulers controlled reasonably substantial and permanent territorial units in a more effective and enduring way than, say, the Polish dukes or Irish petty kings. And the precocious political centralization of England has long been recognized. The contrast seems to be, partly at least, between societies in which kinship formed the basis of social organization and loyalty and those in which political lordship was relatively more important than kinship. In Wales, for example, the lands and grazing rights of the freemen were organized on a clan basis.[32] At this period, too, the blood-feud was still an important part of Welsh life. The Welsh Laws contain a complex schedule of compensations for injuries and murder, resembling the Anglo-Saxon wergeld system.[33] In England, on the other hand, the Anglo-Norman monarchy had taken homicide out of the realm of private compensation and feud and subjected it to the processes of royal justice. This process had not gone so far among the Welsh. As Gerald said, 'They love their kindred above all things and they sharply avenge any injury or disgrace to their blood. For they are of vengeful spirit and their anger is bloody. They are ready to avenge not only new and recent injuries but even old and ancient ones as if they were urgent.'[34]

It seems at first paradoxical that, in addition to characterizing the outlying peoples as internally divided and politically fragmented, the chroniclers and ethnographers of western Europe also considered tyranny to be prevalent among them. Yet the contradiction is only apparent. The tyranny which Adam of Bremen, Helmold, Gerald of Wales, and the others described was not a firmly established absolutism. It was an arbitrary, bloody, and, in the last analysis, desperate tyranny. It was, in fact, a consequence of the lack of ordered polity. The Irish kings, Gerald wrote, 'obtained the monarchy only by force and arms'.[35] Adam and Helmold both mentioned the multiplicity of tyrants among the Danes and Swedes, and Helmold related this to the frequency of civil wars among those peoples.[36] Otto of Freising explicitly contrasted the ways of the Magyar kings with those of the German emperors. When a Magyar count offended the king, he wrote, 'No sentence is requested by the prince from his peers, as is the custom amongst us, and the accused is allowed to make no excuse, but the prince's will alone is universally regarded as sufficient cause.'[37] For Otto, the antithesis was between a kingship moderated by the advice of the king's natural counsellors, and that of an unbridled autocracy; on a more philosophical level, between reason and will.

This question of tyranny highlights one of the central characteristics that the Anglo-Normans and Germans attributed to the Celts and Slavs: wilfulness, lack of reason, lawlessness. The core of their description of the barbarian was not so much concerned with the economic level of the peoples involved, nor with their political organization, but rather with their moral and psychological qualities. This is what Gunther of Pairis had to say about the Poles:

> A people whose culture is crude;
> Terrible of face, with a frightening brutality in their customs.
> They rage with a horrible sound, they are ferocious, threatening,
> Quick of hand, lacking in reason, used to plundering.
> They scarcely behave like men, their cruelty is worse than the horror of
> wild beasts,
> Impatient of laws, eager for slaughter,
> Shifting, inconstant, quick, slippery, deceptive.
> Unaccustomed to keep faith with masters or love their neighbours,
> Uninstructed in the moving feelings of piety.[38]

Many examples of such ideas could be given: Adam writing about the Baltic and Scandinavian peoples, Helmold on the Slavs, Otto of Freising on the Bohemians and Magyars, Gerald of Wales and other Anglo-Norman writers on the Celtic peoples—all stress their ferocity, cruelty, and bloodthirstiness, their faithlessness and disregard for good laws and customs.

There is more to this than simple defamation. Some sense can be made of these charges when we consider the political context in which they occurred. In virtually all the regions under consideration, especially in the Celtic west and Slavic east, military conquest and colonization were in progress. The Anglo-Norman aristocracy, under the general aegis of the English crown, was pushing into Wales and Ireland; the Germans were conquering and colonizing across the Elbe and along the Baltic coast. In these circumstances the native peoples might find that a temporary surrender or agreement was inevitable. But, naturally enough, as soon as the political situation changed, if the enemy dispersed his forces or if he was distracted by civil war at home, then a reassertion of independence would follow. It was this process that the Anglo-Normans and Germans insisted upon referring to as 'rebellion' and 'breach of faith', and this of course contributed to the barbarians' reputation for faithlessness.

Another component of the situation was the difficulty of dealing with politically fragmented peoples. When the king of England or the duke of Saxony made political arrangements with the Irish or Slavs, the two parties involved were not strictly equivalent. The king of England could arrange terms which would be binding on all his subjects. No Irish king could commit all Irishmen in this way. Henry II's dealings with both the Irish and the Welsh show the difficulty he had appreciating that their political pattern was not the one he was familiar with in France or England. As W.L. Warren has observed, 'Wales lacked an internal government with which treaty regulations could be concluded.'[39] In both Ireland and Wales Henry attempted to recognize one particular ruler as overlord of all the others, and to receive fealty from him. The other Irish kings or Welsh princes did not see the situation in quite the same way. Hence, when the complaint of barbarian 'faithlessness' and 'perjury' is heard, it is important to realize that the parties with whom the agreement was originally reached might not actually have the authority to make arrangements binding on other groups or chiefs. This is a situation which has many historical parallels, most strikingly with the relations between the early settlers and Indians in America.

The ferocity and warlikeness ascribed to the barbarian are more difficult to explain. Certainly, there are economic and political circumstances to consider. Raiding and plundering were important in the economy of these undeveloped regions. Gerald said that the Welsh 'live by plunder, theft, and brigandage'.[40] According to Helmold 'the Slavs of the Baltic excel in secret raids. Up to recent times the habit of brigandage was so strong among them that, neglecting opportunities for agriculture, they turned their hand to naval expeditions, placing their greatest hope of wealth in their ships.'[41] Rustling, piracy, and slaving were more important in the economy of the Celts and Slavs than among Anglo-Normans and Germans, whose leaders had by this time moved on to surer ways of acquiring the economic surplus.

Moreover, the Celtic and Slav peoples had much more to lose in the struggles they were engaged in against Anglo-Norman or German invaders than did any of the western European military class in their own wars. When Capetians fought Angevins or Guelph fought Ghibelline, the stakes involved were political predominance and seigneurial income. In the Celtic and Slavic worlds, defeat at the hands of the invaders often meant the replacement of the native populace. Helmold wrote that, after the Count of Holstein rebuilt the stronghold of Plön in 1156 and erected a town around it, 'the Slavs who lived in the surrounding towns left and Saxons came and lived there and gradually the Slavs failed in the land'.[42] In these circumstances it is not surprising that warfare in these frontier regions was more ruthless than elsewhere. 'French warfare', wrote Gerald, 'is very different from Welsh and Irish warfare... In France soldiers are captured; here they are beheaded. There they are ransomed; here they are killed.'[43] The development of rules of war between opponents from the same class and cultural background in western Europe was not extended to battles with barbarians.

These considerations may help us to understand why the barbarians were characterized as cruel and ferocious. We are left, however, with an enigma. It is not impossible that there was an objective truth at the core of the picture and that the development of political order in Western Europe had led to the creation of societies in which violence was less frequent, or, at least, more regulated, than elsewhere. But the estimation of levels of violence is problematic. It is very likely that the Welsh free tribesman, for all his acquaintance with plundering and the blood-feud, might view French or German society, with their pogroms, massacres of heretics, punitive criminal law, and continual internal warfare, as no less cruel or ferocious than his own. Both central western European society and the societies of the peoples around this central core were very violent by modern European peacetime standards. Perhaps the chief distinction between them was in the forms the violence took.

One of the ways in which the Anglo-Normans and Germans justified their expansionism was by using religion as a validation for their actions, and a religious element formed an integral part of their picture of the barbarian. Here a distinction must be drawn between the situation in the Celtic west, which was Christian, and in Eastern and Baltic Europe, where large numbers of pagans survived throughout the period. The Slav tribes between the Elbe and Poland, Baltic peoples such as the Prussians and Lithuanians, and a considerable proportion of the Scandinavians were pagan in the twelfth century. German expansion could be, and was, portrayed as a crusade, from the Wendish Crusade of 1147 to the conquests of the Teutonic Knights in the thirteenth and fourteenth centuries.

Conversely, the Slav peoples equated conversion to Christianity and political submission to the Germans. Helmold described how Gottschalk, a prince of the Slav Abodrites, was converted to Christianity. After his death his son had to be installed in power by Saxon arms 'because, since he was born of Christian parents and was a friend of the Saxon dukes, his people regarded him as a betrayer of their liberty... The Slavs strove to defend their liberty with such obstinacy that they preferred to die rather than become Christians or pay tribute to the Saxon dukes.'[44] Religious and political allegiance seemed to the Abodrites simply two sides of one coin.

Both Adam and Helmold gave quite detailed accounts of the temples, gods, and rites of the Swedes and Slavs respectively, and their comments enable us to see how barbarian paganism appeared to the Germans. Adam of Bremen's picture of paganism among northern peoples was that of domination by superstition and sorcery. 'The whole of the barbarian world (tota barbaries)', he wrote, 'abounds with sorcerers.'[45] In Courland on the east Baltic coast, 'every house is full of diviners, augurers and necromancers'.[46] The men who dwelt north of the Arctic Circle knew everything that was going on in the world, and could catch whales, 'through their magic arts and incantations'.[47] This fearful account of a world under the shadow of black magic existed alongside a condescension to pagan credulity. Adam wrote that Unwan, Archbishop of Hamburg-Bremen in the early eleventh century, ordered churches to be repaired 'from the groves which our marsh-dwelling people used to frequent with such foolish reverence'.[48] When Christian missionaries visited Denmark, the Danes, 'just like barbarians, asked for a wondrous sign'.[49] Adam saw something childish in this emphasis on an external sign.

A connection was also traced between paganism and ferocity. Adam said that the Courlanders were 'a very cruel people because of their great cult of idolatry',[50] and when Helmold described the conversion of some of the Rani he said, 'This rude and animal-like people were turned from their innate wildness to the religion of the new conversion'.[51] The link in the Germans' minds between cruelty and non-Christian beliefs was also shown in their accounts of pagan cults. Both Adam and Helmold claimed that human sacrifice was practised.[52] Whatever the truth of these statements—and they are not intrinsically improbable—human sacrifice formed a natural culmination to the picture of barbarian savagery.

An interesting fact emerges from comparison of pagans and Celts. While the Celts could not be called pagans, they were criticized as being the next worst thing—very bad Christians, semi-pagans. It is clear that some kind of religious deficiency was a crucial part of the concept 'barbarian'. If the people involved happened to be Christian, then clearly they could not be good Christians. Gerald said the Irish were 'most uninstructed in the rudiments of the faith'[53] and complained that they did not pay tithes or enter church reverently. The same points had been made about the converted Slavs. John of Salisbury described the Welsh as 'ignorant of divine law and the institutions of the church. This people are rude and untamed, they live like animals and despise the Word of Life; they nominally profess Christ but deny him in their life and customs.'[54] St. Bernard, writing about the Irish, said they were 'shameless in their customs, uncivilized in their ways, godless in religion, barbarous in their law, obstinate as regards instruction, foul in their lives: Christians in name, pagans in fact'.[55]

This argument, that the Celtic peoples were virtually pagan, was employed in the same way as the Germans used the actual paganism of some of the Slavs—as a justification for conquest. Perhaps the best-known example is Ireland. Papal approval was given to the Anglo-Norman invasion of Ireland because it has been portrayed as a religious mission. In 1172 Pope Alexander III wrote to Henry II that he had heard how the King had conquered 'with God's aid, that Irish people, who put aside the fear of God and wander unbridled through the rough and dangerous ways of vice and cast aside the observance of the Christian faith and of virtue and who slaughter each other in mutual massacres...' (It is interesting to note, in this statement, mention both of semi-paganism and internal strife—two parts of the characterization of the barbarian.) The Pope urged Henry 'to recall the Irish, through your power, to the observance of the Christian faith'.[56] It was politically useful for the Anglo-Normans and Germans to be able to adopt a high moral tone towards these peoples they were attacking. It improved morale, provided a justification for aggression, and reinforced feelings of superiority held by the invaders. Some kind of religious deficiency was attributed to the barbarians and became an integral part of the ethnographic characterization.

One of the failings that the clerical, ethnographic writers ascribed to these peoples was that of sexual immorality. Clearly this type of charge is common between antagonistic groups and often reveals more about the accusers' repressions than about the behaviour of those criticized. But in this case there was more to it than this. Adam of Bremen said of the Swedes, 'they know no moderation in joining with women. Each according to his powers has two or three or more at the same time; rich men and chiefs have them without number. Sons born from these unions are deemed legitimate. But the punishment for rape or adultery is death.'[57] Clearly the accusation was not one of indiscriminate promiscuity. As has been mentioned, Gerald criticized the Welsh for incest, trial marriages, and allowing the illegitimate to inherit,[58] and there is the enormous chorus of Anglo-Norman outrage at Irish marriage customs: 'they exchange wives with each other' (Lanfranc), 'men change their wives just like one gets a new horse' (Anselm); 'They have as many wives as they wish' (Roger of Howden).[59] The Bretons did not escape this general denunciation. 'In Brittany', wrote 'William of Poitiers, 'each knight produces fifty, since each has ten or more wives, like the ancient Moors.'[60] Polygamy, divorce, marriage within the prohibited degrees—i.e. 'incest'—these were the targets of criticism.

As ecclesiastical reformers strove to enforce the rule of indissoluble, monogamous marriage, they encountered not only the intransigence of the aristocracies of France, Germany, and England, but also, among the barbarians beyond, extremely resistant and sometimes very well formulated bodies of custom operating on a different view of marriage. The struggle over marriage customs in Wales and Ireland has been fully discussed in Chapter 2, and the clash between the vigorous canon law of the twelfth century and the secular customs of native societies was not limited to this part of Europe. As in the case of the Celtic west, wherever ecclesiastics faced barbarous marriage practices their criticism became entangled with the process of conquest, colonization, and resistance. The rhetoric of church reformers blended with the hostile characterization of the chroniclers and ethnographers.

So far, the common characterizations of the Celts, Scandinavians, and Slavs have appeared almost entirely negative. Writers ensconced within Anglo-Norman or German society have been described as looking out at a world which was economically backward, dominated by a rough, pastoral way of life; politically fragmented, mauled by civil wars and bloody tyrants; inhabited by fierce, lawless raiders, who could not be trusted; given over to superstition and black magic; pagan or semi-pagan; indulging in human sacrifice and sexual excess. If this were all, then it might be objected that the picture was simply composed of racial prejudice and malicious libel. But barbarian society was presented much more precisely and specifically than that, and even the criticisms and misunderstandings of the ethnographic writers reveal certain coherencies. If we turn to the (rather fewer) good qualities that were ascribed to the barbarians, further striking similarities occur.

Here are three passages from these writers:

> No one in this race is a beggar. For everyone's household is common to all. They prize liberality, especially generosity, before all other virtues. Here the courtesy of hospitality is enjoyed by all in turn so much that it neither has to be offered or requested by travellers. For all that travellers entering the house have to do is to hand over their weapons for safe keeping and then straightaway they are offered water. If they permit their feet to be washed they are received as guests. Offering water for the feet constitutes an invitation to hospitality amongst this people.

> This people exhibits the most perfect hospitality and they show reverence to their parents. No one is ever found lacking or has to beg among this people. For when sickness or age makes any of them weak, he is assigned to be cared for by his heir, with the utmost kindliness. The courtesy of hospitality and care for parents have first place among the virtues for the people.

> This people are especially notable for their hospitality. It is a serious matter to refuse shelter to travellers, so they even compete amongst themselves as to who will be worthy to receive the guest. They perform every kindly duty to their guests, permit them to stay as long as they wish, and then send them on to the houses of friends.

The first passage is Gerald writing about the Welsh,[61] the second Helmold on the Slavic Rani,[62] the third Adam on the Swedes.[63] Something as specific as a reputation for hospitality, particularly when found in conjunction with so many hostile characterizations, really does seem to support the case that Germans and Anglo-Normans saw around them societies which did have much in common; and, conversely, that the Germans and Anglo-Normans differed from these other peoples in the same way.

The trait of hospitality interlinked with the other, less positive, characterizations. In a wilder and less developed countryside, mutual aid was more important. The fact that there were fewer people made more generous hospitality feasible. Absence of money meant that no commercialized hospitality, inns and hostels, existed. It may also be true that a fragmented and kin-based social structure required a formal ethos of hospitality to sustain necessary transactions which would otherwise founder for lack of a niche. An Anglo-Norman or German traveller could probably call on tenurial or institutional connections for support while on his journey, and his kin network would be geographically far-flung. In more localized and less developed regions such networks of support would not exist. A final reason to be considered is that suggested by some comments of Walter Map. 'The Welsh', he wrote, 'retain such great respect for generosity and reverence for hospitality that before the third day no one asks of a guest they have received where he comes from or who he is.'[64] In a society in which blood-feuds predominated it was possibly safer not to ask too many questions about the strangers you entertained.

The case of hospitality shows that certain qualities of barbarians might be held up for approval and used as a standard to criticize the writer's own society. This was rather the way that Tacitus had presented the Germans in his Germania[65]—the simple virtues of the barbarians were intended to shame the degeneracy of the Romans. The eleventh- and twelfth-century chroniclers and ethnographers were all churchmen, and their code of virtues, not surprisingly, put a high valuation on abstinence and moderation. Adam described the simple life of the Icelanders, 'desiring nothing more than nature grants them', sharing everything with great charity. Even before their conversion, he said, 'they, by natural law, were not so divergent from our own observance'.[66] Barbarian moderation was sometimes used to criticize the greed and indulgence of the Anglo-Normans or Germans. Gerald thought that, although the Welsh were prone to glut their appetites when given the chance, 'none of them gives their fortune into the hands of money lenders, on account of their own vicious gluttony and drunkenness, as you can see the English do'.[67] Adam wrote, 'The Prussians do not value gold and silver. They have many exotic furs and skins, whose odour has passed on to our world the lethal poison of pride. The Prussians regard these things as dung—much to our discredit, I say.

We pant after a coat of marten-skin by fair means or foul, as if it were the highest blessing.'[68]

Another aspect of this admiration was a more secular, indeed military, appreciation of the toughness of these peoples as soldiers. Gerald praised the Welsh for their ability to endure cold and hunger on campaign,[69] and Adam described the Norwegians as 'powerful soldiers, unsoftened by any luxury'.[70] The economic backwardness of these peripheral areas of Europe had its compensations.

The men of England, France, and Germany, particularly the clerical writers with some experience of the peripheral areas, all noted common features of the societies around them. This seems to suggest that England, France, and Germany themselves had crucial common features. The accounts of Adam of Bremen, Helmold, and Gerald of Wales throw light back into their own faces as well as outward into the barbarian darkness.

Having tried to sketch in this picture as cogently as possible, a few qualifications must be made. I have already mentioned that not all the qualities referred to were ascribed to all the peoples being discussed—pastoralism is probably the clearest example of this. Another vital point is that these 'peripheral' societies were not themselves static. Indeed, the accounts written about them resulted from the process of western European expansionism which was putting pressure on them. During the twelfth and thirteenth centuries, the societies of the Celtic West, the Scandinavian North, and Slavic East were undergoing crucial developments. Often these developments led to them becoming more like the societies of central western Europe. For example, Wales, during the course of the thirteenth century, developed into a small feudal state under the Llywelyns. They pursued political centralization, took the blood-feud out of the hands of the kindred, and encouraged proto-urban development.[71] In eastern Europe the kingdoms of Poland, Bohemia, and Hungary were to become integral parts of Latin Christendom. The line between these western Europeans who saw themselves as fully civilized and the barbarians beyond was fluid.

Another group of qualifications is of a different nature, dealing with the influence of literary traditions on the ethnographic writers. Characterizations of barbarian peoples had been handed down from classical antiquity and may have had importance. Adam of Bremen, for example, used parts of Tacitus' *Germania*.[72] This should not be overemphasized, however. In the classical tradition the Hyperboreans, that is, the dwellers in the north, were renowned for hospitality, but this was taken as confirmatory evidence by, for example, Adam of Bremen. It was not the sole basis for his assertions. One body of classical material, which had been growing, snowball-like, since Herodotus, might be thought to have relevance here: the descriptions of monstrous creatures. Many of these stories were incorporated into medieval ethnographic accounts. It is, however, always possible to make a distinction between informed, if distorted, accounts of barbarians and the wilder realms of fantasy beyond. Adam of Breman provides a good case. His account of the peoples who lived around the Baltic shores nearer to Saxony, the Slavs, Balts, and Scandinavians, is informed and plausible. The more remote the region he describes, the more fantastic the inhabitants become—Amazons, dog-heads, green men, cannibals.[73] Even here there was a limit: 'There are many other monsters in those parts, as we are told by sailors, but this seems scarcely credible to us.'[74] It is as if there were three concentric circles: one, our world, where there is no need for generalizing description, since everything is taken for granted; the second, outer ring where the barbarians live, peoples whose strange customs prompt us to record them; the third, outermost ring, where the principles of order dissolve and all our fears, fantasies, and projections become real.

A final, perhaps minor, qualification, is that the term 'barbarian' can be used simply as an epithet of abuse. The French often used it of the Germans.[75] It did not, however, have the far broader connotations, the almost sociological picture of barbarism, under discussion here.

What is the broader significance of twelfth-century ideas of the barbarian? The portrayal of the barbarian feeds into the whole fabric of western European civilization in two ways. It had a stimulating effect on the ethnographic tradition. It left a 'damnable heritage' (damnosa hereditas) in the field of colonial experience. Having lost touch with most of the achievement of Greek and Roman ethnographers, medieval writers had very much to build up their own tradition. The contribution of the eleventh- and twelfth-century writers on ethnographic subjects was very great. To be brief, their main achievements were a new emphasis on detail, a sense of a society as an organic whole, and a skilful use of comparative method.[76]

Compared with the earlier fragments prefaced to chronicles and the like, these accounts give us real knowledge of everyday details. Helmold and Adam gave detailed descriptions of pagan rites, for example, and from Gerald we can even learn how the Welsh cleaned their teeth. There is a new naturalistic precision, alongside the more generalized comments about the country or the moral qualities of the inhabitants. More striking even than this development is the way in which some twelfth-century ethnography shows an awareness of how many different aspects of a people's life are interrelated in an organic way. Gerald's Descriptio Kambriae, the high point of twelfth-century ethnography, portrayed a society which was, in every way, anthropologically plausible. Economic, political, military, and psychological characteristics were described in such a way as to emphasize, implicitly, their interrelatedness. Gerald interwove different strands in a unified picture of the Welsh.

The final point, the comparative method, has already been touched upon. Adam's comparison of the Norwegian pastoralists with the Arabs and biblical patriarchs is a case in point. Classical literature provided much material to be used in this way. When William of Poitiers compared Breton polygamy with ancient Moorish practices, his source for the latter was Sallust.[77] One of the scholia in Adam's History compared Scandinavian burial practices with those of the ancient Romans and the Indians, Indian practices being known through the fourth-century grammarian Servius.[78]

Perhaps more important than the simple comparison of current barbarian practices with those of other, ancient or contemporary peoples was the realization that the way the barbarians lived might illuminate the past society of the civilized peoples themselves. This was an insight which the Greek and Roman writers had developed, but it had been lost sight of. Adam of Bremen thought that, before their conversion, the Saxons had practised a form of pagan religion identical to that still followed by the Slavs and Swedes of his own day.[79] While Christianization was a process which created a sharp break in a people's self-perception, other less dramatic changes were also noticed. As has been mentioned, William of Newburgh observed that 'Ireland is divided into many kingdoms, in the manner of early England...'[80] This appreciation of different stages of development received its most comprehensive formulation in Gerald of Wales' Topographia Hibernica:

> The Irish people are a wild and woodland people (gens silvestris); an inhospitable people; a people getting their living from animals alone and living like animals; a people who have not abandoned the first mode of living—the pastoral life. For when the order of mankind progressed from the woods to the fields and from the fields to towns and gatherings of citizens, this people spurned the labours of farming. They viewed the treasures of the city with no ambition and refused the rights and responsibilities of civil life. Hence they did not abandon the life of woods and pastures which they had led up to then.[81]

The concepts behind this passage—the ladder of evolution of human societies and the persistence of primitive survivals—would not be out of place in nineteenth-century anthropological thought. Nor are they complete strangers in the twenty-first century.

The dark side of the picture requires little demonstration. During the course of their eleventh- and twelfth-century expansion, the peoples of central western Europe encountered societies which were poorer, less well organized, and of a different mould from their own. Their ideological, or cultural, response to this was to create a hostile stereotype to salve their consciences and justify their conquests. The descent of these ideas is direct. Perhaps the clearest example is the case of Ireland. The picture that the Anglo-Normans built up of the native Irish in the twelfth century was still at work among their Elizabethan descendants. And the prejudices the English acquired in the course of their colonial experience in Ireland were exported by them and brought to bear on their colonial experience throughout the world.[82]

The attempt by twelfth-century European writers to delineate the face of the barbarian thus resulted in a striking intellectual achievement, but also produced an ideological weapon which has not yet lost its cutting edge.

GERALD'S ETHNOGRAPHIC ACHIEVEMENT

THE PATH TO THE 'DESCRIPTIO KAMBRIAE'

Gerald's reputation as a writer and scholar rests largely upon his Irish and Welsh works. The number of manuscripts surviving from the medieval period indicates their popularity.[1] Medieval translations and abridgements were made,[2] and printed editions appeared in the sixteenth and early seventeenth centuries.[3] Since that time these works have been easily accessible to scholars, and further translations and editions continue to appear.[4] The interest in these works is due partly to their importance as indispensable narrative sources for times and places which are not well represented by other such sources—our knowledge of the Anglo-Norman invasion of Ireland, for example, would be only a pale shadow of what it is without the Expugnatio Hibernica[5]—but they also represent an attempt to do something new, to write detailed accounts of lands and peoples. The Topographia Hibernica and, in particular, the Descriptio Kambriae were original attempts at topographical and ethnographical writing, and, in structure, scope, and detail, represented new departures.

A preliminary sketch of the previous history of ethnographic writing will enable us to grasp the full originality of Gerald's work. The roots of Western ethnography and anthropology are to be found in the intellectual ferment of ancient Greece.[6] As the Greeks colonized the Mediterranean and Black seas, they came into contact with dozens of different peoples at different levels of development. Greek society lacked a strong priestly caste and possessed a tradition of secular literacy. Hence Greek reflections on the diversity of peoples were only minimally influenced by conservative religious forces. By the fifth century BC Herodotus had produced the first (and, perhaps, the greatest) major work of Greek ethnography. It is ambitious in scope, comparative in approach, and remarkably free of moral or national prejudice. It is a tribute to the curious and intelligent ear and eye of the man who wrote it.

Later Greek and Roman scholars developed a tradition that can be called at once ethnographic and anthropological. The ethnographers tended to concentrate on detailed descriptions of specific peoples. Tacitus' Germania is the

perfect example of such an ethnographic monograph.[7] More general questions
of human variability were dealt with by the exponents of climatic determinism,
a doctrine which was forcefully formulated in the Hippocratic Airs, Waters and
Places of the later fifth century BC and was continually repeated throughout antiquity.[8] Other writers tended to concentrate on drawing a picture of
primitive man and on analysing the ladder of human development. Indeed,
one of the major achievements of classical anthropology was the creation of a
naturalistic, evolutionary account of human history. The elements of such an
account were present in the fifth and fourth centuries BC and achieved striking
expression in the poetry of Book V of Lucretius' De Rerum Natura.[9]

Ancient Greek and Roman writers thus created an impressive ethnographic
tradition. From Herodotus to Tacitus, a solid body of material relating to foreign peoples had been built up, often based on detailed, first-hand observation.
Conceptual categories were developed and at least a beginning was made on
anthropological theory. This material, however, did not reach the medieval west.
Instead, broken fragments and disconnected and sensationalized pieces of it
were transmitted via the late Roman and early medieval encyclopaedists. Pliny,
Solinus, and Isidore were read in the twelfth century; Herodotus, Lucretius,
and Tacitus were not. Fragments of theory and snippets of fact survived in this
way, but no models of procedure or approach were transmitted intact. Despite
the numerous examples of classical influence in individual motifs, the Latin
west had to recreate its ethnography.

The germs of this new creation are to be found in history and chronicle.
It was conventional in this genre for the introduction of a new people into
the narrative, or sometimes even the reference to a king of a certain people,
to prompt a brief description of the geography and customs of the people
concerned. Greek and Roman historians had already used this technique. For
instance, at the beginning of chapter XVII of the Bellum Iugurthinum, Sallust
interrupted his account of Jugurtha's career with the words, 'My subject seems
to call for a brief account of the geography of Africa and some description of
the nations there with which the people of Rome has had wars or alliances.'[10]
Chapters XVII-XIX then give a very brief account of African geography and
the various races who had inhabited the region. The same idea of providing
a mise en scène for a historical narrative motivated the first chapter of Bede's
Ecclesiastical History. Twelfth-century chroniclers employed the device. Otto
of Freising prefaced his narrative of campaigns against the Magyars in the Gesta
Friderici with a chapter giving a summary account of the location and terrain
of Hungary, the appearance of the people and their dwellings, and, as might
be expected from an uncle of Barbarossa, a more detailed report on political
and military practices.[11]

Writing of this kind must have provided some sort of stimulus to Gerald's
own work. He borrowed from the encyclopaedists and the set-piece descrip-

tions of the historians. The opening chapters of the Topographia Hibernica, for example, contain quotations from Solinus, Isidore, and Bede's Ecclesiastical History. Yet Gerald went far beyond such sources. His achievement is all the more striking in the light of the fragmentation and, indeed, almost total disappearance of the classical ethnographic tradition. He had no formal models, such as the Germania could have provided, and there was no body of writing accessible to the twelfth-century west dealing with early man or the variety of races.[12] Much of the classical anthropological and ethnographical tradition was lost for ever, and most of what survived was not to receive general currency again in western Europe until the fifteenth or sixteenth centuries. Yet, even without the support of such a tradition, Gerald was able to write a detailed and coherent ethnographic monograph, the Descriptio Kambriae. The very idea of taking the description of a single people as the central theme of a piece of writing was innovative. Whatever motifs or patterns the historians might have offered in their ethnographic excursus, the Descriptio Kambriae was cast in a form that had not been attempted for over a thousand years.

Gerald's progress towards the monograph form took place in several stages. His first extant work, the Topographia Hibernica, showed a strong interest in ethnographic material as an important element in the general description of a country. Book III of the Topographia Hibernica had as its subject 'the first inhabitants of this land and the arrival and disappearance of the various nations in order; the nature and customs of the Irish people, who inhabit the land up to the present; and foreign invasions'.[13] Gerald evidently thought that a topographia should include information on the customs and appearance of the inhabitants. This third book contained much besides ethnography, but it was a first step in Gerald's attempt to organize ethnographic material.

After completion of the Topographia Hibernica, Gerald continued to treat Irish material, but from a different angle. The Expugnatio Hibernica is a narrative of recent Irish history. Gerald's continuing ethnographic interests are witnessed, however, in the Itinerarium Kambriae of about 1191, the account of his own journey through Wales in 1188. The form lent itself naturally to observations on local history and topography, and Gerald also crammed in various stories and notes on the customs of the inhabitants—methods of warfare[14] and divinatory practices,[15] for example.

Such material points forward to the Descriptio Kambriae of 1194, Gerald's fourth work on Irish and Welsh topics, and the one which is, in many respects, the most satisfying as a literary creation and most exciting in conception. He took as his subject 'the description of our Wales and the nature of the people, truly foreign and distinct from other nations'.[16] The Descriptio Kambriae has a thematic unity which the earlier works cannot match and is well organized, comprehensive, and precise. In the absence of the definitive Topographia Britannica, which Gerald envisaged but did not produce,[17] the Descriptio

Kambriae stands as his highest achievement in this field. The opportunity and stimulus for the writing of the Descriptio were provided by Gerald's own mixed ethnic background and the complexity of twelfth-century Wales. As the Anglo-Normans penetrated and settled Wales, a 'frontier society' was created which provoked reflection on ethnic diversity. Similar situations elsewhere in Europe, as on the lower Elbe, produced similar results.[18] Yet, although the stimulus for ethnography was provided by conquest and ethnic conflict, Gerald's own motives for writing the Descriptio Kambriae are far from simple.

There is no doubt that he was attempting 'objective' description, in some sense of the phrase. He labelled the work a descriptio, and referred several times to the need for impartiality. Impartiality did not mean abstaining from moral judgements, but recording both vices and virtues. After describing the good points of the Welsh, he felt that 'suitable order demands' that, *more historico*, he treat their bad points.[19] The phrase *more historico* indicates how he viewed the Descriptio Kambriae. In the absence of an ethnographic tradition, ethnographic writing appeared as a kind of history, both to its audience and its practitioners. As history, it was bound by an obligation to describe both the vices and virtues of the people it took as a subject. Gerald asked for 'pardon for telling the truth, without which no history deserves authority or even truly to be called history'.[20] The only model Gerald mentioned explicitly was Gildas, partly because he too wrote about the Britons, but also because of his reputation for historical impartiality. 'Gildas... *more historico*', he wrote, 'did not fail to mention the vices of his people, because of his love of the truth'.[21]

We can press the question of Gerald's motivations and intentions in writing the Descriptio Kambriae further than his desire to write 'objective ethnography'. To be sure, he had a conception of accuracy and a real curiosity—the Irish and Welsh works would not otherwise exist—but there were other forces shaping their production. In the twelfth century there were no institutional supports which would further ethnographic description for its own sake. Gerald's intentions and motives in writing the works have to be seen in the context of the institutions which did affect him: his family, the clerical order, royal service.

In terms of family and country, it was Gerald's own claim that the Descriptio Kambriae was inspired by local piety. 'Since noble histories of other regions, produced by eminent authors in times past, have come forth into the light,' he wrote, 'we have deemed it neither useless nor unpraiseworthy to unfold the secrets of our region, for the favour of the country and posterity, and to bring from the shadows glorious deeds not yet recorded in any worthy work.'[22] Rather than go over the well-trodden paths of classical legend, 'I have preferred to proclaim the poor history of our region, which others have almost entirely ignored until now, with my efforts, not ungrateful to kin and country (industria nostra parentibus et patriae non ingrata).'[23] 'First I have arranged to illuminate, with my literary efforts, my country and the neighbouring regions, lest I should appear ungrateful to my native soil (ne natali ingratus solo viderer).'[24]

Several of Gerald's works were motivated, partly at least, by local loyalties and attachments. The Expugnatio Hibernica can be seen as a family epic.[25] The saints' lives he wrote in the 1190s were the products of local attachments to the cathedrals where he held prebends. The Itinerarium Kambriae contains much material relating to Gerald's family and the countryside in which he grew up and which he knew so well—accounts of St. David's and Brecon and the famous description of Manorbier. Nor were patriotic motives for the writing of history unknown in the twelfth century. William of Tyre wrote his history of Outremer pressed by 'a most compelling love for my country (urgentissimus... amor patriae)'.[26] But the invocation of local feeling to account for the composition of the Descriptio Kambriae creates problems.

The work is mainly about 'Welsh Wales', and if it is about Gerald's *parentes* and *patria*, it is so only in a very special sense. As Michael Richter has observed, 'It would be difficult to find genuine patriotic motives in his writing'.[27] Yet, although Gerald's associations were much more with the Marcher than the Welsh elements in his blood, the Descriptio Kambriae contains passages which show real sympathy with the Welsh. The ambiguity of Gerald's feelings is symbolized by the three remarkable last chapters of the Descriptio Kambriae: 'How the Welsh should be conquered', 'How, once conquered, they should be governed', and 'How they can resist and rebel'.[28] The advice on how to conquer and rule the Welsh is not, in itself, surprising. It is a commonplace that ethnographic observations have often served the interests of conquerors or colonizers. The line between anthropologist and spy has not always been clear.[29] Half a century or so after the writing of the Descriptio Kambriae, John of Plano Carpini produced his Ystoria Mongalorum, an ethnographic monograph as impressive as Gerald's, 'in order to reveal the Mongols' intentions and plans to the Christians, so that they will not be able to rush upon them unawares...'[30] Here the intention was defensive rather than aggressive, but, again, it is 'applied anthropology'[31]—knowledge of Mongol society, and particularly, of course, their military affairs, would enable Christian Europe to defend itself better.

Gerald's position was not so straightforward, at least in Wales. In Ireland he was more clearly one of the invaders and colonizers; hence his chapters in the Expugnatio Hibernica on 'How the Irish are to be conquered' and 'How they are to be governed'[32] are not balanced by any advice to the native people. The Topographia Hibernica, too, justifies and glorifies the Anglo-Norman invasion.[33] But in Wales Gerald could feel, at times, a closer identification with the native inhabitants. This tentative identification is extremely well illustrated by Gerald's choice of name for his *patria*. He consistently used Kambria in preference to Wallia. On several occasions he wrote 'Kambria nunc adulterino vocabulo Wallia dicitur' or something similar.[34] He knew that Wallia came from the Old English word for 'foreigner' and regarded it as 'a barbarous appellation (barbara nuncupatio)'.[35] Wallia and Wallenses were the usual terms employed by English writers in the twelfth century, and so by using Kambria and Kambrenses Gerald distanced himself from the English usage and expressed some kind of identification with Wales. On the other hand, Kambria and Kambrenses were not the usual words that the Welsh used of themselves. Gerald's idiosyncratic usage can be seen in his rewriting of Rhigyfarch's Life of St. David, where he systematically substituted Kambrenses for the more usual Britones. The word Kambria, a latinization from the vernacular Cymri, the term by which the west Britons referred to themselves, is first recorded in the tenth century, and denotes Strathclyde and (modern) Cumbria. Geoffrey of Monmouth took it as the old name for Wales and invented Kamber, son of Brutus, to explain it.[36] Kambria and its derivatives 'were... felt as imposing and literary'.[37] In his preference for Kambrenses over both Wallenses and Britones, rejecting both what the English called the Welsh and what the Welsh called themselves, Gerald was attempting to create a terminology for his own peculiarly ambiguous ethnic and national position—he belonged to Wales but was not Welsh. In this sense his traditional appellation, Giraldus Cambrensis, is entirely appropriate.

Thus, despite the fact that the Descriptio Kambriae was written by a royal clerk active in the pacification of Wales, and dedicated to Hubert Walter, Archbishop of Canterbury and Justiciar of England, it is about 'our Kambria'[38] and contains such passages as the moving words of the Welsh lord defending the integrity of his people: 'No other people, I believe, than this Welsh race nor any other language will answer in the Day of Judgement before the Supreme Judge for this corner of the earth'.[39] Hence Gerald can claim that the Descriptio Kambriae is a product of local piety while, at the same time, the work has clear affinities with the 'applied anthropology' of ethnographers working for political and military purposes.

The work's moral overtones and implications are as tangled as its political stance. Gerald was an ecclesiastic and a moralist and the very structure of the Descriptio Kambriae is based upon moral polarities. Book I includes 'things consonant with virtue which can be assembled and expounded to their praise and honour', while Book II is entitled 'Unpraiseworthy Things'.[40] Description and moral evaluation are thus assimilated; virtue and vice are analytical, or at least organizational, tools. Yet there is no simple, ultimate moral purpose in the Descriptio Kambriae. It was not a work of moral exhortation addressed to the Welsh, nor is it, like the Gemma Ecclesiastica Gerald wrote four years later, a work of pastoral care for the clergy in Wales. At times it does hold up the Welsh as a model of certain virtues which the English lack—temperance, especially—and it then has a tone reminiscent of the Germania. Even if the Welsh were occasionally greedy, Gerald asserted, nevertheless they did not get entangled with money-lenders through gluttony and drunkenness, like the English.[41] But this contrast of the natural abstinence of a less civilized people with the self-indulgence of a more civilized race is hardly the raison d'être of the work.

There is also surprisingly little emphasis on the idea of 'moral causation'. The belief that the social ordering of the world, patterns of success and failure, of power and weakness, might be explained as consequences of moral behaviour was a commonplace in the twelfth century,[42] but has only a small place in the Descriptio Kambriae. Gerald's statement that the Britons lost Britain to the Saxons because of their sins[43] is an isolated reference. At other times he stressed the fact that moral behaviour was shaped by the environment. Discussing sodomy, for example, he wrote that the absence of the vice among the Welsh of his own time was due to their poverty and exile—sodomy was a vice of luxurious societies—not to their virtue.[44] But he believed the effects of poverty to be two-edged: 'For just as poverty tends to extinguish many vices, so, in the meantime, many things contrary to the virtues spring from it'.[45] In both cases, he was presuming that moral dispositions were shaped by non-moral conditions. Even when attacking Welsh 'incest', marriage within prohibited degrees, he realized the social function of such marriages in patching up feuds within the kindred and in preserving good blood.[46] Gerald's moralism does not dominate the Descriptio Kambriae; it is always tempered by his awareness of the importance of social and physical factors in human behaviour.

Gerald's motives and intentions in writing the Descriptio Kambriae can be seen to be mixed and inconsistent. He was writing for fame and for the favour of princes—although less and less hopefully.[47] He saw himself fulfilling some kind of debt of local piety. He wrote a set-piece account of how the Anglo-Norman kingdom might subdue the Welsh. As an ecclesiastic and moralist, he introduced ethical judgements into the picture, but not in any simple or dominating way. Finally, most important, mingled with these diverse hopes and purposes, we have a clear, curious, and critical eye, capable of producing one of the major ethnographic works of the pre-modern period.

DE GENTIS MORIBUS

Neither the theory nor the vocabulary of ethnographic description were in any way formalized in the twelfth century. The basic unit with which Gerald dealt was an ethnic one: gens (most often), natio, or populus. The Welsh formed a gens; so did the English and the Irish. This is straightforward. The Marchers, however, were also a gens—'a gens raised in the March of Wales'.[48] Hence, although common language and descent were the clearest criteria for what constituted a gens, there were ambiguous areas. The Marchers, of Norman descent and French speech but living in Wales, were perhaps a gens in the process of formation.

Gerald's discussion of the common origin of the Welsh, Cornish, and Bretons reveals what aspects of social life might provide evidence of ethnic relationship. He was aware of their common descent, but saw that this was attested by common cultural features as well as by the bare fact of kinship. One such feature was language: 'Cornwall and Brittany employ a very similar language, which is almost entirely comprehensible to the Welsh, on account of their original harmony.'[49] He realized that some developments of the language had occurred since the time of that 'ancient idiom of the British tongue',[50] but was aware of the historical significance of the mutual comprehensibility of the Brittonic languages.

Certain social practices which were shared by the Bretons and the Welsh also pointed to their common origin. Among the 'unpraiseworthy' aspects of Welsh society Gerald placed the inheritance of ecclesiastical benefices and the readiness of the Welsh to marry within the prohibited degrees. He knew, from reading the Epistolae of Hildebert of Le Mans, that these practices were also prevalent among the Bretons: 'From this it is possible to be certain that both vices have been common from ancient times to this whole people (toti huic genti), on that side of the sea and on this side.'[51] Here Gerald stressed the common nature of the Welsh and Bretons to such an extent that he called them one gens.

The concept of ethnic relationship, centred upon common descent, thus had linguistic and social ramifications. A passage from the Topographia Hibernica illustrates the kinds of similarities which demonstrated common descent. After explaining that the Irish are called Scoti, Gerald wrote, 'The northern part of the island of Britain is also called Scotia, because it is inhabited by a people originally descended from these men [i.e. the Irish]. The affinity of language and dress, of arms and customs, even to this day, proves this (Quod tam linguae quam cultus, tam armorum etiam quam morum, usque in hodiernum probat affinitas).'[52] Here we have four categories: lingua; cultus—here probably 'dress' and 'appearance' rather than 'manner of living' or 'culture';[53] arma, an important category in Gerald's analysis, as we shall see; and mores.

Problems and methods of identifying the ethnic group, the gens so central to the very conception of the Descriptio Kambriae, thus lead imperceptibly into the general problem of classifying social phenomena. The four terms just mentioned—lingua, cultus, arma, and mores—might serve as a shorthand guide to the categories Gerald employed in his ethnographic descriptions. The first three are not problematic. Language is an obvious badge of group identity and, especially when used by a linguistic observer as intelligent as Gerald, provided helpful clues to past history and ethnic affiliation.[54] Dress, in a period of highly differentiated regional costume, and methods of treating hair and beard, were of similar importance. *Arma*, including methods of warfare, considerations of terrain, and even social structure as well as simple weaponry,[55] was of basic importance: these societies probably expended as much energy in war as in agriculture. *Mores* is not so straightforward, and must be analysed briefly.

Gerald sometimes used the word in company with two others. In the Descriptio Kambriae, after describing the geography of Wales and discussing her princes and the etymology of the name, he turned to the Welsh people themselves; chapter viii is entitled 'De gentis hujus natura, moribus et cultu'.[56] This is practically identical wording to the heading of Book III, chapter x of the Topographia Hibernica, which introduces the ethnographic description: 'De gentis istius natura, moribus et cultu'.[57] A people could thus be described from three different viewpoints: nature, customs, and appearance. *Mores*, therefore, form a fundamental category of social description, distinct from natura. The core meaning of *mores* is fairly clear. It is 'social practices, or ways of doing things, characteristic of a people'. The Welsh practice of partible inheritance, for example, was a *mos*.[58] The purchase of girls from their parents was another.[59] Gerald referred to the Welsh singing in choirs 'as is the custom among this people (sicut huic genti mos est)'.[60] Wearing the hair long,[61] arranging the head-dress in a certain way,[62] and holding the right hand out to swear an oath[63] were all *mores*.

The emphasis of the word *mores* is usually, as these examples show, on behaviour, upon the external aspect rather than upon interior, mental characteristics. Yet the word can approach this psychological sense, too. When a 'Welshman entered into a trial period of cohabitation to test the *morum qualitas* of his prospective wife,[64] it is hard to see where the dividing line could be drawn between *mores* as behaviour and *mores* as disposition. Gerald described the Irish in these words: '*Hi mores*: neither strong in war nor trustworthy in peace'.[65] Military weakness and untrustworthiness are hardly 'customs'; Gerald was referring to the Irish character, in the same way as he regarded the boldness and readiness of the Marchers as *mores*. Obviously, to him mores sometimes included the psychological characteristics of a people and this usage approaches the semantic area of the modern 'moral'.

A passage in the Topographia Hibernica shows how Gerald's use of the term *mores* covered a spectrum from 'customs' to 'morals', from ethnography to ethics. He was very interested in the transmission and diffusion of *mores*, and in the Topographia Hibernica he argued that geographical isolation was the reason for Irish barbarism. 'Since behaviour is moulded by social contact (cum a convictu mores formentur),' he wrote, quoting his master, Peter the Chanter,[66] 'as they are so remote from the ordinary world in these far-off parts, as if in another world, and so cut off from virtuous and obedient peoples (modestis et morigeratis populis), they know and are accustomed to only that barbarism in which they were born and raised and which they embrace like a second nature.'[67] The characteristics of the Irish could thus be explained by lack of contact with other peoples. Yet such contact, in Gerald's view, did not necessarily lead to the civilizing of the Irish. When the Anglo-Normans came to Ireland, in fact, the reverse process occurred. They picked up Irish treachery and faithlessness. A moral version of Gresham's Law was at work: 'wicked company corrupts good morals'.[68]

In passages of this kind, Gerald showed both a sense of social process, an awareness of the importance of cultural contact, and the moralism of a rigorous ecclesiastic. His use of quotation exemplifies this. Gerald borrowed the phrase 'behaviour is moulded by social contact' from Peter the Chanter, who had used it in the context of individual moral behaviour, and gave it a more general, social meaning. Peter had in mind the dangers represented by 'bad company'; Gerald was thinking of how races develop their specific traits. Yet he continued to use such ideas in a moral sense too. 'Behaviour is moulded by social contact and "he who touches pitch will be defiled by it"', he wrote, describing the 'infectiousness' of Irish treachery.[69] A biblical moralism informed his idea of cultural contact.

The concept *mores* thus included a predominant external and a subordinate internal sense, and ranged a spectrum from 'social practice' to 'moral quality'. It has various semantic siblings. *Consuetudo* is often almost synonymous with the more external, social sense of *mos*. *Ritus* is a word with both a very general meaning, so that roughly made clothes can be described as 'put together *barbarico rite*'[70] but also has a meaning close to 'rite' or 'ritual'. Gerald used it, for example, in connection with blood-brotherhood and royal inauguration.[71] *Mos, consuetudo*, and *ritus* form a closely related trio.[72]

This group of concepts relates largely to unconscious social processes and can be distinguished on one side from more conscious, learned habits and, on the other, from the innate or the natural. There is little in the Irish and Welsh works about conscious learning—the general focus is on unconscious, osmotic social processes—but there is one isolated reference which may be significant. This occurs in Gerald's discussion of 'the ancient foundations of the faith' in Wales. He described certain peculiar religious practices, such as breaking off the first corner of a loaf to give to the poor and sitting down to eat in threes, in honour of the Trinity. These, he said, dated back to the mission of Saints Germanus and Lupus in the fifth century. 'From their teaching, they hold these lessons even up to today (Ab eorundem... doctrina, haec... usque in hodiernum diem documenta tenuerunt).'[73] These peculiarities, unlike royal inaugurations or the inheritance of benefices, are not *ritus*, *mores*, or *consuetudines*—they are *documenta* springing from *doctrina*. To a modern eye there would be no clear reason for such a distinction. Yet Gerald seems to have felt that good religious practices, especially those stemming from the impeccable authority of a bishopsaint, were not assimilable to secular customs. They inhabited a separate world, a world of consciousness and grace. Such, at any rate, is an interpretation that the difference in terminology might suggest. So, on one side of 'custom', there is self-awareness and learning.

On the other side is nature. Sometimes what is natural means innate mental dispositions. 'Nature', wrote Gerald, 'gives to all of them [the Welsh]... boldness of speech and assurance in response.'[74] But *natura* is a Protean word, as the discussion of miracles and marvels in Part II has indicated, and the line between nature and custom often blurs. Habits become natural: 'From long exile and poverty, the nature of this people [the Welsh] could have been perverted into worse usages';[75] 'the long abuse of a wicked custom (*consuetudinis*) could be converted into nature'.[76] In discussing Irish treachery, as mentioned above, Gerald wrote, 'even strangers become entangled in this vice of the country, which is, as it were, innate and extremely contagious'.[77] In these statements, nature turns to worse usages through social causes; customs turn into nature; and there is a vice which both, in a sense, innate and highly contagious. Gerald's sense of the effects of nature, as geography, upon social forms, is discussed below, but here it is worth simply noting the fluidity of the boundary between the innate and the natural, on the one hand, and custom on the other.

The storehouse of concepts and terms which Gerald had available was, therefore, not poorly stocked; nor were these concepts crude or inadequate. Yet in many ways they were unsystematic and their contours look unfamiliar to us. Distinctions between inner and outer, natural and social, were asserted but transgressed. His terms were not technical. Indeed, there is a fluidity and suggestiveness about the conceptual apparatus of Gerald's ethnographic works that sets them apart from the increasingly strict definitions of the schools. They are imprecise, but they represent a living and responsive vocabulary. There is no doubt that the verbal and conceptual building blocks for ethnographic description were available in the twelfth century.

What makes Gerald's Irish and Welsh works unique is the acuteness of his observation and the detail of his description. The Descriptio Kambriae is a world away from the ethnographic commonplaces catalogued by the encyclo-paedists and, unlike most twelfth-century historians, Gerald allowed himself the space to describe the smallest details of everyday life. Given the scope of the Gesta Friderici, for example, Otto of Freising could only attempt a thumbnail sketch of the Magyars and was able to touch on only the most salient ethno-graphic features.[78] Gerald, by reinventing the ethnographic monograph, was able to go much further into microcosmic description.[79] His account of how the Welsh cared for their teeth is a good example: 'Both sexes take greater care of their teeth than any people I have seen. They make them like ivory by continually rubbing them with green hazel and cleansing them with a woollen cloth. In order to look after them they abstain from hot food, always eating cold or lukewarm food.'[80] However, his attempt to write a detailed account of the ways of a foreign people was sometimes hampered by technical problems. For example, when he tried to recreate in words the implement that the Welsh used for reaping, he was frustrated by the limitations of verbal description:

> They do not use sickles for reaping but employ more readily a medium-sized iron implement, shaped like a knife, which is loosely and flexibly bound with two rods at the ends. But since
>
> 'Things imparted through the ears enliven the mind more slowly
> Than things placed before our trustworthy eyes',
>
> you will understand the method better by seeing than by hearing.[81]

It is not often that Gerald reached the limits of verbal description in this way. The fact that he did so is a sign, in itself, that he was attempting to deal with new subjects on a level of technical detail that was rare.

Other ethnographic writers of the Middle Ages had similar feelings about the inadequacy of words for describing the artefacts of alien societies. William of Rubruck, Franciscan missionary among the Mongols in the 1250s, in his account of the Mongols' houses and wagons, sighed, 'The married women make beautiful wagons for themselves, which I don't know how to describe to you except through an illustration—indeed, I would illustrate everything for you, if I knew how to draw.'[82] Problems of visualization were, of course, frequent for writers in the didactic tradition of Latin prose, and it was only the development of the diagram and illustration which resolved these problems. European exploratory expeditions from the sixteenth century onwards commonly included an artist to record both the natural history and the inhabitants of distant regions. It is worth noting that Gerald himself tried his hand at one form of visual aid, the map,[83] and may have been responsible for the archetypes of the illuminations which appear in some manuscripts of the Topographia Hibernica.[84] Normally, however, Gerald's verbal powers were adequate to the material; expression and observation were in harmony.

ARMS AND LIBERTY

The society Gerald presented in the Descriptio Kambriae strikes us as a coherent and plausible social world. We are not confronted with an assemblage of discordant practices or presented with a random mixture of anecdote and moral judgement. It is anthropologically plausible, for Gerald had a strong, if often implicit, sense of how various component social practices fitted together into a whole, and of how societies could be characterized by distinctive qualities or by the way they had adapted to a particular physical environment. Classical ethnographers, and those early medieval encyclopaedists who referred to ethnographic data, had certain traditional categories into which they fitted their material. It is reasonably certain that they would deal with geography, language, dress, diet, dwellings, warfare and marriage customs, and, especially in the case of Christians writing about pagans, religious rites and burial practices.[85] Gerald covered all these traditional topics and went beyond them, both in the detail of his description and in the scope of his account. He added to this comprehensiveness an implicit feeling for the distinctiveness and unity of the society he was describing.

Gerald began his description systematically, with the material basis of the society. The first seven chapters of the Descriptio Kambriae discuss, among other things, 'the quality and quantity of the land' and include a gazetteer of the rivers of Wales, the princely courts, the bishoprics, and the mountains.[86] This is a prelude to the account of the people themselves. He characterized their economic activities briefly but clearly, emphasizing, as we have seen,[87] the pastoralism of the Welsh: 'Almost the entire population is fed from flocks, barley, milk, cheese, and butter. They eat a lot of meat but little bread.'[88] 'They do not have orchards or gardens... Their fields are mainly used for pasture...'[89] Not only was their agriculture largely pastoral, but their economy as a whole was less developed and less complex than that of England or France: 'They do not trouble themselves with trade, navigation or crafts.'[90] In some crucial areas they were, in fact, dependent on their corn-growing and manufacturing neighbour; Gerald referred to 'trade in iron, cloth, salt, and corn, through which they are accustomed to be supported from the resources of England'.[91] This general level of economic development was reflected in the low density of population, the absence of towns, and the simple nature of the dwellings—although Gerald the moralist praised this last feature as evidence of an admirable austerity, rather than despising it as an indicator of poverty: 'They do not live in towns, villages, or castles,' he wrote, 'but cling to the woods like hermits. It is their custom to raise on the edge of the woods not great, high palaces or sumptuous and superfluous buildings of stone and mortar, but wattle huts, sufficient for one year's use, involving only moderate effort and cost.'[92] From the point of view of England or France, it was reasonable to characterize the Welsh by their 'poverty'.[93]

Upon these economic foundations a particular kind of social structure had been raised. It was clan-based and politically decentralized, although, as has been emphasized,[94] by no means static. Welsh society in the twelfth and, especially, the thirteenth century was in the process of transformation. Nevertheless, the clan basis was still very important, and many of Gerald's observations make this clear.

One characteristic of Welsh society that struck him was that all free members of the clan were trained warriors. 'This whole people', he wrote, 'are dedicated to war. For here not only the nobles, but the whole people are trained in arms. When the war trumpet sounds the country dweller rushes to arms from the plough as swiftly as the courtier from the hall.'[95] Here was a crucial distinction between the clan-based Welsh society and the feudal society of the Anglo-Normans. Gerald's contrast is overdrawn, since, in keeping with the well-nigh total invisibility of the lower classes throughout his work, he completely omitted any mention of the Welsh taeogs, bondsmen forming a substantial minority of the population.[96] Yet his point about warlike training in Welsh and English society seems accurate. In Wales 'communities of free pastoralists'[97] did exist and made their living from stock-rearing and raiding. In Anglo-Norman England there was a clear, indeed an increasingly sharp, line between a military upper class and a peasant population who worked the land and were untrained in war—bellatores and laboratores.

Gerald devoted a lot of space to discussion of methods of warfare. This interest may have a partly autobiographical explanation; he belonged to the world of bellatores as well as that of the oratores.[98] Yet the discussion of Welsh warfare in the Descriptio Kambriae reflected more than the seasoned observations of the son of a Marcher family. His analysis of Welsh military tactics can be seen as a keystone linking various other aspects of his description. On one hand, it is clear that these tactics were a consequence of the terrain, and so Gerald's description of warfare interlocks with his description of the geography of Wales. On the other hand, Welsh social structure was moulded into a certain shape by the requirements of military technology and organization, and this relationship comes out clearly from Gerald's analysis. At a further level, Gerald was also aware of the way a people's psychological characteristics were influenced by both military organization and social structure. His analysis of the Welsh is a complex in which his account of military matters has a central place.

Gerald must have had firsthand acquaintance with the heavy cavalry of France and England, since he had been in the entourage of Prince John in Ireland in 1185 and was with Henry II in France in 1188-9. What struck him first when considering the Welsh warriors was their lightness and speed in comparison with the mailed horsemen of the Angevins:

> It is worth noting that the Welsh, on many occasions, do not fear to engage naked with men clad in iron, unarmed with armed men, on foot with cavalry. They often emerge victorious from these conflicts simply because of their agility and spiritedness...They use light weapons which do not impede their agility: small mail-coats, handfuls of arrows, long lances; helmets, shields, and (more rarely) iron greaves. The more noble ride to war on swift, well-bred horses which are born in Wales, but most of the people go into battle on foot, because the terrain is marshy and uneven. The foot soldiers, however, easily become horsemen, if time or place dictates either flight or pursuit.[99]

The Welsh method of waging war was clearly related to the terrain of Wales. It had both advantages and disadvantages when faced with armoured, mounted men. The initial attack of the Welsh could be terrifying, Gerald observed, but, if they encountered stiff resistance, then they could soon be put to flight. 'Their battles are all either pursuits or routs', he wrote. 'A lightly armoured people, trusting in agility rather than strength, cannot sustain conflict on the level plain, hand to hand contest for victory or manful struggle, for very long.'[100] However, they were as easily stirred up to fight again as they were induced to retreat; they were expert at guerrilla war. 'It is easy to win a battle against them,' Gerald said, 'but difficult to win the war.'[101]

Gerald distinguished 'French warfare' (*Gallica militia*[102]) from 'Welsh and Irish warfare'. The former, he argued, was quite inappropriate to Welsh conditions:

Although the Flemings, Normans, Coterelli, and Bragmanni[103] are excellent soldiers in their own lands and well trained in war, nevertheless it should be known that French warfare is very different from Welsh and Irish warfare. In their lands there are level plains, armour is an honour, and it is stability which conquers; here are rugged woodlands, armour is a burden, and victory is won through agility. There soldiers are captured; here they are beheaded. There they are ransomed; here they are killed.

Therefore, just as that heavy, elaborate armour of linen and iron both protects and adorns the knights when battle is joined on level ground, so light armour is far superior when it is a matter of single combat in enclosed spaces—woods or marshes—where the site is more suitable for footmen than horsemen...

In such elaborate armour it is difficult to dismount from the high, curving saddles; it is even more difficult to remount, and most difficult of all to go on foot, when there is need... We assert that there is doubtless need for armoured men and might—when it is a matter of fighting against heavily armoured troops who rely on strength and force of arms and fight on level ground and obtain victory by might. But against light, agile men, in broken country, lightly armoured troops, who are trained in such conflicts, should be employed.[104]

The *Gallica militia* was a product of the plains of northern France, where heavily armoured cavalry made military sense. The expense of fitting out an armoured horseman and the consequences of this fact for the development of feudal society have often been discussed.[105] However, the relatively slight investment represented by Welsh war equipment meant that military technology did not drive such a deep fissure into Welsh society as it did in contemporary feudal Europe. Welsh society was by no means egalitarian, but a greater proportion of the population than elsewhere enjoyed libertas. In Gerald's eyes training in arms and libertas were intimately connected. For example, one way in which he thought the defence of the March might be assured was by giving 'the soldiers and citizens, the servants, too, and the whole people' training in arms; this would imbue them with libertas and superbia (self-respect).[106]

For Gerald, the liberty of the Welsh seemed to be one of their most striking characteristics, and sharply distinguished them from the English, for whom he had little respect:

> They are zealous in defence of their country and liberty; they fight for their country, they strive for liberty; for these things it seems sweet to them not only to fight, but even to give up their lives.[107]

> Because the Welsh are not oppressed with heavy burdens or worn down by servile works or troubled with any seigneurial exactions (nec laboriosis oneribus opprimuntur, nec servilibus operibus atteruntur, nec dominorum exactionibus ullis molestantur), they can hold their heads high and repel wrongs. This is the source of their great boldness in defence of their country, and it is because of this that this people are always ready at arms for resistance. For there is nothing that stirs, encourages, and summons men's hearts to worthiness like the joyfulness of liberty; nothing depresses and discourages like the oppression of servitude.[108]

This 'joyfulness of liberty' (libertatis hilaritas) is a psychological, almost moral, quality which is a consequence of the rough egalitarianism of pastoral, clan society. If we grant the invisibility of the bond taeogs in their farming villages, then Gerald's picture was not grossly inaccurate, particularly if we remember that the whole picture must be seen in contast to Anglo-Norman society. There is a complex pattern relating the pastoralism, the terrain, the military technology, the social structure, and the psychological characteristics of the Welsh. When Gerald wrote of Welsh boldness of speech, it is possible to see the implicit ties connecting this quality with the other features he described: 'Nature has given them all, the least of the common people as well as the chief men, a boldness in speech and readiness of response before princes and magnates concerning every matter.'[109] It is the same libertatis hilaritas which the servile, tongue-tied English so clearly lacked.

Gerald admired the independence of the Welsh free clansmen and praised the simplicity of their life, while being aware of their economic backwardness. As one of the well-born, he despised the servile class in his own society and admired the 'aristocratic' virtues of courage, outspokenness, and independence that he saw in this clan-based society. Gerald's attitude to the Welsh has something of the same tone as that of a Victorian gentleman explorer towards the Bedouin.

Yet, like those Victorian travellers, Gerald was also aware of the price of libertas. He was a harsh critic of the continual internecine quarrels of the Welsh, their violence and political particularism. The society he knew in England and France had deeper class fissures and a servile and downtrodden peasantry, but he also thought that it had succeeded better in coping with problems of political and social order.[110] 'It is characteristic of them', he wrote of the Welsh, 'to pursue plunder and to live by theft, robbery, and brigandage, not only from foreign and hostile peoples but also among themselves.'[111] 'More than any other nation, this people are ambitious to root up boundary ditches, to move boundary stones, and to overstep limits and to occupy lands or extend them in every way possible... the result of this is litigation in court and quarrels, killings, burnings, and frequent fratricides.'[112]

He traced this internecine strife to certain social institutions. The Welsh practice of partible inheritance (cyfran in Welsh) between brothers, legitimate and illegitimate, stood in marked contrast to the primogeniture of the Anglo-Normans. Gerald attributed much of the friction within kindreds to this inheritance practice.[113] He also criticized the custom of putting out princes' sons to aristocratic foster-families. He thought this simply encouraged the ambitions of the foster-fathers: 'After the father's death each of them strives and schemes with all his might to raise his own foster-son and have him preferred above all the rest. Because of this grave disturbances often arise in their lands, with many killings, fratricides, and frequent blindings of brothers.'[114] Gerald lived through times when the activities of the sons of the Lord Rhys in South Wales and the sons and grandsons of Owain Gwynedd in the north fully justified this analysis.[115] In his opinion, kin loyalty and blood feud were characteristic features of Welsh life.[116] The combination of dissension within the kin, consequent upon inheritance practices, and the ethos of kin loyalty, led to curious results: 'They love their brothers more when they are dead than when they are alive. For when they are alive, they harry them to death, but when they are dead if killed by others, they avenge them with all their power.'[117]

The institutional feature which epitomized the discord and internal strife of Welsh society, embodying it at its highest level, was the refusal of the Welsh to acknowledge a single prince. Gerald had a deep admiration for the Capetians and had served the Angevins and knew their power; the inability of the Welsh to produce a similar centralizing dynasty seemed to him, as already observed,[118] their major political weakness. This sentiment, great propaganda for the house of Gwynedd in its attempt to centralize and feudalize Wales, is clearly an integral part of Gerald's whole attitude to Welsh society. Political disunity was, in a sense, the other side of libertas. The pastoral kin-based society of Welsh Wales produced men who could hold their heads high but was also perpetually embroiled in bloody feud and disunity. The arable, feudal societies ruled by the

Angevins and Capetians were characterized by oppressiveness and class divisions but could guarantee at least a minimum of social and political order.

CLIMATE, HISTORY, AND LANGUAGE

Gerald's picture of the Welsh was thus detailed and coherent and this detail and coherence represent a major achievement. In the field of theory he was not such a trail-blazer. His talents were for vivid description of the particular rather than rigorous or systematic theorizing, and we should not look to his works for major developments in what might be called 'anthropological theory'. Nevertheless, he did attempt to apply general explanations for some of the phenomena he described. These are advanced briefly and sometimes allusively, but provide evidence for his presuppositions about the forces that shaped human society.

Geographical influences were, as we have seen, important in Gerald's explanation of social and cultural characteristics. He related the continued independence of the Welsh, compared with the subjugation of the Cornish, to the natural defensibility of Wales. Wales was:

> a land well fortified by high mountains, deep valleys, huge forests, waters, and marshes, so that from the time when the Saxons first occupied the island, the remnants of the Britons, who had withdrawn into these parts, have not been completely conquered either by the English, or, later, by the Normans. But those who betook themselves to the southern corner, which received its name from Duke Corineus [i.e. Cornubia, Cornwall], were not able to resist so well because the land was not so well protected.[119]

Gerald's use of concepts of environmental influence, however, went further than this. He believed that climatic influences could leave a permanent imprint upon a race. In the Descriptio Kambriae he discussed Welsh 'boldness in speech', and commented that they shared this gift with the Romans and the French. The English, however, their kinsmen from Saxony, and the Germans did not possess it. The explanation for this difference, Gerald argued, could not lie in the fact that the English were an enslaved people, since the Saxons and Germans were free, but still marked by this tongue-tied reticence.

> Therefore the Saxons and Germans contracted this coldness of nature from the cold, polar regions to which they belong. The English, too, although they have been distant from those regions for a long time, nevertheless possess inseparably, as part of their original nature, both an exterior quality, paleness, and an interior one, coldness, from the same cause—the wet, cold nature of their complexion.

The Britons, however, on the contrary, coming from the hot, sun-burnt shore of Troy, although they came to these temperate regions...bear from their origin both, externally, that dark colour, related to the land, and internally, a natural heat from the dry humour, the source of their confidence.[120]

The theory that the climate influenced both the physical and psychological character of peoples was an ancient one. It had been formulated in the Hippocratic writings and was a commonplace among ancient authors.[121] Isidore summed up the theory in the following words:'Psychological diversity and the size, colour and appearance of men are caused by the different skies they are born under (Secundum diversitatem enim caeli et facies hominum et colores et corporum quantitates et animorum diversitates existunt).'[122]

Gerald made use of the theory in the Topographia Hibernica as well as in the Descriptio Kambriae. He wrote several chapters devoted to a comparison of 'the West' (which included Ireland and probably, in fact, referred to western Europe as a whole) and 'the East' (the Holy Land and adjacent regions). The different climates of these two regions had formed very contrasting types of people. In the east 'thanks to the more subtle air, the people, who are small in body, are powerful in intellectual subtlety. Because of this, they tend to conquer with poison rather than force and to be strong in cunning rather than in war.' In the west we find 'a people less clever, but stronger'. 'There a clever people, here a strong people. There they fight with poison, here with force. There cunning, here Mars. There study of wisdom, here of eloquence...'[123] This particular characterization, in which hot climates produced clever, indeed cunning men, who were physically small, while colder regions were inhabited by strong, warlike types who were less subtle, went back to at least the fifth century BC. It is found in the Hippocratic Airs, Waters and Places,[124] occurred in Aristotle,[125] and was frequently repeated. Gerald's belief in climatic theory explains certain references in his work which might otherwise be cryptic. For instance, he wrote that the Welsh were 'a people of subtle and acute mind...This whole nation, in general, is very shrewd and clever, more than other peoples living in a western clime (occiduo climate).'[126] The force of occiduo climate depends upon the general context of climatic theory.

Climatic influence was one of the most general physical causes available to a twelfth-century thinker for explanatory purposes. It was rivalled in generality only by astral determinism. Indeed, the two theories could be closely interdependent since the qualities of the different places were sometimes attributed to the different stars and planets. Albertus Magnus gave memorable formulation to this connection between geographical and astral influence when he wrote, 'wise philosophers teach us to regard the qualities of places like second stars (considerare virtutes locorum quasi stellas secundas...)'.[127] But astral determinism was a doctrine with which Gerald apparently felt no sympathy, although he did not warn against it explicitly like Nequam.[128]

Despite its appeal as a broad and convincing theory, and its basis in empirical fact, the employment of climatic explanations led to some intellectual problems. For instance, Gerald seems to have been unclear in his own mind whether Welsh boldness and English reticence were entirely attributable to a climatic origin or not. On one hand, he refuted the idea that the servitude of the English might explain their lack of confidence and forthrightness by bringing in the case of the Germans. If the Germans were reticent and free, he argued, then reticence had to have causes other than servitude. But he was also aware of the social causes of Welsh boldness and, as we have seen, specifically linked libertas and superbia with the right to bear and use arms. He presented both social and climatic reasons for the differences between the two peoples.

Another problem of climatic theory was its static nature; Gerald believed that the characteristics implanted by climate were permanent. Despite the migration of the English to a more southerly zone (he presumably saw Germany as north of England) and despite the move of the Britons from the Mediterranean to Britain, they had retained the qualities which were implanted in them by the climate of their original homes. The question springs to mind, of course, that if climatic conditions were sufficient to create the ethnic characteristics in the first place, why were they not able to alter those characteristics? This is a problem that would continually trouble the proponents of climatic theory, perhaps most crucially when African slaves began to be brought into northern climates,[129] but Gerald left it unresolved. He sometimes wrote as if nature could be influenced by social customs.[130] English servitude again provides an example: 'The English have been slaves and subjects for a long time and now are slaves naturally, as it were; it would not surprise me if they refused to abandon the long custom of their servile condition, which has possibly turned into something like nature (longa suae servilis conditionis consuetudine, quae tanquam in naturam converti potuit).'[131] The contradictions between this position and the climatic explanation are clear: one theory is social and dynamic, the other physical and static.

While it was difficult to reconcile climatic theory with explanation in social terms, a passage in the De Principis Instructione shows that it could be ingeniously integrated with the traditional religious themes of sin, heresy, and the devil's temptation of mankind. The diabolic cunning of heretics, Gerald argued, was shown by the way they tempted men to those sins which their climatic conditioning rendered most attractive to them. So Muhammad suggested polygamy to the Arabs 'since he knew that easterners are lustful, impelled and urged to this by the heat of the region'. The contemporary Cathars 'use the same technique of the Old Enemy to deceive men nowadays; for in these cold zones, where cold constricts and makes men greedy, they recommend avarice to men, suggesting and legislating that tithes are not to be given to priests nor offerings made to churches'.[132] The devil's technique is thus to vary the nature of heresies according to the known weaknesses of men of a particular climate, offering to legitimize their characteristic vices. Climatic theory was frequently used to argue that human laws should vary according to the differing natures of men in different climates, but Gerald's point here is more unusual. It shows that, despite its apparent physical and deterministic overtones, there is nothing in climatic theory which is intrinsically irreconcilable with a traditional religious viewpoint.

Clarence Glacken wrote, 'no exhaustive examination has ever been made of theories of geographical influence in the Middle Ages; such a study would not be rewarding since it would only tediously and repetitiously accumulate examples of a few basic ideas...'[133] Gerald's use of such theories supports Glacken's judgement. He used the concept of climatic determinism intelligently and sometimes originally, but it did not serve as a structuring device in his work, nor did it lead him to ask new questions or develop new approaches. He is really more interesting when discussing the impact of social forces, such as demography, economic activity, or foreign contact, on a people's way of life. The connection between the poverty of the Britons and their freedom from certain luxurious vices, such as homosexuality, has been mentioned,[134] and it is in his willingness to trace links of this kind that Gerald's strength lies. It was more innovative and fruitful to see moral disposition as the changing product of social and economic forces than as a permanent effect of climate.

Gerald's impressiveness in the *Descriptio Kambriae* also stems from his use of a comparative and historical approach. He highlighted Welsh practices by contrasting them with other peoples', illuminated them through comparisons, and was willing to analyse change over time. Such contrasts and comparisons sometimes led him to striking discoveries and insights.

Gerald drew on various sources for his comparisons—contemporary peoples, especially those now classified as 'Celtic', and peoples of the past known to him through his reading. Any description is implicitly comparative, and on several occasions Gerald made points about the Welsh which depend on such implicit comparisons. The distinctiveness of the fact that all the Welsh clansmen bore arms was emphasized by such phrases as 'Non... hic, ut alibi...'[135] In discussing Welsh disregard for oaths, Gerald wrote 'they think little of oaths, which are inviolable among other peoples'.[136] The practices which he took as norms were those of his own society—Anglo-Norman and also, perhaps, French. Indeed, in a letter written in 1198 he contrasted England, a *regio composita*, with Wales, a *regio barbara*.[137]

His comparisons were often less normative and more specific. He compared the Welsh habit of part-singing, for example, to that of the north of England. He also attempted to distinguish them. The Welsh practice had arisen indigenously and was now 'second nature', while the northern English practice was, he thought, the result of Viking influence.[138] Gerald concentrated most of his attention on comparisons with other Celtic peoples. He recognized the common descent of Welsh, Cornish, and Bretons.[139] He did not make such an explicit claim for the Irish and Scots, but drew several comparisons between these people and the Welsh, regarding, for example, music[140] and language.[141] He observed that the music of Scotland, Wales, and Ireland had much in common, both in form and in terms of the instruments used: 'It is to be noted that Scotland and Wales, the former on account of propagation (propagatio), the latter on account of its neighbourhood (affinitas) and travel to and fro (commeatio), strive to imitate Ireland in music.'[142] Propagatio, affinitas, and commeatio are concepts which can serve quite adequately in such a preliminary analysis of cultural diffusion.

His experience in Wales and Ireland, plus knowledge drawn from books, had given Gerald real insight into the ethnic and social patterns of Europe's 'north-western fringe'. Moreover, his reading of the classics and history enabled him to develop a historical sense of those peoples. Caesar, Lucan, and Gildas, in particular, provided information about the Britons which he used to build up this historical dimension. Sometimes the point was relatively simple, as when, after describing the Welsh practice of wearing a moustache, Gerald wrote, 'And they observe this custom not from recent times, but from antiquity and for long ages, as can be inferred from the book of Julius Caesar's deeds, which he himself wrote. There you will find these words: the British race "shaved in every part of the body except the upper lip".'[143] This example shows how Gerald combined the classics and his own observation to indicate a striking continuity.

A far more complex instance is the discussion of the bravery of the Britons or Welsh.[144] Gerald's argument here was scholastic. He produced two competing authorities and proceeded to resolve them. Gildas had written that the British 'were not powerful in war'.[145] On the other hand, the great Julius Caesar had, in Lucan's words, 'shown a terrified back to the pursuing Britons'.[146] Moreover, the story of Belinus and Brennius' conquests, Constantine's British birth (Helenae nostrae filius), the exploits of Aurelius Ambrosius and of 'our famous, I won't say fabulous, Arthur' would all lead one to believe that the British were brave enough. Yet, 'e diverso', Gildas, a Briton himself, had not praised their bravery, but had to describe their defeat at the hands of barbarian invaders. Gerald resolved the issue through historical and critical methods.[147] The expedition to the continent of the fourth-century usurper Maximus, famous in Welsh legend down to Gerald's own day,[148] had drained the Britons of 'the whole strength of the armed youth of Britain'. Before Maximus the Britons had been strong, able, in fact, to attack Rome. But their recovery from the depopulation resulting from his expedition was slow. Gildas wrote during this period of weakness. Eventually, however, the Britons increased in numbers and recovered their earlier boldness. In this way the authorities could be reconciled: 'Let the times be differentiated and the writings will agree'.[149] In a century conspicuous for the attempt to reconcile authorities in law and theology, Gerald used similar techniques to render human history comprehensible.

He made a final point: he recorded that the Welsh of his own day said that Gildas omitted any praise of Arthur from his work because of a feud between Arthur and Gildas' family. It is a sensible explanation for an omission which has troubled Arthurian scholars ever since, although it is not strictly compatible with the argument about depopulation which Gerald advanced. The two explanations revolve around two different principles—one seeking to harmonize the sources by arguing for a real historical change, the other relying on a critique of the sources to render the discrepancy only apparent. Gerald thought the latter explanation worth recording, but made no comment upon it.

Gerald used past writers on the Britons and attempted to reconcile them with each other and with his own observations in a way very similar to that in which he dealt with what the encyclopaedists had to say about natural history.[150] His dealings with both show the same respect for authorities, coupled with a critical ability. If possible, Gerald advanced arguments that saved his sources, but there was a tough core of his own personal observation which he would not sacrifice. He used the harmonizing techniques of the theologians and lawyers, and extended them to include his own experience of the human and natural world.

He did not think that the historical processes which affected Welsh success in war had ceased in his own day. He saw change in the contemporary situation, too, and explained the political and military factors which governed the balance between Welsh and Anglo-Norman in the eleventh and twelfth centuries. Whenever the English kings were free of French entanglements, he claimed, they could defeat the Welsh. Harold's successes in the 1060s had shown this, and the effect of his campaigns had been so great that the Welsh had been unable to recover during the entire reigns of the first three Norman kings. But three developments had led to their revival in the late twelfth century, Gerald's own day: their growth in numbers, the preoccupation of the Angevins with their French domains, and the fact that, as they came into contact with the Anglo-Normans at court and as hostages, the Welsh learned their military techniques.[151]

Observations such as these show Gerald's qualities as an interpreter of social and political forces. He was not content simply to discuss the question of whether the Welsh were brave and successful in war or not. Rather, he advanced a sophisticated scheme, in which all sorts of demographic, military, and political factors were employed to explain British or Welsh success and failure at different times. His explanations were not monocausal. Indeed, he can be criticized more often for entertaining too many, mutually exclusive, solutions. He had a precision and concreteness which were not common in the twelfth century. When, for example, he described the ways in which the Welsh became acquainted with Anglo-Norman military technique at close quarters, he was specific in mentioning attendance at court and service as hostages—two very important ways in which pre-modern societies gained knowledge of each other.

Gerald's achievements as a detailed and comparative observer, with a developed historical sense, were, perhaps, crowned by his observations on language. While it is hyperbole to call him 'the father of comparative philology',[152] it is clear that he was deeply interested in language and noticed some things about it which were quite original. His linguistic interests reflected both an acute ear and his training in grammar and rhetoric. He was interested in music and analysed and compared Irish and Welsh musical technique.[153] In the Topographia Hibernica he went from this subject to a long discussion on 'the benefits and effects of music', on David as the superlative musician, and on the etymology of the word 'music';[154] and he recommended these chapters as his most successful.[155] He revered music; 'Among all the most joyful things', he wrote, 'nothing pleases or delights men's feelings more'.[156] His sympathy for music led naturally to an appreciation of the musical qualities of language. His training had also given him an analytical insight into the structure and nature of language and linguistic effects. The two strands, a musical ear and an understanding of rhetoric, combined. For instance, the chapter in the Descriptio Kambriae on 'the intellectual acuteness and subtlety' of the Welsh covered both instrumental music, rhythmical songs, and alliteration.[157] The discussion of alliteration shows his lively ear and the natural way in which he used a comparative approach. He gave examples of Welsh, English, and Latin alliteration; the French, to his surprise, did not use it. Welsh and English alliteration, he said, was not an artistic contrivance, but a custom based on long usage. Gerald's mixed national origin and his education enabled him to compare Welsh and English verses with passages from Virgil, and to make assertions about the nature of French poetry.

A natural interest for such a linguistically complex mind was the etymology and translation of words from different tongues. The Descriptio Kambriae contains many examples of the translation of Welsh proper names and technical terms into Latin or, occasionally, English. For example, he referred to 'Ereri... quae Anglice Snaudune dicuntur, id est Nivium Montes',[158] talked of the 'nobiles qui Kambrice Hucheilwer, quasi superiores viri, vocantur',[159] and gave the etymology of Cantref: 'Cantaredus... id est Cantref, a Cant quod est centum et Tref, villa, composito vocabulo, tam Britannica quam Hybernica lingua dicitur'.[160] There are many cases of this kind. Gerald not only considered the origins of individual words but also characterized dialects and linguistic change in general. He regarded northern Welsh as 'more delicate, elegant, and praiseworthy' than other Welsh dialects, but thought that the clumsy dialects of Cornwall and Brittany were closer to the original tongue. In the same way, Wessex English, especially as spoken in Devon, was both clumsy and yet close to 'the nature of the original tongue', while northern English had many Danish and Norwegian borrowings. Proof of this was to be found in the similarity of twelfth-century Devon dialect to the Old English works of Bede, Rabanus, and Alfred.[161] Arguments like this reveal Gerald's linguistic acuteness. He believed languages developed from a state in which they were unformed (incomposita) to one in which they were more elegant (ornatior), saw that linguistic change might take place at different rates in different regions, understood the influence of foreign settlement on language, and, perhaps most striking of all, used Anglo-Saxon writings to substantiate his argument. If he was not 'the father of comparative philology', he was, without doubt, a comparative philologist.

His most remarkable insight in linguistics has already been analysed by scholars.[162] Briefly, he noticed the similarities between certain languages of the Indo-European group. In one case he listed the words for 'salt' in seven languages—Greek, Latin, Welsh, Irish (here, characteristically, he was inaccurate), French, English, and Flemish—and pointed out their similarities. He commented on the shift from 'h' to 's' between Greek and Latin, a fact he could have got from his grammars. He observed similarities between several Latin and Welsh words, many of which are now recognized as loan words dating from the Roman occupation.[163] As a linguistic theorist and observer, he probably went as far as a gifted individual could go, when no institutional resources or developed science existed to guide and support him. Early modern scholarship discredited some of the premises upon which his linguistic theories were based—notably the descent of the Welsh from the Trojans, who picked up Greek on their way from Troy to Britain. But he did notice genuine similarities between Greek and Welsh, and, in the absence of an alternative theory, migration was a plausible explanation. Given the limitations of twelfth-century thought and knowledge, Gerald made a major contribution to ethnographic writing.

EPILOGUE

Gerald's writings are varied and personal enough to convey a strong sense of his individuality. Certain traits are very striking and have been commented upon by virtually every scholar who has studied Gerald. His vanity, in particular, has been singled out, and there is no doubt that he was both boastful and almost hysterically sensitive to slights or rejection. He was prone to pomposity and, like most vain people, humourless. He took himself very seriously, and had no sense of proportion when others did not.

This earnestness about himself was matched by a certain authoritarianism in his religion. It is sometimes difficult to remember that Gerald died only a few years before St. Francis. The saint's spirituality, with its emphasis upon feeling, its interiority, and its sense of pathos, stands worlds apart from Gerald's hard and formal religion. Indeed, not only was Gerald very far away from Franciscan feeling, he also seems to have been untouched by the 'humanizing' elements of twelfth-century spirituality—spiritual friendship (amicitia), and a new warmth and delicacy in devotion. His God was a judge and a lord, not a father, let alone a friend. His writings stressed God's power and inscrutability. Gerald, in some ways, exhibited a 'pre-twelfth-century' spirituality.

This stern picture of God was accompanied by a great rigour towards the body. His polemics against clerical incontinence and his pervasive anti-feminism have an angriness of tone that suggests his own need for control. Some passages in the Gemma Ecclesiastica exhibit a violent loathing for the body and physical processes. The impression one receives of Gerald is that of a man of considerable intrinsic sexuality who, both by conscious training and by sublimation, successfully redirected these energies into other activities. This goes some way to explain the need he felt for models by which to define himself. The more insecure, threatened, and divided he felt, the more important it was that he has some picture of himself, as man of letters or man of God, indispensable royal servant or brilliant academic, to give him an anchor. This tendency was exacerbated by the disappointments of his life, and, in the retrospective writings of his later years, he tried to justify himself, to paint his past in its most glowing colours in order to redeem the present.

His career represents a tangle of discordant ideals and interests. His intellectual and expressive powers led him to a very high evaluation of literature. He had a sense of letters as a vocation and an almost classical concept of reputation (fama) as the writer's reward. But, as we have seen, he was susceptible to an alternative model of literary activity, a religious one, based on spiritually profitable reading and the writing of theology. His time at Paris had offered him yet another image of the intellectual, expounding the techniques of rhetoric or problems of law in the schools. These different emphases, scholastic, traditional religious, and humanist, were unreconciled.

Gerald was not only an intellectual. He was an active and energetic man, interested in the exercise of power and authority. He prided himself on his activities as an ecclesiastic and an administrator, as a royal servant and an indefatigable litigant. Until his retirement to Lincoln in 1207, he had spent few periods of literary activity in seclusion from the world. The Irish and Welsh works, for example, were produced while he was involved in the busy life of the court. Periods of study were interspersed with administration, travel, and lawsuits. Yet, in Gerald's own eyes, his urge to activity and power never found adequate fulfilment. His innate energy, his Paris training, and his experience in ecclesiastical and royal government did not win him the rich bishopric he desired.

Here, once more, we return to Gerald's ambiguous national position. His mixed Welsh and Norman blood and his Marcher sympathies put a millstone around his neck. He was frustrated at every turn and barred from the active power to which he aspired, because his Welsh and Marcher connections made the central government suspicious. Yet it was just this ambiguous position which enabled him to write the innovative topography and ethnography he did. His experience of a divided society stimulated his powers of observation—ethnographic consciousness springs, by definition, from an awareness of difference. His education took him away from the society into which he had been born and provided him with the cultural tools to describe it. At the same time it gave him ideals and aspirations which it would be difficult to realize in that society. His consciousness and articulateness sprang from the same divisions, between races, between educated and uneducated, that hamstrung his own career. In a sense, his political failure was the price of his intellectual achievement.

APPENDIX I

The purpose of this appendix is to provide a convenient summary of information rather than to present the results of exhaustive original research. Much of the material, especially the dating of manuscripts, is compiled from the work of others.

A. Topographia Hibernica. Gerald's first major work and his most popular. Dimock, the Rolls Series editor, distinguished four recensions, plus later versions incorporating material possibly by Gerald (Op., v, pp. xi–xxviii).

1st recension:
Cambridge, University Library Mm. 5.30 (late 12th cent.); Peterhouse 181 (15th cent.); St. Catherine's College L. v. 87 (13th cent.); London, British Library, Harleian 3,724 (13th cent.).
This recension was begun before Gerald left Ireland in May 1186, and completed before March 1188, when he presented a copy to Archbishop Baldwin. It was probably the recension Gerald recited at Oxford in 1187 or 1188 (Itin., p. 20; De Rebus, pp. 72-3).

2nd recension:
Cambridge, Corpus Christi College 400 (13th cent.). London, British Library, Add. 44,922 (incomplete) (13th cent.); Add. 34,762 (intermediate between 1st and 2nd recension) (13th cent.). London, Westminster Abbey (No. 23 in Robinson and Jones' catalogue) (13th cent.). Oxford, Bodleian, Rawlinson B. 483 (13th cent.).
The second recension was written before Henry II's death in July 1189 (Op., v, p. lii).

3rd recension:
London, British Library, Arundel 14 (13th cent.); Royal 13. B. viii (illustrated, incomplete) (13th cent.); Add. 33,991 (intermediate between 2nd and 3rd recension) (13th cent.). Oxford, Bodleian, Rawlinson B. 188 (13th cent.).

4th recension:
Cambridge, University Library Ff. 1.27 (illustrated) (13th cent.). Paris, Bibliothèque Nationale, Lat. 4846 (14th cent.).
'Late editions':
London, British Library, MS Cotton Cleo. D. v. (14th cent.); Harleian 4,003 (14th cent.); Royal 13. A. xiv (14th cent.). London, Lambeth Palace 622 (15th cent.). Oxford, Bodleian, Laud Misc. 720 (illustrated) (13th cent.). Paris, Bibliothèque Nationale, Lat. 4126 (14th cent.).

It is not possible to date these later recensions. Gerald was busy correcting and enlarging the Top. up to within a few years of his death (Epistola ad Capitulum Herefordense, written after 1220, Op., i. 409).

There are three other copies of the Top. It has not proved possible to discover which recension they represent: Aberystwyth, National Library of Wales 3074D (14th cent.); Douai, Bibliothèque Municipale 887 (13th cent.); Dublin, National Library of Ireland 700 (13th cent.). The general nature of the additions in the later recensions of the Top. is discussed above, pp. 145-6, 151-2.

There are excerpts from the Top. in three fourteenth-century manuscripts: Cambridge University Library, Mm. 2. 18. London, British Library, MS Cotton, Claud. E. viii; Royal 14. C. vi.

In the fourteenth century an abbreviated version was made by Philip of Slane, Prior of Cork: London, British Library, Add. 19,513.

There is a fourteenth-century Provençal translation of this: London, British Library, Add. 17,920.

There are several sixteenth- and seventeenth-century transcripts of the Top.:
London, British Library, MS Cotton, Faust. C. iv (17th cent.); Harleian 359 (16th cent.); Harleian 551 (an English trans.) (16th cent.); Harleian 1,757(16th cent.). Oxford, Bodleian, Bodley 511 (16th cent.); Tanner 2 (16th cent.).

B. Expugnatio Hibernica. Dimock distinguished first, second, and 'later' editions (Op., v, pp. xxix—xlvii), but Brian Scott, in his edition, has argued for a gradual development of the text from a group of manuscripts representing an early stage, through a group representing 'a slight and gradual evolution of the text' (Exp., ed. Scott and Martin, p. xl) to a final group (Dimock's 'later edition') containing Gerald's 'extensive reworking of the text' (ibid.). He calls the first two groups the α text, the third group the β text:

α text. Early Stages:
Douai, Bibliothèque Municipale 887 (13th cent.). London, British Library, Royal 13. B. viii (13th cent.); Add. 34,762 (very incomplete) (13th cent.). London, Lambeth Palace 371 (13th cent.). Oxford, Bodleian, Rawlinson B. 188 (13th cent.).
This recension was completed in the summer of 1189 (Exp., ed. Scott and Martin, pp. xvi-xvii).

α text. Developed Form:
Cambridge, University Library, Ff. 1. 27 (14th cent.); Add. 3392 (imperfect) (14th cent.). Dublin, National Library of Ireland 700 (13th cent.). London, British Library, Harleian 177 (an abbreviated version) (13th cent.).
Dimock thought this recension might represent the 'second and corrected edition' sent to King John with the dedicatory letter of 1209 (Op., v, p. lx). However, if the Symbolum Electorum can be dated to c.1199 (see below, pp. 178), then this developed form of the α text must date from the 1190s, since all of the many excerpts from the Exp. in the Symbolum Electorum are from this version.

β text:
Aberystwyth, National Library of Wales 3074 (13th cent.). London, British Library, MS Cotton, Cleo. D. v (14th cent.); Harleian 4003 (14th cent.); Royal 13. A. xiv (14th cent.); Royal 14. C. xiii (14th cent.). London, Lambeth Palace 622 (15th cent.).
Brian Scott argues that this version is from Gerald's hand (Exp., ed. Scott and Martin, pp. lii-lxx).

There are excerpts from the Exp. in two fourteenth-century manuscripts: London, British Library, MS Cotton, Claud, E. viii; Royal 14. C. vi; and a few leaves in a thirteenth-century hand in: Oxford, Bodleian, Rawlinson D. 125.

An Anglo-Irish translation of the Exp. was made in the fifteenth century, probably from a Latin version close to the abbreviated Harleian 177. Various versions are extant:

Dublin, Trinity College 575 (15th cent.); Trinity College 593 (16th cent.). London, British Library, Add. 40,674 (15th cent.). London, Lambeth Palace 598 (15th cent.); Lambeth Palace 623 (15th cent.). Oxford, Bodleian, Rawlinson B. 490 (15th cent.).

Trinity College 575 and Rawlinson B. 490 were edited by F.J. Furnivall, The English Conquest of Ireland (Early English Text Society, original series 107, 1896). The two Lambeth manuscripts were printed in Calendar of the Carew Manuscripts (Book of Howth. Miscellaneous), ed. J.S. Brewer and W. Bullen (London, 1871). An Irish abridgement was also made: Dublin, Trinity College 1298 (15th cent.); this was edited by Whitley Stokes, 'The Irish Abridgement of the Expugnatio Hibernica', English Historical Review, xx (1905). There are also some sixteenth- and seventeenth-century transcripts of the Exp.:

London, British Library, Harleian 310 (17th cent.); Harleian 359 (16th cent.); Harleian 551 (an English trans.) (16th cent.). London, Lambeth Palace 248 (16th cent.).

C. Itinerarium Kambriae: Dimock distinguished three recensions, c.1191, c.1197 and c. 1214 (Op., vi, pp. xxxiii-xxxix). There is no reason to differ from his conclusions.

1st recension:

Cambridge, University Library Ff. 1. 27 (13th cent.); London, British Library, Royal 13. B. viii (13th cent.); Oxford, Bodleian, Rawlinson B. 188 (13th cent.).

2nd recension:

London, British Library, Add. 34,762 (13th cent.).

Dimock did not know this manuscript and had to base his 2nd recension on a sixteenth-century transcript, Harleian 359.

3rd recension:

Aberystwyth, National Library of Wales 3024 (13th/14th cent.); London, British Library, MS Cotton, Domit. I (13th cent.).

There are extracts in a fourteenth-century manuscript: London, British Library, Harleian 912.

Several sixteenth-century transcripts exist:

Cambridge, Corpus Christi College 400. London, British Library, Harleian 359; Harleian 551 (English translation); Harleian 1757; Lansdowne 229 (extracts); Royal 13. B. xii. Oxford, Bodleian, Rawlinson B. 471 (extracts).

D. Descriptio Kambriae: Dimock distinguished two recensions, c.1194 and c.1215 (Op. vi, pp. xxxix-xlii).

1st recension:

London, British Library, MS Cotton, Nero D. viii (15th cent.); MS Cotton, Vitell. C. x (14th cent.); Royal 13. C. iii (15th cent.).

2nd recension:

Aberystwyth, National Library of Wales 3024 (13th/14th cent.); London, British Library,

Cotton MS, Domit. I (13th cent.).

There are extracts in the fourteenth-century manuscript: London, British Library, Harleian 912.

There are many sixteenth- and seventeenth-century transcripts, several including only Book II, since Book I was printed in 1585:

Cambridge, University Library Ff. 1. 27 (16th cent.); Corpus Christi College 400(16th cent.); Trinity College o. 5. 24 (Book II) (17th cent.). London, British Library, MS Cotton, Vitell. E. v (fragments) (16th cent.); Harleian 359 (excerpts) (16th cent.); Harleian 551 (16th cent.); Harleian 1757 (Book II) (16th cent.); Royal 13. B. xii (16th cent.); Sloane 1691 (17th cent.); Sloane 1710 (Book II) (17th cent.); Sloane 4785 (Book II) (17th cent.). Oxford, Bodleian, Rawlinson B. 471 (extracts) (16th cent.).

E. Vita Galfridi Archiepiscopi Eboracensis. This survives in a single manuscript. The latest dateable events it describes took place in June 1193 (pp. 415-17), and it was probably written not long afterwards.

Cambridge, Corpus Christi College 390 (13th cent.).

F. Saints' Lives. Gerald wrote five hagiographic works, of which four probably date from the mid and late 1190s:

(1) Vita Sancti Davidis. There is only one extant manuscript, but Wharton printed a text from a now destroyed Cottonian manuscript, Vitellius E. vii (Anglia Sacra, 2 vols., London, 1691). Michael Richter, 'The Life of St. David by Giraldus Cambrensis', Welsh History Review, iv (1968-9), thinks the Life was written in the 1190s, after Gerald's retirement from court. This would make good sense. Excerpts were included in the Symbolum Electorum, which probably dates from c. 1199.

London, British Library, Royal 13. C. i (15th cent.).

(2) Vita Sancti Ethelberti. Again, there is only one extant manuscript, but extracts from the Vitellius E. vii text were printed in AASS, May, v. This Life is also represented in the Symbolum Electorum and may be connected with a period of residence at Hereford c. 1195.

Cambridge, Trinity College B. 11. 16 (14th/15th cent.).

(3) Vita Sancti Karadoci. This does not survive, but its preface is preserved in the Symbolum Electorum (see below), ff. 90^r-92^r. The preface is virtually identical with that of the 2nd recension of the Vita Sancti Remigii, but marginal additions in the Symbolum Electorum text have been incorporated in the Vita Remigii text. Gerald took the Vita Karadoci to Rome in 1199 (Inv., p. 177). The text printed in C. Horstman (ed.), Nova Legenda Anglie (2 vols., Oxford, 1907) i, 174-7, may well descend from Gerald's Life.

(4) Vita Sancti Remigii. Dimock makes the case for a first recension, c. 1198, of which no manuscripts survive (although the original preface is in the Symbolum Electorum), and a second recension, c. 1213, preserved in the one extant manuscript (Op., vii, pp. x-xv).

Cambridge, Corpus Christi College 425 (early 13th cent.).

(5) Vita Sancti Hugonis. Dimock dates the first two Books c. 1213, and the third, dealing with later miracles, c. 1213-19 (Op., vii, pp. xlix-li). Cambridge, Corpus Christi College 425 (early 13th cent.).

G. Gemma Ecclesiastica. Gerald presented this work to Innocent III in 1199 (De Rebus, p. 119). It refers to the death of Maurice de Sully, Bishop of Paris, which took place in September 1196 (pp. 32-3), and is usually dated c. 1197. Reference to the death of the Paris theologian Simon of Tournai (pp. 148-9) might suggest that the text of the Gemma as we have it is a later recension, since Simon's death has been dated to 1201 (J. Warichez, Les 'Disputationes' de Simon de Tournai, Spicilegium Sacrum Lovaniense, xii (1932), p. xxxiii). However, the authority for this, Matthew Paris, is hardly to be relied upon for so precise a dating half a century after the event (Chronica Majora, ed. H.R. Luard, 7 vols. (RS, 1872-83), ii. 476-7). The fact that Gerald lists the Gemma with his later works (e.g. Inv., Spec. Duorum) in all three lists of his writings (Op., i. 415, 422; De Jure, p. 334) might also argue for a later recension. Gerald was, however, extremely vague on matters of chronology. The sole manuscript is:

London, Lambeth Palace 236 (13th cent.).

H. Symbolum Electorum. This is a collection of Gerald's favourite compositions. The full version, of which only one manuscript exists, contained four parts: letters, poems, selections from the Top. and Exp., prefaces. The letters all date from before 1199 and no excerpts are included from works known to have been written after the St. David's case, 1199-1203. It seems defensible to assign the compilation of the Symbolum Electorum to c. 1199, just before the cause célèbre diverted Gerald's energies from literary activity. If this is the case, we have a valuable guide to his existing opus c. 1199. This includes the Irish and Welsh works, Vita Galf., the saints lives (except the Vita Hug.), and the Gemma. There is no problem in dating any of these to before 1199. The only doubt which might be raised springs from the inclusion in the Symbolum Electorum of all four prefaces from the De Principis Instructione. However, although the text of the Prin. as we now have it dates from c. 1217, Gerald worked on it for many years and there is no compelling objection to the existence of a complete, short draft of all three books c. 1199. The passage in the 'Praefatio Prima' (Inc. 'De principis instructione tractatum edere...') which refers to Prince Louis and was probably written in 1216-17 (Prin., pp. 6-7), is absent from the Symbolum Electorum text of the preface.

Cambridge, Trinity College R. 7. 11 (13th cent.).

I. Invectiones. This work was begun at Rome in 1200 but not completed until 1216. Book VI was copied from the De Rebus. See Michael Richter's introduction to the Speculum Duorum. One manuscript exists:

Rome, Vatican Library, Cod. Reg. Lat. 470 (13th cent.).

J. Speculum Duorum. Composed over the period 1208-16, it is found in the same manuscript as the Invectiones. Again, see Richter's introduction.

K. De Rebus a Se Gestis. This was written after 1208, since it refers to Meiler fitzHenry as 'Hiberniae tunc justiciarius' (p. 7), and Meiler left the post in 1208, but before 1216, since part of the Invectiones was copied from it. Over 200 chapters of Book III are missing in the only known copy:

London, British Library, MS Cotton, Tib. B. xiii (13th cent.).

L. De Jure et Statu Menevensis Ecclesie. This work mentions the Invectiones, Speculum Duorum, and De Principis Instructione (pp. 333-4) in a list of Gerald's works, but does not refer to the Speculum Ecclesie. It was, therefore, probably composed c. 1218. Two

versions, one very much abridged (possibly by Gerald himself), survive:
Cambridge, Corpus Christi College 400 (abridged) (13th cent.); London, British Library,
MS Cotton, Dom.,V (13th cent.).
The abridged version also survives in a sixteenth-century transcript:
London, British Library, MS Cotton,Vitell. E. v.
Extracts are to be found in London, British Library, Harleian 544 (16th cent.).
Some pages from the Corpus manuscript not printed in the Rolls Series were edited by
H.E. Butler, 'Some New Pages of Giraldus Cambrensis', Medium Aevum, iv (1935).

M. De Principis Instructione. As discussed above (p. 62) the composition of this work
extended from the early 1190s to c.1217. One manuscript survives:
London, British Library, MS Cotton, Julius B. xiii (14th cent.).

N. Speculum Ecclesiae. This work was envisaged as early as c.1191 (Itin., p. 47) but not
completed until very late in Gerald's life. The text mentions the Fourth Lateran Council
of 1215 (p. 94), and the preface must have been composed after 1219 (see R.W. Hunt,
'The Preface to the Speculum Ecclesiae of Giraldus Cambrensis',Viator, viii, 1977). It
survives in the same damaged manuscript as the De Rebus (above).

O. Poems. There are three distinct groups of poems, found in three separate manuscripts.
In all cases there is a very slight overlap of material. The first group consists of the poems
in the Symbolum Electorum. These include the Cosmographia and other verses probably
dating from Gerald's student days. The other two manuscripts contain quite distinct mate-
rial, with the exception of the exchange between Gerald and Simon de Fresne, Canon
of Hereford (Op., i. 378-80, 382-4; R.W. Hunt, 'English Learning in the Late Twelfth
Century', in Essays in Medieval History, ed. R.W. Southern (London, 1968), pp. 121-2).
The poems in the Vitellius manuscript were copied from the Corpus manuscript:
Cambridge, Corpus Christi College 400 (13th cent.); London, British Library, MS Cotton,
Vitell. E. v. (16th cent.); London, Lambeth Palace 236 (13th cent.).

P. Short Pieces. There are a few short pieces that had an independent circulation.

(1) De Giraldo Archdiacono Menevensi. This is, in fact, an extract from the Invectiones
(bk. IV, ch. ix), but is also found separately:
Cambridge, Trinity College R. 7. 11 (15th cent.). London, British Library, Harleian 359
(16th cent.); Harleian 544 (16th cent.).

(2)-(3) Epistola ad Stephanum Langton and Epistola ad Capitulum Herefordense de
Libris a Se Scriptis. Both of these mention the Speculum Ecclesie and are therefore
after c. 1220:
London, Lambeth Palace 236 (13th cent.).

(4) Catalogus Brevior Librorum Suorum. This mentions the De Principis Instructione
but not the De Jure and is therefore dateable to c.1217.

(5) Retractiones. This mentions the Invectiones and the De Rebus and probably dates
from about the same time as the Catalogus Brevior. Both works are usually found
together.
Cambridge, Corpus Christi College 400 (16th cent.). London, British Library, MS

Cotton, Domit. I (13th cent.); MS Cotton, Vitell. E. v. (16th cent.); Harleian 359 (16th cent); Harleian 544 (16th cent.).

One manuscript has only the Retractiones, although it promises the Catalogus Brevior also in its heading: Cambridge, University Library, Ff. 1. 27 (16th cent.).

Q. Lost Works

(1) Mappa Kambriae. See above, pp. 112, 158 and 228, n. 83.

(2) De Fidei Fructu Fideique Defectu. Presumably written in the decade c.1205-15 (Op., i. 423; De Jure, p. 334).

(3) De Philosophicis Flosculis. An early work discussing the tides (Top., p. 79).

APPENDIX II

This poem was printed in Gerald's Opera (i. 374-7) from the defective sixteenth-century manuscript, British Library, Cotton MS, Vitellius E. v. A complete text, supplying the missing seven lines and title, and giving some better readings, can be found in Cambridge, Corpus Christi College MS 400, and it is printed here for ease of reference, as it is discussed in some detail in the text (above, pp. 83-5). The Corpus book consists of three manuscripts, a thirteenth-century Topographia Hibernica, a sixteenth-century Descriptio Kambriae (with the Retractationes and Catalogus Brevior) and a thirteenth-century De Jure, with an appended collection of Gerald's poems. The poem welcoming Prince Louis is on pp. 115-16. I have given significant variants from the Vitellius manuscript (V). Sections, for which I have left a line, are indicated by alternate red and blue capitals in the manuscripts.

Epigramma metricum nuper editum ex versu virgiliano tamquam themate carmen
   incipiens

> Nocte pluit tota, redeunt spectacula mane.
> Nubes et nebulas nescit amena dies.
> Diffugiunt tenebre tenebrosi temporis auctor
> Dum fugit et rutilat lux nova sole novo.
> Servilis rabies iam cessat, libera dantur   5
> Tempora, solvuntur anglica colla iugo.
> Gaudeat anglorum gens quam sub fine dierum
> Gratia respexit summa favore pio.
> Gaudeat et pronis semper cervicibus illi
> Serviat ex cuius gaudia sumpsit ope.   10
>
> Prodiit ex L. P. set et L. post prodiit ex P.
> Inclita dum gratos dat genitura gradus,
> Germine felici tres triplicante gradus.
> Utque bono melior sic ex meliore virescens
> Optimus et florens fructificansque magis.   15
> Tempora sic prolis fecundant facta parentis
> Ut prosit meritis ad pociora bonis.
>
> Pax datur hinc profugis, timor hinc terrorque tirannis.
> Iuris libra viget religioque viret,
> Morum nobilitas, armorum gloria, cervix   20
> Libera, cena sub hiis sobria, recta fides.

Sensit Otho tumidus, pathari sensere duoque
Reges arrogonus, anglicus, arma ducum.
Hispani paveant paveantque incredulus affer,
Damascus paveat ense domanda ducum.   25
Sobria strenuitas francorum classis habundans
Anglica gaza reis causa pavoris erunt.

Urbs igitur cesset animos turbare feroces
Prona quibus quondam colla subacta dedit.
Illa laborat ad hoc, ut Christi sponsa tirannis   30
Serviat et servi libera colla premant.
Hii vero ut cleri lacrimas populique dolores
Armis abstergant arma manusque movent.
Pre cunctis igitur regnis te lingua canora,
Francia flos orbis, laudet, honoret, amet.   35

Absit ut ecclesie princeps aversus ab illis
Esse velit per quos erigit ipsa capud.
Hic etenim populus, hic gaudet clerus honore.
Hic studium martis hicque minerva viget.
Leges hic iuste, princeps pius inque regendo   40
Vix punire volens et ferus esse dolens.
Per francos fiet petri quod cimba resurget,
Gaudia quod redeant pristina monte syon.

Roma memor recolat privati lumine pape
Digna quod a francis ulcio sumpta fuit.   45
Hoc quoque quod terre cuncte sublataque petri
Predia per francos sunt revocata petro.
Gratus ad hec igitur petri successor habenas
Iusticie leni sub pietate regat.
Sit pape pietas modus atque modestia mulcens,   50
Sit pater ipse pius, triste rigor nimius.
Membra suo capiti male iam prescisa coherent.
Triste rigor nimius, sit pater ergo pius
Saucia sanantur sed non* prescisa, resectus
Palmes non reviret, sit pius ergo pater.   55
Iudicio prestat clemencia, mitigat iras
Mens pia, mens lenis, sit modus ergo patri.
Lene fluit nilus, syloes fluit unda silenter.
Lenis alit flammas, grandior aura necat.
Tempore mitescunt posita feritate leones,   60
Tempore leniri tigris et ursa solent.
Micior in multos sentencia danda rebelles
Asperitas animos immoderata facit.

Det pater omnipotens ut sub moderamine iusto
Anglia servili gaudeat absque iugo.   65

Ille gubernator summus de munere cuius
Quicquid in orbe pium, quicquid ubique bonum,
Det duo, quod capiti sua sint conformia membra
Et gens anglorum principe tuta bono.
Felices oculi, felicia tempora tandem.   70
Post mala tanta quibus ista videre datum.

Applicuit thanetos vox vite, preco salutis,
Et luctum removens leticiamque ferens.
Hinc data corporibus libertas, hinc animabus.
Frendet ob hoc pharao, flet sua dampna sathan.   75
Felix ille locus cuius se littore primum
Suscepit tanti lator uterque† boni.
Liberat hic animas, hic corpora; gratus utrique
Sit grex anglorum, liber utroque iugo.
Exilio rediens insignis martir ibidem   80
Applicuit proprium morte sacrando solum.
Sic igitur fundans, sic formans, sic et adornans.
Hic christi sponsam litus adivit idem.
Non ergo exigua, non est exilis habenda
Insula tam claris preradians titulis.   85

Mirum que rome modicos sentencia pape
Non movet, hic regum sceptra movere parat.★
Que minimos minime censura cohercet in urbe,
Sevit in orbe fremens celsaque colla premens.
Cui male sublatus rome non cederet ortus,   90
Nititur ad nutum flectere regna suum.
Explicit.

BIBLIOGRAPHY

A. MANUSCRIPTS (EXCLUDING THOSE MENTIONED ONLY IN APPENDIX I)

Cambridge, Corpus Christi College 400.
        Trinity College R. 7. 11.
        University Library Ff. 1. 27.
London, British Library, MS Cotton, Tiberius B. xiii.
               Harleian 4751
               Royal 13. B. viii.
               Vitellius E.v.
Oxford, Bodleian Library, Bodley 764.
           Laud Misc. 642.
           Laud Misc. 720.
           Rawlinson B. 188.

B. PRINTED PRIMARY SOURCES

ADAM OF BREMEN, Gesta Hammaburgensis Ecclesiae Pontificum, ed. B. Schmeidler, Scriptores Rerum Germanicarum in Usum Scholarum (Hanover, 1917).
——, Gesta... Pontificum, ed., with a German translation, by W. Trillmich in Quellen des 9. und 11. Jahrhunderts zur Geschichte der Hamburgischen Kirche und des Reiches (Berlin, 1961).
ADAM OF EYNSHAM, Magna Vita Hugonis, ed. D.L. Douie and Dom Hugh Farmer (2 vols., London, 1961-2).
ADELARD OF BATH, Quaestiones Naturales, ed. M. Müller, Beiträge zur Geschichte der Philosophie des Mittelalters, xxxi (1934-5).
ALAIN DE LILLE, Textes Inédits, ed. M.-T. d'Alverny, Études de Philosophie Médiévale, lii (1965).
ALBERTUS MAGNUS, Opera Omnia, ed. A. Borgnet (38 vols., Paris, 1890-99).
ALEXANDER NEQUAM, De Naturis Rerum, ed. T. Wright (RS, 1863).
Ancient Laws and Institutes of Wales, ed. Aneurin Owen (London, 1841).
Aristoteles Latinus (Union Académique Internationale, Corpus Philosophorum Medii Aevi, Rome, 1951-).
AUGUSTINE, Civitas Dei (Corpus Christianorum, Series Latina xlviii, 1955).
——, Confessions, ed. P. Knöll (CSEL, xxxiii, 1896).
——, Contra Faustum, ed. J. Zycha (CSEL, xxv, 1891).
——, De Diversibus Quaestiones LXXXIII, ed. A. Mutzenbecher (Corpus Christianorum, Series Latina xliv A, 1975).

——, De Genesi ad Litteram, ed. J. Zycha (CSEL, xxviii, part I, 1894).

——, Sermones (PL, xxxviii).

AVICENNA LATINUS, ed. S.Van Riet (2 vols., Louvain, 1968-72).

BARTOLOMAEUS ANGLICUS, De Proprietatibus Rerum (Lyons, 1480).

BEDE, Historia Ecclesiastica, ed. C. Plummer (2 vols., Oxford, 1896).

BEDE, Opera de Temporibus, ed. C.W. Jones (Mediaeval Academy of America Publication, xli, 1943).

ST. BERNARD, Vita Sancti Malachiae, ed. A. Gwynn, in Sancti Bernardi Opera, ed. J. Leclerq and H.M. Rochais, iii (Rome, 1963).

BERNARD SILVESTER, Cosmographia or De Mundi Universitate, ed. P. Dronke (Leiden, 1978), tr. Winthrop Wetherbee (New York, 1973).

——, Experimentarius, ed. M.B. Savorelli, Rivista Critica di Storia della Filosofia, xiv (1959).

——, Mathematicus (PL, clxxi).

The Bestiary, ed. M.R. James (Roxburghe Club, 1928).

The Black Book of Limerick, ed. J. MacCaffrey (Dublin, 1906).

The Black Book of St. David's, ed. J.W. Willis-Bund (Cymmrodorion Record Series, No. 5, 1902).

BOETHIUS, The Consolation of Philosophy, ed. S.J. Tester (Loeb Classical Library, 1973).

Brut y Tywysogyon or The Chronicle of the Princes. Red Book of Hergest Version, ed. Thomas Jones (Board of Celtic Studies, History and Law Series, no. 16, Cardiff, 1955).

CAESARIUS OF HEISTERBACH, Dialogus Miraculorum, ed. J. Strange (2 vols., Cologne, etc., 1851).

CALCIDIUS, Timaeus Calcidius, ed. J.H. Waszink, Corpus Platonicum Medii Aevi, iv (London, 1962).

Calendar of Documents Relating to Ireland, ed. H.S. Sweetman (5 vols., London, 1875-86).

The Calendar of the Gormanston Register, ed. J. Mills and M.J. McEnery (Dublin, 1916).

Canterbury Professions, ed. Michael Richter (Canterbury and York Society, lxvii, 1973).

Cartularium Prioratus Sancti Johannis Evangelistae de Brecon, ed. R.W. Banks (London, 1884).

Charters of Gilbertine Houses, ed. F.M. Stenton (Lincoln Record Society, xvii, 1922).

Chartularies of St. Mary's Abbey, Dublin, ed. J.T. Gilbert (RS, 1884).

Chronica de Gestis Consulum Andegavorum, ed. P. Marchegay and A. Salmon, Chroniques d'Anjou, i (Paris, 1856).

The Chronicle of Signy, ed. L. Delisle, Bibliothèque de l'Ecole des Chartes, lv (1894).

CLAREMBALD OF ARRAS, Life and Works of Clarembald of Arras, ed. N.M. Häring (Toronto, 1965).

Concilia Magnae Brittaniae et Hiberniae, ed. D. Wilkins (4 vols., London, 1737).

Councils and Ecclesiastical Documents Relating to Great Britain and Ireland, ed. A.W. Haddan and William Stubbs (3 vols., Oxford, 1869-78).

Curia Regis Rolls, xii (HMSO, 1957).

DANIEL OF MORLEY, Philosophia or Liber de Naturis Inferiorum et Superiorum, ed. K. Sudhoff (Archiv für die Geschichte der Naturwissenschaften, viii, 1918).

Dialogus de Scaccario, ed. C. Johnson (London, 1950).

Early Yorkshire Charters, xi, ed. C.T. Clay (Yorkshire Archaeological Society Record Series, 1963).

Episcopal Acts Relating to Welsh Dioceses, 1066-1272, ed. J. Conway Davies (2 vols., Cardiff, 1946-8).

SEXTUS POMPEIUS FESTUS, De Verborum Significatu, ed. W.M. Lindsay (Teubner, 1913).

FREDERICK II, De Arte Venandi cum Avibus, ed. C.A. Willemsen (2 vols., Leipzig, 1942).

GEOFFREY OF MONMOUTH, Historia Regum Britanniae, ed. Acton Griscom (London, 1929).

GERALD OF WALES, The Autobiography of Giraldus Cambrensis, tr. H.E. Butler (London, 1937).

——, Expugnatio Hibernica, ed. A.B. Scott and F.X. Martin (Dublin, 1978).

——, Invectiones, ed. W.S. Davies, Y Cymmrodor, xxx (1920).

——, The Jewel of the Church, tr. J.J. Hagen (Leiden, 1979).

——, The Journey through Wales/The Description of Wales, tr. L. Thorpe (Harmondsworth, 1978).

——, Opera, ed J.S. Brewer, J.F. Dimock, and G.F. Warner (8 vols., RS, 1861-91).

——, Speculum Duorum, ed. Y. Lefèvre and R.B.C. Huygens. Gen. ed., Michael Richter (Cardiff, 1974).

——, The Topography of Ireland, tr. J.J. O'Meara (Dundalk, 1951).

——, 'Giraldus Cambrensis in Topographia Hibernie. Text of the First Recension', ed. J.J. O'Meara, Proceedings of the Royal Irish Academy, lii, sect. c (1948-50).

——, Vita Ethelberti, ed. M.R. James, 'Two Lives of St. Ethelbert, King and Martyr', English Historical Review, xxxii (1917).

GERVASE OF TILBURY, Otia Imperialia, ed. G.G. Leibnitz, Scriptores Rerum Brunsvicensium (3 vols., Hanover, 1707-11), i.

Die Gesetze der Angel-Sachsen, ed. F. Lieberman (3 vols., Halle, 1898-1916).

Gesta Regis Henrici Secundi Benedicti Abbatis, ed. W. Stubbs (2 vols., RS, 1867).

Gesta Stephani, ed. K.R. Potter, new edn. with intro, and notes by R.H.C. Davis (Oxford, 1976).

GILDAS, De Excidio et Conquestu Britanniae, ed. T. Mommsen, MGH, Auctores Antiquissimi, xiii (1898).

'GLANVILL', Tractatus de Legibus, ed. G.D. Hall (London, 1965).

GREGORY THE GREAT, Regula Pastoralis (PL, lxxvii).

GREGORY OF NAZIANZUS, Oratio Apologetica (PG, xxxv).

GUNTHER OF PAIRIS, Ligurinus, ed. C.G. Dümge (Heidelberg, 1812) (PL, ccxii).

HELMOLD OF BOSAU, Cronica Slavorum, ed. B. Schmeidler, Scriptores Rerum Germanicarum in Usum Scholarum (Hanover, 1937).

——, Slawenchronik, ed. with a German translation by H.H. Stoob (Darmstadt, 1963).

HILDEBERT OF LE MANS, Epistolae (PL, clxxi).

L'Histoire de Guillaume le Maréchal, ed. P. Meyer (3 vols., Société de l'Histoire de France, 1891-1901).

Historical Manuscripts Commission, Reports on Manuscripts in Various Collections, i (1901), 246-50 (late 13th-century account of the Welsh and the Edwardian wars).

HONORIUS AUGUSTODUNIENSIS, Gemma Animae (PL, clxxii).

HUGH OF FLEURY, Historia Ecclesiastica (excerpts), in MGH, Scriptores, ix, and PL, clxiii.

The Irish Cartularies of Llanthony Prima and Secunda, ed. E.St.J. Brooks (Irish Manuscripts Commission, Dublin, 1953).

ISIDORE OF SEVILLE, Etymologies, ed. W.M. Lindsay (2 vols., Oxford, 1911).

Itinera et Relationes Fratrum Minorum Saeculi XIII et XIV, ed. P.A. van den Wyngaert, Sinica Franciscana, i (Quaracchi, 1929).

Itinerarium Regis Ricardi, ed. W. Stubbs, Chronicles and Memorials of the Reign of Richard I (2 vols., RS, 1864-5), i.

JEROME, Epistolae (PL, xxii).

JOCELYN OF FURNESS, Vita Sancti Patricii, in AASS, March, ii. 540-80.

JOHN BLUND, Tractatus de Anima, ed. D.A. Callus and R.W. Hunt, Auctores Britannici Medii Aevi, ii (London, 1970).

JOHN OF GARLAND, De Triumphis Ecclesiae, ed. T. Wright (Roxburghe Club lxxii, 1856).

JOHN OF PLANO CARPINI, Ystoria Mongalorum (see Itinera et Relationes...).

JOHN OF SALISBURY, Entheticus, ed. Ronald E. Pepin, 'The "Entheticus" of John of Salisbury: A Critical Text', Traditio, xxxi (1975).

——, Historia Pontificalis, ed. M. Chibnall (London, 1956).

——, The Letters of John of Salisbury, i, The Early Letters (1153-1161), ed. W.J. Millor and H.E. Butler, revised by C.N.L. Brooke (London, 1955).

——, Metalogicon, ed. C.C.J. Webb (Oxford, 1929).

——, Policraticus, ed. C.C.J. Webb (2 vols., Oxford, 1909).

The Latin Texts of the Welsh Laws, ed. Hywel D. Emanuel (Cardiff, 1967).

The Laws of Hywel Dda (the Book of Blegywryd), ed. Melville Richards (Liverpool, 1954).

Letters of Henry III, ed. W.W. Shirley (2 vols., RS, 1862-6).

Llyfr Iorwerth, ed. Aled Rhys Wiliam (Cardiff, 1960).

The Mabinogion, tr. J. Gantz (Harmondsworth, 1976).

MANEGOLD OF LAUTENBACH, Liber contra Wolfelmum, ed. W. Hartmann, MGH (1972).

MARIUS, On the Elements, ed. Richard C. Dales (Berkeley, 1976).

Materials for the History of Thomas Becket, ed. J.C. Robertson (7 vols., RS, 1875-85).

Moralium Dogma Philosophorum, ed. J. Holmberg (Uppsala, 1929).

ORDERICUS VITALIS, Ecclesistical History, ed. M. Chibnall (6 vols., Oxford, 1969-). ORIGEN, Contra Celsum, ed. M. Borret (5 vols., Paris, 1967-76), and PG, xi.

——, In Numeros Homilia, tr. Rufinus ed. W.A. Baehrens, Griechischen Christlichen Schriftsteller, xxx (Leipzig, 1921).

OTTO OF FREISING, Ottonis et Rahewini Gesta Friderici I Imperatoris, ed. G. Waitz, Scriptores Rerum Germanicarum in Usum Scholarum (Hanover, 1912).

——, Die Taten Friedrichs, ed., with a German translation, F.-J. Schmale (Berlin, 1965).

PAUL THE DEACON, Historia Langobardorum, MGH, Scriptores Rerum Langobardorum.

PETER ABELARD, Sic and Non, ed. Blanche Boyer and Richard McKeon (Chicago, 1976-7).

PETER OF BLOIS, Opera (PL, ccvii).

PETER THE CHANTER, Verbum Abbreviatum (PL, ccv).

——, Summa de Sacramentis, ed. J.A. Dugauquier (Analecta Mediaevalia Namurcensia, iv, vii, xi, xvi, xxi, 1954-67).

PETER COMESTOR, Historia Scholastica (PL, cxcviii).

PETER LOMBARD, Sententiae in IV Libris Distinctae, i, Spicilegium Bonaventurianum, iv (Grottaferrata, 1971).

PHILIP, PRIOR OF ST. FRIDESWIDE'S, Historia Miraculorum Sanctae Frideswidae, AASS, Oct., v

Physiologus, ed. F. Sbordone (Milan, 1936).

Physiologus Latinus, ed. F.J. Carmody (Paris, 1939).

Pipe Rolls: 31 Henry I (HMSO, 1929), 17 and 18 Henry II (Pipe Roll Society, 1893-4), 3-4 Richard I to 5 John (Pipe Roll Society, 1926-38).

PLATO, see CALCIDIUS.

PLINY THE ELDER, Naturalis Historia, ed. H. Rackham, W.H.S. Jones, and D.E. Eichholz (Loeb Classical Library, 10 vols., London, 1938-63).

Pontificia Hibernica, ed. Maurice P. Sheehy (2 vols., Dublin, 1962).

RALPH OF COGGESHALL, Chronicon Anglicanum, ed. J. Stevenson (RS, 1875).

RALPH OF DICETO, Opera Historica, ed. William Stubbs (2 vols., RS, 1876).

RAOUL GLABER, Historiarum Sui Temporis Libri V, ed. M. Prou, Les Cinq Livres de Ses Histoires (Paris, 1886).

Register of the Abbey of St. Thomas, Dublin, ed. J.T. Gilbert (RS, 1889).

Registrum Epistolarum Fratris Johannis Peckham Archiepiscopi Cantuariensis, ed. C.T. Martin (3 vols., RS, 1882–5).

RHIGYFARCH, Life of St. David, ed. J.W. James (Cardiff, 1967).

ROGER OF HOWDEN, Chronica, ed. William Stubbs (4 vols., RS, 1868–71).

ROGER OF WENDOVER, Flores Historiarum, ed. H.G. Hewlett (3 vols., RS, 1886–9).

Rotuli Chartarum, ed. T.D. Hardy (London, 1837).

RUFINUS, Orationum Gregorii Nazianzeni Novem Interpretatio, ed. A. Engelbrecht (CSEL, xlvi, 1910).

Sacrorum Conciliorum Nova et Amplissima Collectio, ed. J.D. Mansi (31 vols., Florence and Venice, 1757–98).

SALLUST, Bellum Iugurthinum, ed. J.C. Rolfe (Loeb Classical Library, revised edn., 1931).

SERVIUS, Servii Grammatici qui Feruntur in Vergilii Carmina Commentarii, ed. G. Thilo and H. Hagen (3 vols. in 4 parts, Leipzig, 1878–1902).

SOLINUS, Collectanea Rerum Memorabilium, ed. T. Mommsen (Berlin, 1895).

The Statutes of Wales, ed. Ivor Bowen (London, 1908).

De Successione Episcoporum et Gestis Eorum, Videlicet Bernardi et David Secundi, ed. Michael Richter, Bulletin of the Board of Celtic Studies, xxii (1967).

SUGER, Vita Ludovici Grossi Regis, ed. H. Waquet, Vie de Louis VI le Gros (Paris, 1929).

TACITUS, Germania, ed. J.G.C. Anderson (Oxford, 1938).

THIERRY OF CHARTRES, Commentaries on Boethius by Thierry of Chartres and His School, ed. N.M. Haring (Toronto, 1971).

THOMAS AQUINAS, Scriptum Super Libros Sententiarum, ed. R.P. Mandonnet and M.F. Moos (4 vols., Paris, 1929–47).

——, Summa Theologica, ed. P. Caramello (4 vols., Rome, 1948).

Translatio Sancti Alexandri (MGH, Scriptores, ii).

USAMAH IBN-MUNQIDH, An Arab-Syrian Gentleman and Warrior... Memoirs of Usamah Ibn-Munqidh, ed. P.K. Hitti (New York, 1929).

Veterum Epistolarum Hibernicarum Sylloge, ed. James Ussher (Dublin, 1632 and 1696), in Ussher's Works, ed. C.R. Elrington, iv (Dublin, 1847).

VINCENT OF BEAUVAIS, Speculum Naturale, in vol. i of Speculum Maius (3 vols., Venice, 1591).

Vita Sancti Patris Basilii Magni, in L. Surius, De Probatis Sanctorum (8 vols., Cologne, 1576–81), i.

WALTER MAP, De Nugis Curialium, ed. M.R. James (Oxford, 1914).

WALTER OF ST. VICTOR, Contra Quatuor Labyrinthos Franciae, ed. P. Glorieux, Archives d'histoire doctrinale et littéraire du moyen âge, xix (1952).

Welsh Medieval Law, ed. A.W. Wade-Evans (Oxford, 1909).

WILLIAM OF CONCHES, Glosae super Platonem, ed. E. Jeauneau (Paris, 1965).

——, Philosophia Mundi (PL, clxxii).

WILLIAM OF MALMESBURY, Gesta Regum, ed. W. Stubbs (2 vols., RS, 1887–9).

WILLIAM OF NEWBURGH, Historia Rerum Anglicarum, ed. R. Howlett, Chronicles of the Reigns of Stephen, Henry II and Richard I (4 vols., RS, 1884–9), i–ii.

WILLIAM OF POITIERS, Gesta Willelmi, ed. R. Foreville, Histoire de Guillaume le Conquérant (Paris, 1952).

WILLIAM OF RUBRUCK, Itinerarium (see Itinera et Relationes...)

WILLIAM OF ST. THIERRY, De Erroribus Guillelmi de Conchis (PL, clxxx).

WILLIAM OF TYRE, Historia Rerum Transmarinarum (PL, cci).

C. SECONDARY WORKS—PUBLISHED

ALCOCK, LESLIE, 'Some Reflections on Early Welsh Society and Economy', Welsh History Review, ii (1964-5).

APPLEBY, J.T., England without Richard 1189-1199 (London, 1965).

BALDWIN, J.W., Masters, Princes and Merchants. The Social Views of Peter the Chanter and His Circle (Princeton, 1970).

BATE, A.K., 'Walter Map and Giraldus Cambrensis', Latomus, xxxi (1972).

BERGES, W., Die Fürstenspiegel des Hohen und Späten Mittelalters (Stuttgart, 1938).

Bibliotheca Hagiographica Latina, ed. Socii Bollandiani (2 vols., Brussels, 1898-1901).

BINCHY, D.A., 'The Linguistic and Historical Value of the Irish Law Tracts', Proceedings of the British Academy, xxix (1943).

BLOCH, MARC, Feudal Society, tr. L.A. Manyon (2nd edn., London, 1962).

BORST, ARNO, Der Turmbau von Babel (4 vols. in 6 parts, Stuttgart, 1957-63).

BOUTEMY, A., 'Giraud de Barri et Pierre I Chantre', Revue du moyen âge latin, ii (1946).

BROOKE, C.N.L., 'The Archbishops of St. David's, Llandaff and Caerleon-on-Usk', in Studies in the Early British Church, ed. Nora K. Chadwick, et al. (Cambridge, 1958).

——, 'Gregorian Reform in Action: Clerical Marriage in England, 1050-1200', Cambridge Historical Journal, xii (1956), revised in Brooks's Medieval Church and Society (London, 1971).

BROOKS, E.ST.J., 'An Unpublished Charter of Raymond le Gros', Journal of the Royal Society of Antiquaries of Ireland, 7th ser., ix (1939).

BROWN, P., 'Society and the Supernatural: A Medieval Change', Daedalus (Spring 1975).

BRUNEL, CLOVIS, 'David D'Ashby, Auteur Méconnu des Faits des Tartares', Romania, lxxix (1958).

CALLUS, D.A., 'The Introduction of Aristotelian Learning to Oxford', Proceedings of the British Academy, xxix (1943).

CANNY, NICHOLAS P., 'The Ideology of Colonisation: from Ireland to America', William and Mary Quarterly, 3rd ser., xxx (1973).

CHENEY, C.R., From Becket to Langton (Manchester, 1956).

CHENU, M.-D., Nature, Man and Society in the Twelfth Century, tr. Jerome Taylor and Lester K. Little (Chicago, 1968).

COLE, A. THOMAS, Democritus and the Sources of Greek Anthropology (Middletown, Conn., 1967).

COULTER, CORNELIA C., AND F.P. MAGOUN, JNR., 'Giraldus Cambrensis on Indo-Germanic Philology', Speculum, i (1926).

COURCELLE, P., La Consolation de philosophic dans la tradition littéraire (Paris, 1967).

DAVIES, J. CONWAY, 'Giraldus Cambrensis, 1146-1946', Archaeologia Cambrensis, xcix (1946-7).

——, 'The Kambriae Mappa of Giraldus Cambrensis', Journal of the Historical Society of the Church in Wales, ii (1952).

DAVIES, REES, 'Race Relations in Post Conquest Wales', Transactions of the Honourable Society of Cymmrodorion (1974-5).

DAVIES, R.R., 'The Survival of the Blood Feud in Medieval Wales', History, liv (1969).

DE GAIFFIER, B., Études critiques d'hagiographie et d'iconologie (Subsidia Hagiographica, xliii, Brussels, 1967).

DE LUBAC, H., Surnaturel, Études Historiques (Paris, 1946).

DE VOOGHT, P., 'La Notion philosophique du miracle chez S. Augustin dans le De Trinitate et le De Genesi ad Litteram', Recherches de Théologie Ancienne et Médiévale, x (1938).

——, 'La Théologie du miracle selon S. Augustin', Recherches de Théologie Ancienne et Médiévale, xi (1939).

DOUIE, DECIMA L., Archbishop Pecham (Oxford, 1952).

DRONKE, PETER, 'Peter of Blois and Poetry at the Court of Henry II', Mediaeval Studies, xxxviii (1976).

DUBY, GEORGES, 'Les "Jeunes" dans la société aristocratique dans la France du Nord-Ouest au XIIᵉ siècle', Annales (1964); also in Duby's Hommes et structures du moyen âge (Paris, 1973).

——, Medieval Marriage. Two Models from Twelfth-century France, tr. E. Forster (Baltimore, 1978).

——, The Early Growth of the European Economy, tr. H.B. Clarke (London, 1974).

DUCKETT, GEORGE, 'Evidences of the Barri Family of Manorbier and Olethan', Archaeologia. Cambrensis, 5th ser., vii (1891).

EKWALL, E., Etymological Notes on English Place Names (Lund, 1959).

ELLIS, T.P., Welsh Tribal Law and Custom in the Middle Ages (2 vols., Oxford, 1926).

EVANS-PRITCHARD, E.E., The Nuer (Oxford, 1940).

EYTON, R.W., Court, Household and Itinerary of King Henry II (London, 1878).

FLAHIFF, G.B., 'Deus non vult: A Critic of the Third Crusade', Mediaeval Studies, ix (1947).

FREEMAN, E.A., History of the Norman Conquest (6 vols., Oxford, 1867-79).

GALBRAITH, V.H. 'The Literacy of the Medieval English Kings', Proceedings of the British Academy, xxi (1937), and in Studies in History, selected by Lucy S. Sutherland (London, 1966).

GLACKEN, CLARENCE J., Traces on the Rhodian Shore (Berkeley, 1967).

GODDU, A.A. AND R.H. ROUSE, 'Gerald of Wales and the Florilegium Angelicum', Speculum, lii (1977).

GRANSDEN, A., 'Realistic Observation in Twelfth Century England', Speculum, xlvii (1972).

GRANT, ROBERT M., Miracle and Natural Law in Graeco-Roman and Early Christian Thought (Amsterdam, 1952).

GREGORY, T., Anima Mundi. La Filosofia di Guglielmo di Conches e la Scuola di Chartres (Florence, 1955).

——, 'L'Idea di Natura nella Filosofia Medievale Prima dell'Ingresso della Fisica di Aristotele—II Secolo XII', in La Filosofia della Natura nel Medioevo. Atti del Terzo Congresso Internazionale di Filosofia Medioevale, 1964 (Milan, 1966).

——, 'La Nouvelle Idée de nature et de savoir scientifique au XIIᵉ siècle', The Cultural Context of Medieval Learning, ed. J.E. Murdoch and E.D. Sylla (Dordrecht and Boston, 1975).

——, Platonismo Medioevale. Studi e Ricerche (Rome, 1958).

GWYNN, AUBREY, 'The First Synod of Cashel', Irish Ecclesiastical Record, lxvii (1946). ——, 'Lanfranc and the Irish Church', Irish Ecclesiastical Record, lvii (1941) and lviii (1941).

——, 'St. Anselm and the Irish Church', Irish Ecclesiastical Record, lix (1942).

——, 'St. Malachy of Armagh', Irish Ecclesiastical Record, lxx (1948).

——, The Twelfth Century Reform, A History of Irish Catholicism, ii (i), (Dublin, 1968).

HANDELSMAN, M., 'La role de la nationalité dans l'histoire du moyen âge', Bulletin of the International Committee of Historical Studies, ii (1929-30).

HASKINS, C.H., 'Henry II as a Patron of Literature', in Essays in Medieval History Presented to T.P. Tout, ed. A.G. Little and F.M. Powicke (Manchester, 1925).

——, Studies in the History of Medieval Science (2nd edn., Cambridge, Mass., 1927).

HAYS, R.W., 'Rotoland, Subprior of Aberconway, and the Controversy over the See of Bangor 1199-1204', Journal of the Historical Society of the Church in Wales, xiii (1963).

HELBLING-GLOOR, B., Natur und Aberglauben im Policraticus des Johannes von Salisbury (Zurich, 1956).

HERON-ALLEN, EDWARD, Barnacles in Nature and in Myth (London, 1928).

HODGEN, MARGARET T., Early Anthropology in the Sixteenth and Seventeenth Centuries (Philadelphia, 1964).

HOLMES, U.T., 'Gerald the Naturalist', Speculum, xi (1936).

HOLT, J.C., Magna Carta (Cambridge, 1965).

HOWELL, MARGARET, Regalian Right in Medieval England (London, 1962).

HUGHES, K., The Church in Early Irish Society (London, 1966).

HUNT, R.W., 'English Learning in the Late Twelfth Century', Transactions of the Royal Historical Society, 4th ser., xix (1936), reprinted in Essays in Medieval History, ed. R.W. Southern (London, 1968).

——, 'The Preface to the Speculum Ecclesiae of Giraldus Cambrensis', Viator, viii (1977).

JOLLIFFE, J.E.A., Angevin Kingship (2nd edn., London, 1963).

JONES, G.R., 'The Distribution of Bond Settlements in North-West Wales', Welsh History Review, ii (1964-5).

——, 'The Tribal System in Wales', Welsh History Review, i (1961).

JONES, THOMAS, 'Gerald the Welshman's Itinerary through Wales and Description of Wales', National Library of Wales Journal, vi (1949-50).

——, Gerallt Gymro/Gerald the Welshman (dual language, Cardiff, 1947).

JONES, W.R., 'The Image of the Barbarian in Medieval Europe', Comparative Studies in Society and History, xiii (1971).

JORDAN, WINTHROP D., White Over Black (Chapel Hill, N.C., 1968).

KNOWLES, DAVID, 'Some Enemies of Giraldus Cambrensis', Studia Monastica, i (1959).

LACOMBE, GEORGE, Aristoteles Latinus (2 parts and supplement, Rome, 1939-61).

LAWN, B., The Salernitan Questions (Oxford, 1963), expanded version I Quesiti Salernitani, tr. A. Spagnuolo (Salerno, 1969).

LE GOFF, J. AND E. LE ROY LADURIE, 'Mélusine maternelle et défricheuse', Annales, xxvi (1971) and (in part) in Le Goff's Pour un autre moyen âge (Paris, 1977).

LEMAY, RICHARD, Abu Ma'shar and Latin Aristotelianism in the Twelfth Century (Beirut, 1962).

LIEBESCHÜTZ, H., Medieval Humanism in the Life and Writings of John of Salisbury (London, 1950).

LLOYD, J.E., A History of Wales (2 Vols., 3rd edn., London, 1939).

LODGE, J., The Peerage of Ireland (London, 1754).

MACKINNON, H., 'William de Montibus: A Medieval Teacher', Essays in Medieval History Presented to Bertie Wilkinson, ed. T.A. Sandquist and M.R. Powicke (Toronto, 1969).

McCULLOCK, F., Medieval Latin and French Bestiaries (Chapel Hill, N.C., 1960).

McKECHNIE, W.S., Magna Carta (2nd edn., Glasgow, 1914).

MARKUS, R.A., 'Augustine, God and Nature', in Cambridge History of Later Greek and Early Medieval Philosophy, ed. A.H. Armstrong (Cambridge, 1967).

MINIO-PALUELLO, L., Opuscula: the Latin Aristotle (Amsterdam, 1972).

MORRIS, COLIN, The Discovery of the Individual (London, 1972).

MÜLLER, KLAUS E., Geschichte der Antiken Ethnographie und Ethnologischen Theoriebildung, i (Wiesbaden, 1972).

NELSON, LYNN H., The Normans in South Wales, 1070-1171 (Austin, Texas, 1966).

NICHOLLS, KENNETH, Gaelic and Gaelicised Ireland in the Middle Ages (Dublin, 1972).

O'DOHERTY, J.F., 'A Historical Criticism of the Song of Dermot', Irish Historical Studies, i (1938).

OFFERMANNS, D. (ed.), Der Physiologus nach den Handschriften G und M (Beiträge zur Klassischen Philologie, xxii, 1966).

OTTE, JAMES K., 'The Life and Writings of Alfredus Anglicus', Viator, iii (1972).

OTWAY-RUTHVEN, J., A History of Mediaeval Ireland (London, 1968).

OWEN, HENRY, Gerald the Welshman (London, 1889, revised edn. 1904).

PÄCHT, OTTO AND J.J.G. ALEXANDER, Illuminated Manuscripts in the Bodleian Library, Oxford (3 vols., Oxford, 1966—73).

PALMER, A.N., 'The Portionary Churches of Mediaeval North Wales', Archaeologia Cambrensis, 5th series, iii (1886).

PARENT, J.M., La Doctrine de la Creation dans l'École de Chartres (Paris, 1938).

PIERCE, T. JONES, Medieval Welsh Society (Cardiff, 1972).

——, 'Einion ap Ynyr (Anian II), Bishop of St. Asaph', Flintshire Historical Society Publications, xvi (1957).

POWICKE, F.M., 'Gerald of Wales', Bulletin of the John Rylands Library, xii (1928); reprinted in his The Christian Life in the Middle Ages and Other Essays (Oxford, 1935).

REES, W., An Historical Atlas of Wales (London, 1951).

RICHTER, MICHAEL, 'Canterbury's Primacy in Wales and the First Stage of Bishop Bernard's Opposition', Journal of Ecclesiastical History, xxii (1971).

——, 'Gerald of Wales: a Reassessment on the 750th Anniversary of His Death', Traditio, xxix (1973).

——, Giraldus Cambrensis: the Growth of the Welsh Nation (2nd edn., Aberystwyth, 1976).

——, 'The Life of St. David by Giraldus Cambrensis', Welsh History Review, iv (1968-9).

——, 'A New Edition of the So-Called Vita Davidis Secundi', Bulletin of the Board of Celtic Studies, xxii (1967), 245-9.

——, 'Professions of Obedience and the Metropolitan Claim of St. David's', National Library of Wales Journal, xv (1967-8).

RODERICK, A.J., 'Marriage and Politics in Wales, 1066-1282', Welsh History Review, iv (1968-9).

ROUND, J.H., Feudal England (London, 1895, repr. 1964).

ROUSE, R.H. AND M.A., 'The Florilegium Angelicum: Its Origin, Content and Influence', in Medieval Learning and Literature. Essays Presented to R.W. Hunt, ed. J.J.G. Alexander and M.T. Gibson (Oxford, 1976).

ROWE, J.H., 'Ethnography and Ethnology in the Sixteenth Century', (Kroeber Anthropological Society Papers, xxx, 1964).

RUSSELL, J.C., 'The Canonization of Opposition to the King in Angevin England', in Anniversary Essays in Mediaeval History by Students of C.H. Haskins, ed. C.H. Taylor and John L. LaMonte (Boston, 1929).

SANFORD, E.M., 'Giraldus Cambrensis' Debt to Petrus Cantor', Medievalia et Humanistica, iii (1945).

SBORDONE, F., Richerche sulle Fonti et sulla Composizione del Physiologus Greco (Naples, 1936).

SCHNITH, K., 'Betrachtungen zum Spätwerk des Giraldus Cambrensis: De Principis Instructione', in Festiva Lanx (Munich, 1966).

SIKES, E.E., The Anthropology of the Greeks (London, 1914).

SILVERSTEIN, T., 'Daniel of Morley, English Cosmologist and Student of Arabic Science', Mediaeval Studies, x (1948).

——, 'The Fabulous Cosmogony of Bernard Silvestris', Modern Philology, xlvi (1948-9).

SMALLEY, BERYL, The Becket Conflict and the Schools (Oxford, 1973).

——, 'Sallust in the Middle Ages', in R.R. Bolgar (ed.), Classical Influences on European Culture 500-1500 (Cambridge, 1971).

SOUTHERN, R.W., Medieval Humanism and Other Studies (Oxford, 1970).

STENTON, F.M., The First Century of English Feudalism (2nd edn., Oxford, 1961).

STIEFEL, TINA, 'The Heresy of Science: A Twelfth Century Conceptual Revolution', Isis, lxviii (1977).

STOCK, BRIAN, Myth and Science in the Twelfth Century: a Study of Bernard Silvester (Princeton, 1972).

STRAYER, JOSEPH R., 'France: The Holy Land, the Chosen People, and the Most Christian King', Medieval Statecraft and the Perspectives of History (Princeton, 1971).

STUBBS, WILLIAM, 'Learning and Literature at the Court of Henry II,' Seventeen Lectures on the Study of Medieval and Modern History (3rd edn., Oxford, 1900).

SYME, R., Tacitus (2 vols., Oxford, 1958).

TATLOCK, J.S.P., The Legendary History of Britain (Berkeley, 1950).

THOMPSON, E.A., The Early Germans (Oxford, 1965).

THURNEYSEN, R. (ed), Studies in Early Irish Law (Dublin, 1936).

TOOLEY, MARIAN J., 'Bodin and the Medieval Theory of Climate', Speculum, xxviii (1953).

TÜRK, EGBERT, Nugae curialium, le regne d'Henri II Plantagenet, 1154-1189, et l'éthique politique (Geneva, 1977).

VIARRE, Simone, La Survie d'Ovide dans la littérature scientifique des XIIe et XIIIe siècles (Poitiers, 1966).

WALLACE-HADRILL, J.M., Early Germanic Kingship (Oxford, 1971).

WARREN, W.L., Henry II (London, 1973).

——, King John (London, 1961).

WATT, J.A., The Church in Medieval Ireland (Dublin, 1972).

——, The Church and the Two Nations in Medieval Ireland (Cambridge, 1970).

——, et al. (eds.), Mediaeval Studies Presented to Aubrey Gwynn (Dublin, 1961).

WETHERBEE, WINTHROP, Platonism and Poetry in the Twelfth Century (Princeton, 1972).

WILLIAMS, E.A., 'A Bibliography of Giraldus Cambrensis', National Library of Wales Journal, xii (1961-2).

WILLIAMS, GLANMOR, The Welsh Church from Conquest to Reformation (Cardiff, 1962).

WILLIAMS, J.R., 'The Quest for the Author of the Moralium Dogma Philosophorum, 1931-56', Speculum, xxxii (1957).

WILLIAMS-JONES, KEITH, 'Thomas Becket and Wales', Welsh History Review, v (1970-1).

WORSTBROCK, F.J., 'Translatio Artium', Archiv für Kulturgeschichte, xlvii (1965).

WRIGHT, J.K., Geographical Lore at the Time of the Crusades (New York, 1925).

YOUNG, CHARLES C., Hubert Walter (Durham, N.C., 1968).

ZIRKLE, C., 'The Early History of the Idea of the Inheritance of Acquired Characteristics and of Pangenesis', Transactions of the American Philosophical Society, xxxv (1946).

D. SECONDARY WORKS—UNPUBLISHED

BEST, EDWARD E., 'Classical Latin Prose Writers quoted by Giraldus Cambrensis' (Univ. of North Carolina Ph.D. thesis, 1957) (synopsis only consulted).

HUMPHREYS, DOROTHY, 'Some Types of Social Life as Shown in the Works of Gerald of Wales' (Oxford Univ. B. Litt. thesis, 1936).

HUNT, R.W., 'Alexander Nequam' (Oxford Univ. D. Phil. thesis, 1936).

RYAN, MARY T., 'The Historical Value of Giraldus Cambrensis' Expugnatio Hibernica as an Account of the Anglo-Norman Invasion of Ireland' (University College, Dublin, MA thesis, 1967).

SULLIVAN, GERALD J.E., 'Pagan Latin Poets in Giraldus Cambrensis' (Cincinnati Univ. Ph.D. thesis, 1950).

BIBLIOGRAPHY TO THE
NEW EDITION: 1981–2005

There has been only one new *edition* of a work of Gerald's since 1981:
The Life of St. Hugh of Avalon, Bishop of Lincoln 1186-1200, ed. and tr. Richard M. Loomis
(New York, 1985).

Several older *translations* have been reprinted:
The Autobiography of Gerald of Wales, ed. and tr. H.E. Butler (London, 1937, repr. Woodbridge,
2005, with "A Guide to Further Reading" by John Gilllingham).
Concerning the Instruction of Princes, tr. Joseph Stevenson (London, 1858, repr. Felinfach,
1991).
The History and Topography of Ireland, tr. J. J. O'Meara (Penguin Classics, 1982) (a translation
of the first version of the *Topography of Ireland*, originally published in 1951).

The *secondary literature* is, however, quite voluminous and diverse:

BARBER, Richard, "Was Mordred Buried at Glastonbury? Arthurian Tradition at
Glastonbury in the Middle Ages", *Arthurian Literature* 4 (1985), pp. 37-63 (repr. in
Glastonbury Abbey and the Arthurian Tradition, ed. James P. Carley (Arthurian Studies 44
(not 45 as on title page), Cambridge, 2001), pp. 143-59).
BARROW, Julia S., "Gerald of Wales's Great-nephews", *Cambridge Medieval Celtic Studies* 8
(1984), pp. 101-6.
BARTLETT, Robert, "Gerald of Wales", in *The Oxford Dictionary of National Biography*
(Oxford, 2004), pp. 925-8.
———, "Political Prophecy in Gerald of Wales", in *Culture politique des Plantagenêt*, ed.
Martin Aurell (Poitiers, 2003), pp. 303-11.
———, "Rewriting Saints' Lives: The Case of Gerald of Wales", *Speculum* 58 (1983), pp.
598-613.
BEARE, Rhona, "Gerald of Wales on the Barnacle Goose", *Notes and Queries* 242 (1997), pp.
459-62.
BEESTON, A. F. L., "In the Steps of Gerallt Gymro", *Transactions of the Honourable Society of
Cymmrodorion* (1988), pp. 11-28.
BOIVIN, Jeanne-Marie, *L'Irlande au Moyen Âge: Giraud de Barri et la 'Topographia Hibernica'
(1188)* (Paris, 1993).
———, "Le prêtre et les loups-garous: une épisode de la *Topographia Hibernica* de Giraud de
Barri", in *Métamorphose et bestiaire fantastique au Moyen Age*, ed. Laurence Harf-Lancner
(Paris, 1985), pp. 51-69.
———, "Les paradoxes des *clerici regis*: l'exemple, à la cour d'Henri II Plantagenêt, de
Giraud de Barri", in *Le Clerc au Moyen Age* (Aix-en-Provence, 1995), pp. 47-61.
BOULOUX, Nathalie, "Les usages de la géographie à la cour des Plantagenêts dans la seconde
moitié du XIIe siècle", *Médiévales: langue, textes, histoire* 24 (1993), pp. 131-48.
BREEZE, Andrew, "Gerald of Wales's *Expugnatio Hibernica* and Pedro of Cardona (d. 1183),
Archbishop of Toledo", *The National Library of Wales Journal* 29 (1995-6), pp. 337-9.

————, "Gerald of Wales's *Itinerary of Wales* in Medieval Exeter", *Notes and Queries* 243 (1998), pp. 31-3.

————, "Giraldus Cambrenis and Poland", *Bulletin of the Board of Celtic Studies* 34 (1987), pp. 111-12.

BROWN, Elizabeth A. R., "Ritual Brotherhood in Western Medieval Europe", *Traditio* 52 (1997), pp. 357-81 (at pp. 366-70).

BROWN, Michelle, "Marvels of the West: Giradus Cambrensis and the Role of the Author in the Development of Marginal Illustration", *English Manuscript Studies 1100-1700* 10 (2002), pp. 34-59.

BURNETT, Charles, "Arabic Divinatory Texts and Celtic Folklore: A Comment on the Theory and Practice of Scapulimancy in Western Europe", in *Magic and Divination in the Middle Ages: Texts and Techniques in the Islamic and Christian Worlds* (Variorum Collected Studies Series 557, Aldershot, 1996), pp. 31-42 (Essay XIII) (at pp. 33-7).

BURSTYN, Shai, "Gerald of Wales and the Sumer Canon", *Journal of Musicology* 2 (1983), pp. 135-50.

————, "Is Gerald of Wales a Credible Musical Witness?" *Musical Quarterly* 72 (1986), pp. 155-69.

BYNUM, Caroline Walker, "Metamorphosis, or Gerald and the Werewolf", *Speculum* 73 (1998), pp. 987-1013.

CAREY, John, "The Finding of Arthur's Grave: A Story from Clonmacnois?" in *Ildánach Ildírech: A Festschrift for Proinsias Mac Cana*, ed. John Carey, John T. Koch and Pierre-Yves Lambert (Celtic Studies Publications 4, Andover and Aberystwyth, 1999), pp. 1-14.

CASTORA, Joseph C., "The Cistercian Order as Portrayed in the *Speculum ecclesiae* of Gerald of Wales", *Analecta Cisterciensia* 53 (1997), pp. 73-97.

CHAPMAN, Malcolm, *The Celts: The Construction of a Myth* (Basingstoke, 1992) (pp. 185-200).

COHEN, Jeffrey, "Hybrids, Monsters, Borderlines: The Bodies of Gerald of Wales", in *The Postcolonial Middle Ages*, ed. Jeffrey Cohen (Basingstoke, 2000), pp. 85-104.

COLE, Penny J., *The Preaching of the Crusades to the Holy Land, 1095-1270* (Cambridge, Mass., 1991) (pp. 74-8).

COLEMAN, Edward, "Nasty Habits - Satire and the Medieval Monk", *History Today* 43/6 (June 1993), pp. 36-42.

COWLEY, F. G., *Gerald of Wales and Margam Abbey* (Friends of Margam Abbey Annual Lecture, 1982, 2nd ed., 1992).

CRICK, Julia, "The British Past and the Welsh Future: Gerald of Wales, Geoffrey of Monmouth and Arthur of Britain", *Celtica* 23 (1999), pp. 60-75.

DUFOURNET, Jean, "Giraud de Barri et l'Irlande: une grande figure du XIIe siècle", *Le Moyen Age* 101 (1995), pp. 113-19.

ECHARD, Siân, *Arthurian Narrative in the Latin Tradition* (Cambridge, 1998) (pp. 70-5).

EDBURY, Peter W., "Preaching the Crusade in Wales", in *England and Germany in the High Middle Ages*, ed. Alfred Haverkamp and Hanna Vollrath (Oxford, 1996), pp. 221-33.

EMPEY, Adrian, "Gerald of Wales: A Case of Myopia?" in *Contrasts and Comparisons: Studies in Irish and Welsh Church History*, ed. John R. Guy and W.G. Neely (Powys, 1999), pp. 43-53.

English Episcopal Acta 27: York, 1189-1212, ed. Marie Lovatt (Oxford, 2004), introduction, pp. cxxxv-cxxxviii.

EVANS, H. Wyn, "The Bishops of St. Davids from Bernard to Bec", in *Medieval Pembrokeshire*, ed. R. F. Walker (Pembrokeshire County History 2, Haverfordwest, 2002), pp. 270-311 (at pp. 270-90).

EVANS, Michael, "An Emended Joke in Gerald of Wales", *Journal of the Warburg and Courtauld Institutes* 61 (1998), pp. 253-4.

FERRUOLO, Stephen C., *The Origins of the University: The Schools of Paris and their Critics, 1100-1215* (Stanford, 1985) (pp. 168-83).

GAUTIER Dalché, Patrick, "Entre le folklore et la science: la légende des antipodes chez Giraud de Cambrie et Gervais de Tilbury", in *Géographie et culture: La représentation de l'espace du VIe au XIIe siècle* (Variorum Collected Studies Series 592, Aldershot, 1997), pp. 103-14 (Essay XI).

GILLINGHAM, John, "The English Invasion of Ireland", in *Representing Ireland: Literature and the Origins of Conflict, 1534-1660*, ed. Brendan Bradshaw, Andrew Hadfield and Willy Maley (Cambridge, 1993), pp. 24-42 (repr. in *The English in the Twelfth Century: Imperialism, National Identity and Political Values* (Woodbridge, 2000), pp. 145-60).

———, "Henry II, Richard I and the Lord Rhys", *Peritia* 10 (1996), pp. 225-36 (repr. in *The English in the Twelfth Century: Imperialism, National Identity and Political Values* (Woodbridge, 2000), pp. 59-68).

———, "'Slaves of the Normans?' Gerald de Barri and Regnal Solidarity in Early Thirteenth-century England", in *Law, Laity and Solidarities: Essays in Honour of Susan Reynolds*, ed. P. Stafford, J. L. Nelson and J. Martindale (Manchester, 2001), pp. 160-71.

GNEUSS, Helmut, "Giraldus Cambrensis und die Geschichte der englischen Sprachwissenschaft im Mittelalter", in *Language and Civilization: A Concerted Profusion of Essays and Studies in Honour of Otto Hietsch*, ed. Claudia Blank (Frankfurt, 1992), pp. 164-72 (repr. in *Language and History in Early England* (Variorum Collected Studies Series 559, Aldershot, 1996) Essay XI, with identical pagination).

GOLDING, Brian, "Gerald of Wales and the Cistercians", *Reading Medieval Studies* 21 (1995), pp. 5-30.

———, "Gerald of Wales and the Monks", *Thirteenth Century England* 5 (1993), pp. 53-64.

GRESHAM, C. A., "Archbishop Baldwin's Journey through Merioneth in 1188", *Journal of the Merioneth Historical and Record Society* 10/3 (1987-8), pp. 186-204.

HARF-LANCNER, Laurence, "L'Enfer de la cour: la cour d'Henri II Plantagenet et la Mesnie Hellequin", in *L'Etat et les aristocraties (France, Angleterre, Ecosse) XIIe-XVIIe siècle*, ed. Philippe Contamine (Paris, 1989), pp. 27-50.

HARRISON, Julian, "A Note on Gerald of Wales and *Annales Cambriae*", *Welsh History Review* 17 (1994), pp. 252-5.

HAYWOOD, Eric, "'La divisa dal mondo ultima Irlanda' ossia la riscoperta umanistica dell'Irlanda", *Giornale storico della letteratura italiana* 176 (1999), pp. 363-87, esp. pp. 363-6 (although Gerald was not a "monaco gallese"!).

HOWLETT, David, *Cambro-Latin Compositions: Their Competence and Craftsmanship* (Dublin, 1998) (pp. 138-52).

JENSEN, Sonya, "Merlin: Ambrosius and Silvester", in *Words and Wordsmiths. A Volume for H. L. Rogers*, ed. Geraldine Barnes et al. (Sydney, 1989), pp. 45-8.

KAY, Richard, "Gerald of Wales and the Fourth Lateran Council", *Viator* 29 (1998), pp. 79-93.

KNIGHT, Rhonda, "Procreative Sodomy: Textuality and the Construction of Ethnicities in Gerald of Wales's *Descriptio Kambriae*", *Exemplaria: A Journal of Theory in Medieval and Renaissance Studies* 14 (2002), pp. 47-77.

———, "Werewolves, Monsters and Miracles: Representing Colonial Fantasies in Gerald of Wales' *Topographia Hibernica*", *Studies in Iconography* 22 (2001), pp. 55-86.

LAPIDGE, Michael, and Richard Sharpe, *A Bibliography of Celtic-Latin Literature 400-1200* (Dublin, 1985) (pp. 22-8).

LE RIDER, Paule, "A propos de costumes ... De Giraud de Barri au Conte du Graal et à Fergus", *Le Moyen Age* 107 (2001), pp. 253-82.

LEERSSEN, Joseph, *Mere Irish and Fíor-ghael: Studies in the Idea of Irish Nationality, its Development and Literary Expression prior to the Nineteenth Century* (Amsterdam, 1986) (pp. 36–9).

LOOMIS, Richard, "Giraldus de Barri's Homage to Hugh of Avalon", in *De Cella in Seculum*, ed. Michael G. Sargeant (Cambridge, 1989), pp. 29–40.

MAAZ, Wolfgang, "Brotlöffel, haariges Herz und wundersame Empfängnis. Bemerkungen zu Egbert von Lüttich und Giraldus Cambrensis", in *Tradition und Wertung: Festschrift für Franz Brunhölzl zum 65. Geburtstag*, ed. Günther Bernt, Fidel Rädle and Gabriel Silagi (Sigmaringen, 1989), pp. 107-18.

———, "Giraldus Cambrensis", in *Enzklopädie des Marchens 5* (Berlin, 1987), pp. 1255-65.

MANN, Jill, "Giraldus Cambrensis and the Goliards", *Journal of Celtic Studies* 3 (1981), pp. 31-9.

McCAULEY, Barbara Lynne, "Giraldus 'Silvester' of Wales and his *Prophetic History of Ireland*: Merlin's role in the *Expugnatio Hibernica*", *Quondam et Futurus: A Journal of Arthurian Interpretations* 3/4 (1993), pp. 41-62.

MITTMAN, Asa Simon, "The Other Close at Hand: Gerald of Wales and the 'Marvels of the West'", in *The Monstrous Middle Ages*, ed. Bettina Bildhauer and Robert Mills (Cardiff, 2003), pp. 97-112.

MORGAN, Hiram, "Giraldus Cambrensis and the Tudor Conquest of Ireland", in *Political Ideology in Ireland, 1541-1641*, ed. Hiram Morgan (Dublin, 1999), pp. 22-44.

NICHOLS, Stephen G., "Fission and Fusion: Mediations of Power in Medieval History and Literature", *Yale French Studies* 70 (1986), pp. 21-41.

NIELSEN, Robert L., "The Cistercian Chapters of *The Mirror of the Church*", *Cistercian Studies Quarterly* 34 (1999), pp. 19-28.

NIXON, Paul, "Giraldus Cambrensis on Music: How Reliable are his Historiographers?" in *Proceedings of the First British-Swedish Conference on Musicology: Medieval Studies, 1988*, ed. Ann Buckley (Stockholm, 1992), pp. 264-89.

O'LOUGHLIN, Thomas, "An Early Thirteenth-Century Map in Dublin: A Window into the World of Giraldus Cambrensis", *Imago Mundi* 51 (1999), pp. 24-39.

———, "Giraldus Cambrensis and the Sexual Agenda of the Twelfth Century Reformers", *Journal of Welsh Religious History* 8 (2000), pp. 1-15.

———, "Giraldus Cambrensis's View of Europe", *History Ireland* 8:2 (2000), pp. 16-21.

OTTER, Monika, *Inventiones: Fiction and Referentiality in Twelfth-Century English Historical Writing* (Chapel Hill, 1996) (pp. 129-55).

PRYCE, Huw, "British or Welsh? National Identity in Twelfth-century Wales", *English Historical Review* 116 (2001), pp. 775-801 (at pp. 785-90, 797-8).

———, "A Cross-border Career: Giraldus Cambrensis between Wales and England", in *Grenzgänger*, ed. Reinhard Schneider (Veröffentlichungen der Kommission für Saarländische Landesgeschichte und Volksforschung, 1998), pp. 45-60.

———, "Gerald's Journey through Wales", *Journal of Welsh Ecclesiastical History* 6 (1989), pp. 17-34.

———, "In Search of a Medieval Society: Deheubarth in the Writings of Gerald of Wales", *Welsh History Review* 13 (1986-7), pp. 265-81.

RIGG, A. G., *A History of Anglo-Latin Literature 1066-1422* (Cambridge, 1992) (pp. 93-6).

ROBERTS, Brynley F., *Gerald of Wales* (Cardiff, 1982).

———, "Gerald of Wales and Welsh Tradition", in *The Formation of Culture in Medieval Britain: Celtic, Latin, and Norman Influences on English Music, Literature, History, and Art*, ed. Françoise H. M. Le Saux (Lewiston, 1995), pp. 129-47.

ROLLO, David, "Gerald of Wales' *Topographia Hibernica*': Sex and the Irish Nation", *Romanic Review* 86 (1995), pp. 167-90.

ROONEY, Catherine, "The Manuscripts of the Works of Gerald of Wales" (Ph.D. dissertation, Cambridge University, 2005).

St Davids Episcopal Acta 1085-1280, ed. Julia Barrow (Cardiff, 1998), introduction, pp. 5-10.

SPATZ, Nancy, "Evidence of Inception Ceremonies in the Twelfth-century Schools of Paris", *History of Universities* 13 (1994), pp. 3-19 (at pp. 7-10).

STEWART, James, "Gleann na nGealt: A Twelfth-century Latin Account", *Celtica* 17 (1986), pp. 105-11.

————, "*Topographia Hiberniae*", *Celtica* 21 (1990 (Essays in Honour of Brian Ó Cuív)), pp. 642-57.

THOMAS, Charles, "The Artist and the People, a Foray into Uncertain Semiotics", in *From the Isles of the North: Early Medieval Art in Ireland and Britain*, ed. Cormac Bourke (Belfast, 1995), pp. 1-7.

THOMSON, John A. F., "St. Eiluned of Brecon and her Cult", in *Martyrs and Martyrologies*, ed. Diana Wood (Studies in Church History 30, 1993), pp. 117-25.

TYERMAN, Christopher, *England and the Crusades, 1095-1588* (Chicago, 1988) (pp. 156-67).

VERGER, Jacques, "*Plus libris quam linguis*. Giraud de Barri et l'écriture d'après la «Lettre au chapitre de Hereford» (vers 1221)", in *Religions et mentalités au Moyen Age: Mélanges en l'honneur d'Hervé Martin*, ed. Sophie Cassagnes-Brouquet et al. (Rennes, 2003), pp. 499-505.

WADA, Yoko, "Gerald on Gerald: Self-presentation by Giraldus Cambrensis", *Anglo-Norman Studies* 20 (1997), pp. 223-46.

WALKER, David, "Cultural Survival in an Age of Conquest", in *Welsh Society and Nationhood: Historical Essays Presented to Glanmor Williams*, ed. R. R. Davies (Cardiff, 1984), pp. 35-50 (at pp. 47-50).

WELLER, Philip, "Gerald of Wales's View of Music", *Welsh Music History* 2 (1997), pp. 1-32.

WILLIAMS, Glanmor, "An Old Man Remembers: Gerald the Welshman", *Morgannwg* 32 (1988), pp. 7-20.

WOOD, Charles T., "Guenevere at Glastonbury: A Problem in Translation(s)", *Arthurian Literature* 16 (1998), pp. 23-40 (repr. in *Glastonbury Abbey and the Arthurian Tradition*, ed. James P. Carley (Arthurian Studies 44 (not 45 as on title page), Cambridge, 2001), pp. 83-100).

ZIMMER, Stefan, "A Medieval Linguist: Gerald de Barri", *Etudes celtiques* 35 (2003), pp. 313-50.

NOTES

CHAPTER I

1. H. Owen, Gerald the Welshman (London, 1889, rev. edn. 1904).
2. T. Jones, Gerallt Gymro/Gerald the Welshman (dual language, Cardiff, 1947); 'Gerald the Welshman's Itinerary through Wales and Description of Wales', National Library of Wales Journal, vi (1949-50), 117-48.
3. F.M. Powicke, 'Gerald of Wales', Bulletin of the John Rylands Library, xii (1928), 399; reprinted in The Christian Life in the Middle Ages and Other Essays (Oxford, 1935).
4. M. Richter, Giraldus Cambrensis: the Growth of the Welsh Nation (2nd edn., Aberystwyth, 1976).
5. W. Berges, Die Fürstenspiegel des Hohen and Späten Mittelalters (Stuttgart, 1938), p. 144.
6. K. Schnith, 'Betrachtungen rum Spätwerk des Giraldus Cambrensis: De Principis Instructione', Festiva Lanx (Munich, 1966), pp. 53-66.
7. M. Handelsman, 'La rôle de la nationalité dans l'histoire du moyen âge', Bulletin of the International Committee of Historical Studies, ii (1929-30), 242.
8. L'Histoire de Guillaume le Maréchal, ed. P. Meyer (Société de l'Histoire de France, 1891-1901), ll. 5214-15.
9. Gemma, p. 348; Vita Galf., p. 423.
10. Calendar of Documents Relating to Ireland, ed. H.S. Sweetman (London, 1875-86), iii. 10, quoted in J.A. Watt, 'Edward I and the Irish Church', Mediaeval Studies Presented to Aubrey Gwynn (Dublin, 1961), p. 150, n. 71. I see no need to translate linguam as 'race' as is done by J. Otway-Ruthven, A History of Mediaeval Ireland (London, 1968), p. 133.
11. Captures by the Welsh are recorded in 1145 (or 1147), 1189, and 1215: Brut y Tywysogion or The Chronicle of the Princes. Red Book of Hergest Version, ed. T. Jones (Cardiff, 1955), pp. 121-3, 171, 205.
12. Spec. Duorum, p. 36.
13. Inv., p. 93.
14. Printed in E.St.J. Brooks, 'An Unpublished Charter of Raymond le Gros', Journal of the Royal Society of Antiquaries of Ireland, 7th sec., ix (1939), 1677.
15. Itin., p. 34, De Reb., pp. 57-8.
16. For 'Nesta's brood' see Exp., p. 229; Itin., pp. 91, 130; De Reb., pp. 21, 58-60; Brut y Tywsogion, pp. 55-7; and the family tree at the end of this chapter. See also A.J. Roderic, 'Marriage and Politics in Wales, 1066-1282', Welsh History Review, iv (1968-9).
17. See above, pp. 170-1.
18. Itin., pp. 14, 55, 83, 126; De Reb., pp. 76-7. Cf. Prin., p. 83; Becket Materials, iii. 528.
19. Spec. Duorum, p. 132.

20. De Reb., p. 57.

21. Ibid., pp. 80–1, 84.

22. Symb. El., pp. 203, 295; cf. Pipe Roll 3-4 Richard I (Pipe Roll Society, 1926), p. 165.

23. De Reb., p. 60. The Lord Rhys of South Wales is meant.

24. Descr., p. 218-25.

25. Ibid., p. 225, n. 4.

26. pp. 33-45.

27. De Jure, p. 178; cf. Symb. El., p. 308.

28. De Jure. pp. 113-14; cf. ibid., p. 344; Spec. Duorum, p. 18.

29. Exp., pp. 224, 390.

30. Vita Galf., pp. 358, 365, 367.

31. See part III, 'Ethnography', esp. pp. 131-41.

32. Descr., pp. 226-7.

33. Itin., pp. 34-5.

34. This survives in the Symbolum Electorum and is printed in Gerald's Opera, ed. J.S. Brewer, J.F. Dimock, and C.F. Warner (RS, 1861-1891), viii, pp. lvii–lxvii.

35. Exp., p. 267.

36. Ibid., p. 229.

37. Ibid., p. 242.

38. For Wibert see Symb. El., pp. 203-18, 293-301; Spec. Eccl., pp. 156-61; De Reb., pp. 95, 102, 103; and D. Knowles, 'Some Enemies of Giraldus Cambrensis', Studia Monastica, i (1959), 137-41.

39. He received 5d. a day (7.12s.1d. a year) from 1191-2 until midway through 1201-2, when this revenue was reallocated to two other clerks: Pipe Rolls 5 Ric. I, p. 88; 6 Ric. I, p. 136; 7 Ric. I, p. 108; 8 Ric. I, p. 88; 9 Ric. I, p. 195; 10 Ric. I, p. 211; 1 John, p. 215; 2 John, p. 240; 3 John, p. 265; 4 John, p. 273; 5 John, p. 55 (Pipe Roll Society, 1927-38). Cf. Gerald's Opera, i, 435; Rotuli Chartarum, ed T.D. Hardy (London, 1837), p. 105.

40. Symb. El., p. 332.

41. Exp., pp. 351-2.

42. The charter is printed in J. Lodge, The Peerage of Ireland (London, 1754), i.194. The two additional cantreds eventually occupied were Killede and Muscherie-Dunegan, as is made clear in King John's confirmatory charter of 1207 to William de Barri, Philip's son: see Calendar of Documents i (1171-1251), no. 340.

43. William de Barri, Gerald's father, owed a relief of £10 in 1130: Pipe Roll 31 Hen I (HMSO, 1929), p. 137. This would correspond to 2 knights' fees at the rate of 100s. as given in the Leis Willelme, in Die Gesetze der Angel-Sachsen, ed. F. Lieberman (Halle, 1898-1916), i.506; 'Glanvill', Tractatus de Legibus 9.4, ed. G.D. Hall (London, 1965), p. 108); Dialogus de Scaccario 2.10 (ed. C. Johnson (London, 1950), p. 96); and in clause 2 of Magna Carta. F.M. Stenton, The First Century of English Feudalism, 2nd edn. (Oxford, 1961), p. 163, however, warns against too ready an equation of practice and legal principle.

44. Exp., pp. 232, 234-6, and 245 for Robert; ibid., pp. 354, 386 for Robert junior.

45. Ibid., p. 245; cf. p. 297.

46. Ibid., pp. 323-4. v47. Ibid., pp. 324-5.

48. Ibid., pp. 309-10. Meiler's courage is also mentioned at pp. 234-6, 321-2, 330, 354, 355-6.

49. Itin., p. 91.

50. De Reb., pp. 58-60.

51. Exp., pp. 325-6.

52. Ibid., pp. 335-6.

53. Pipe Rolls, 17 Hen II (Pipe Roll Society, 1893-4), pp. 17, 29, 92; 18 Hen. II, p. 49.

54. Exp., p. 383.

55. Gesta Regis Henrici Secundi Benedicti Abbatis, ed. W. Stubbs (RS, 1867), i.137.

56. Ibid., i.221.

57. Exp., p. 335.

58. Ibid., p. 337.

59. Ibid., p. 353.

60. Ibid., p. 338.

61. For reference see Expugnatio Hibernica, ed. A.B. Scott and F.X. Martin (Dublin, 1978), pp. 330-1, n. 294.

62. Exp., pp. 383-4.

63. Ibid., p. 389.

64. e.g. Usama's famous story of how a newly arrived Frank tried to force him to pray in the Christian style, while his Templar friends apologized: An Arab-Syrian Gentleman and Warrior... Memoirs of Usamah Ibn-Munqidh, ed. P.K. Hitti (New York, 1929), pp. 163-4.

65. Exp., pp. 391, 394-5.

66. Ibid., pp. 395-6.

67. Itin., p. 138.

68. Descr., p. 220.

CHAPTER II

1. De Reb., p. 21.

2. Ibid., p. 22.

3. Ibid.

4. e.g. Itin., pp. 218-27.

5. De Reb., p. 50.

6. Exp., pp. 295-6. This was Walter de Barri, Gerald's half-brother. The fact that he set out for the fatal battle from a place where his father was present (Manorbier?) suggests a fight against the Welsh rather than the Irish. Gerald would certainly not have omitted to mention his father's presence in the first wave of Norman invaders of Ireland.

7. See above, p. 25.

8. Georges Duby, 'Les "Jeunes" dans la société aristocratique dans la France du Nord-Ouest au XIIᵉ siècle', Annales xix (1964), reprinted in his collection of articles, Hommes et structures du moyen âge (Paris, 1973).

9. De Reb., pp. 21-2.

10. M. Richter, 'A New Edition of the So-Called Vita Davidis Secundi', Bulletin of the Board of Celtic Studies, xxii (1967), 245-9.

11. The Calendar of the Gormanston Register, ed J. Mills and M.J. McEnery (Dublin, 1916), p. 165, contains Bishop David's charter granting the stewardship of St. David's and various estates to his brother Maurice. The Black Book of St. David's, ed. J.W. Willis-Bund (Cymmrodorion Record Series, No. 5, 1902), p. 138, mentions Bishop David alienating episcopal demesne to provide a dowry for his daughter. Gerald also mentioned some of his uncle's alienations, De Jure, p. 155.

12. c. 1162-1174 according to M. Richter, Giraldus Cambrensis, p. 4. Gerald spent three periods of several years at Paris studying the arts (De Reb., p. 23), and was back in England c. 1174 since he was appointed archdeacon by his uncle David (d. 1176) and had already been active in Wales before the appointment. He was definitely in Paris in 1165

(Prin., p. 292). A very inconsistent story (Vita Rem., p. 69) might suggest that he was in Canterbury in December 1172 or 1173.

13. It has been estimated that approximately one-eighth of the Gemma Ecclesiastica was taken verbatim from the Chanter's Verbum Abbreviatum (PL, ccv): E.M. Sanford, 'Giraldus Cambrensis' Debt to Petrus Cantor', Medievalia et Humanistica, iii (1945); A. Boutemy, 'Giraud de Barri et Pierre le Chantre', Revue du moyen âge latin, ii (1946).

14. J.W. Baldwin, Masters, Princes and Merchants. The Social Views of Peter the Chanter and His Circle (Princeton, 1970).

15. B. Smalley, The Becket Conflict and the Schools (Oxford, 1973), p. 14.

16. Gemma, p. 169.

17. Ibid., p. 335.

18. Ibid., pp. 128-9.

19. Inv., pp. 203-4.

20. Gemma, p. 338.

21. Inv., p. 203.

22. Spec. Eccl., p. 337.

23. Gemma, pp. 118-19.

24. Ibid., pp. 119-20.

25. Ibid., pp. 36-7, quoting Origen, In Numeros Homilia, II, in Rufinus's translation (ed. W.A. Baehrens, Griechischen Christlichen Schrftsteller, xxx (Leipzig, 1921), 9.

26. For English conciliar legislation of the 12th century, see the canons of the councils of Westminster (1102, 1125, 1127, 1138, 1175, 1200), London (1108), and York (1195), most easily accessible in vol. i of Concilia Magnae Brittaniae et Hiberniae, D. Wilkins (London, 1737).

27. For what follows, see De Reb., pp. 23-32.

28. On this archdeacon, Jordan, see The Letters of John of Salisbury, i, The Early Letters (1153-1161), ed. W.J. Millor and H.E. Butler, revised by C.N.L. Brooke (London, 1955), pp. 134-5

29. Descr., p. 214. Also in De Jure, p. 130.

30. De Jure, p. 114. These practices are discussed by J.C. Davies, in Episcopal Acts Relating to Welsh Dioceses, 1066-1272, ii (Cardiff, 1948), 457-68. G. Williams, The Welsh Church from Conquest to Reformation (Cardiff, 1962), pp. 16, 337-44, notes their continuance in the later Middle Ages.

31. De Jure, p. 122 (This passage refers to the situation in 1148, but Gerald states that he believed it still to be true in his own time.)

32. Ibid., p. 128.

33. Ibid., pp. 128-31.

34. Ibid., p. 361.

35. On the portionary church and the related phenomenon of the clas, see A.N. Palmer, 'The Portionary Churches of Mediaeval North Wales', Archaeologia Cambrensis, 5th series, iii (1886); J.E. Lloyd, A History of Wales (3rd edn., London, 1939), i. 205-8; G. Williams, Welsh Church, pp. 17-18; Davies, Episcopal Acts, i (Cardiff, 1946), 69-75. Gerald described a clas at Llanbadarn Fawr, Itin., pp. 120-2.

36. See C.N L. Brooke, 'Gregorian Reform in Action: Clerical Marriage in England 1050-1200', Cambridge Historical Journal, xii (1956), reprinted (revised) in id., Medieval Church and Society (London, 1971). See also Episcopal Acts, ii. 465-8.

37. De Jure, p. 366.

38. Descr., pp. 206-7.

39. Gemma, pp. 157-8.

40. De Jure, p. 114; cf. Spec. Duorum, pp. 110-12, on 'Welsh oaths'.

41. De Jure, p. 114; cf. Descr., p. 206.

42. Richter, Giraldus Cambrensis, p. 11, quoting Mary T. Ryan, 'The Historical Value of Giraldus Cambrensis' Expugnatio Hibernica as an Account of the Anglo-Norman Invasion of Ireland' (University College, Dublin, MA thesis, 1967), p. 15.

43. Top., p. 178; cf. De Reb., pp. 65-6. The constitutions of this synod were confirmed by Urban III (Pontificia Hibernica, ed. M.P. Sheehy (Dublin, 1962), i. 48-52).

44. Especially pp. 164-5 and 170-8. Much of this material is repeated in De Reb., pp. 67-71.

45. Top., pp. 173-6.

46. Ibid., pp. 178-9.

47. Ibid., pp. 164, 170.

48. Ibid., p. 165.

49. Ibid., p. 167.

50. Ibid., p. 164.

51. Ibid., p. 171.

52. On twelfth-century church reform in Ireland, see A. Gwynn, The Twelfth Century Reform, A History of Irish Cotholicism, ii (1) (Dublin, 1968), which conveniently summarizes his views expressed in many articles over the years; these are listed in Watt, Medieval Studies, pp. 502-7. See also the first chapter of J.A. Watt, The Church and the Two Nations in Medieval Ireland (Cambridge, 1970), or the first chapter of the same author's The Church in Medieval Ireland (Dublin, 1972), and the last part of K. Hughes, The Church in Early Irish Society (London, 1966).

53. Similar hostility and misunderstanding, also distinguished by an 'unsympathetic and external viewpoint', was shown earlier in the century by another reforming churchman, St. Bernard. Aubrey Gwynn noted that Bernard's denunciation of Irish practices is an 'example of the way in which Irish customs and traditions were inevitably misunderstood abroad' and reflects his failure to appreciate the Irish situation. Twelfth Century Reform, p. 20. Cf. pp. 21, 27, 39-52 for the way in which St. Bernard interpreted the Irish situation through a French, and Cistercian, lens. 'Bernard', Gwynn observed elsewhere, 'is typically French in his conviction that all life outside and apart from the mainstream of French culture is inevitably rude and barbarous', 'St. Malachy of Armagh', Irish Ecclesiastical Record, lxx (1948), 965. Gwynn points out exaggerations in Bernard's description of the Irish in his notes on Bernard's life of Malachy, Vita Sancti Malachiae in Sancti Bernardi Opera, ed. J. Leclerq and H.M. Rochais, iii (Rome, 1963), 316 nn., 325 nn.

54. See also pp. 140-1.

55. See Georges Duby, Medieval Marriage. Two Models from Twelfth-century France, tr. E. Forster (Baltimore, 1978).

56. Sacrorum Conciliorum Nova et Amplissima Collectio, ed. J.L. Mansi (Florence and Venice, 1757-98), xxii, col. 1035, canon 50.

57. Descr., p. 213. Gerald's computation of degrees is inconsistent. He described the Lord Rhys as marrying his 'cousin in the fourth degree' (Itin., p. 15), but Rhodri ap Owain Gwynedd as marrying his 'cousin in the third degree' (Ibid., pp. 126-7), although the distance between the spouses in both cases was the same—the grandparent of one was the great-grand-parent of the other. No variation in methods of computation will plausibly remove this inconsistency.

58. Itin., pp. 15, 126-7, 133.

59. Letters of John of Salisbury, 135-6.

60. Itin., p. 133.

61. Descr., pp. 213-14.
62. See T.P. Ellis, Welsh Tribal Law and Custom in the Middle Ages (Oxford, 1926), i. 414.
63. Ibid., pp. 414-24. The Welsh laws exist in three versions, the Llyfr Blegywryd or 'Dimetian Code', the Llyfr Cyfnerth or 'Gwentian Code' (this is generally agreed to be a geographical misnomer) and the Llyfr Iorwerth or 'Venedotian Code'. Each contains a section on 'The Laws of Women', in which provision is made for divorce. English translations of the relevant sections of the Llyfr Blegywryd can be found in The Laws of Hywel Dda (the Book of Blegywryd), ed. M. Richards (Liverpool, 1954), pp. 67-72, and of the Llyfr Cyfnerth in Welsh Medieval Law, ed. A.W. Wade-Evans (Oxford, 1909), pp. 235-42. For a translation of the Llyfr Iorwerth one must go back to the 19th-century edition, Ancient Laws and Institutes of Wales, ed. A. Owen (London, 1841), pp. 38-49, although there is a modern Welsh edition, Llyfr Iorwerth, ed. Aled Rhys Wiliam (Cardiff, 1960). The Latin texts are in The Latin Texts of the Welsh Laws, ed. Hywel D. Emanuel (Cardiff, 1967), pp. 141-6, 220-6, 341-7, 469-76.
64. Councils and Ecclesiastical Documents Relating to Great Britain and Ireland, ed A.W. Haddan and W. Stubbs (Oxford, 1869-78), i. 382. Wilkins, in Concilia, i. 475, dates the canons in which this is included to 1173, which is extremely unlikely. Haddan and Stubbs suggest that they are a modified copy of the canons of Westminster, 1175. It has also been suggested that these canons represent a draft prepared for the council of Westminster (C.R. Cheney, From Becket to Langton (Manchester, 1956), p. 77 n. 2).
65. This statement is generally true, but for qualifications see R. Davies, 'Race Relations in Post Conquest Wales', Transactions of the Honourable Society of Cymmrodorion (1974-5), p. 385n, and Ellis, Welsh Law, pp. 451-3.
66. De Jure, p. 130.
67. T.J. Pierce, Medieval Welsh Society (Cardiff, 1972), pp. 295-6; Latin Texts, pp. 67-8, 70-2, 80.
68. Ancient Laws, p. 86. The introduction of primogeniture into Wales can also be seen as a facet of the anglicization of Welsh society. Here again ecclesiastical principles were an adjunct of colonization.
69. See T.J. Pierce, 'Einion ap Ynyr (Anian II), Bishop of St. Asaph', Flintshire Historical Society Publications, xxvii (1957); Williams, Welsh Church, pp. 8-12; Councils, i. 514, no.18. The Statute of Rhuddlan, 1284, decreed 'that bastards from henceforth shall not inherit, and also shall not have portions with the lawful heirs not without the lawful heirs', The Statutes of Wales, ed. I. Bowen (London, 1908), p. 36.
70. This is discussed by D.L. Douie, Archbishop Pecham (Oxford, 1952). Her chapter 6 deals with Pecham's relations with Wales, including his criticisms of Welsh law, hostile characterization of the Welsh, and the visitation. Texts associated with the visitation are printed in Registrum Epistolarum Fratris Johannis Peckham Archiepiscopi Cantuariensis, ed. C.T. Martin (RS, 1882-5), ii. 724-43 and iii. 773-806.
71. Ibid., i. 77.
72. Ibid., i. 136.
73. Ibid., i. 474-6.
74. Historical Manuscripts Commission, Report on Manuscripts in Various Collections, i (1901), 248. Douie, Pecham, p. 252, thought that this document probably originated in the royal household (although cf. ibid., n. 2).
75. Ibid., pp. 249-50, 261-2 (laziness and immorality of Welsh), 265 (English rule), 262 (Protestant clergyman and Irish).
76. On divorce and polygamy within the brehon laws, see the chapters by Nancy Power and August Knoch in R. Thurneysen et al. (ed.), Studies in Early Irish Law (Dublin,

1936), and D.A. Binchy, 'The Linguistic and Historical Value of the Irish Law Tracts', *Proceedings of the British Academy*, xxix (1943), 219-20. Irish customs regarding the prohibited degrees were attacked by 'romanizing' churchmen in the seventh century: Hughes, Church in Early Irish Society, p. 131. Cf. ibid., p. 260. For the persistence of these customs see K. Nicholls, *Gaelic and Gaelicised Ireland in the Middle Ages* (Dublin, 1972), pp. 73-6. 'In no field of life', he writes, 'was Ireland's apartness from the main stream of Christian European society so marked as in that of marriage. Throughout the medieval period... what could be called Celtic secular marriage remained the norm in Ireland.' Watt, Church in Medieval Ireland, pp. 206-8, is much more cautious, but concludes, from sixteenth-century evidence, 'This evidence suggests that in Ireland, as in certain other parts of Europe, local matrimonial usages yielded but slowly to the claims of canon law.' Gwynn, Twelfth Century Reform, pp. 17-18, after summarizing the brehon law on divorce and polygamy, comments, 'Students of Irish history know... that this observance of an older tradition was common as late as the fifteenth and sixteenth centuries.'

77. These letters are printed in Veterum Epistolarum Hibernicarum Sylloge, ed. James Ussher (Dublin, 1632 and 1696), Epp. 26-7,35-6; also in Ussher's Works, ed. C.R. Elrington, iv (Dublin, 1847), pp. 490-3, 520-4. They are discussed by A. Gwynn, 'Lanfranc and the Irish Church', Irish Ecclesiastical Record, lvii (1941), lviii (1941); id., 'St. Anselm and the Irish Church', ibid., lix (1942); and briefly by Hughes, Church in Early Irish Society, pp. 259-62.

78. Gesta Regis Henrici Secundi, i. 28; cf. Roger of Howden, Chronica, ed. w. Stubbs (RS, 1868-71), ii. 31.

79. Top., p. 181.

80. Ibid., p. 108.

81. Ibid., pp. 164-5. Hughes, Church in Early Irish Society, p. 131, mentions a 7th-century church canon which attacked the custom of a man taking his dead brother's widow to wife.

82. See n. 52 above. For the provisions of the first synod of Cashel on marriage, see A. Gwynn, 'The First Synod of Cashel', Irish Ecclesiastical Record, lxvii (1946), 109-22, and id., Twelfth Century Reform, pp. 15-19. For the synod of Kells on marriage, see ibid., p. 60. Hughes, Church in Early Irish Society, pp. 51, 53-4, 131, mentions earlier attacks on Irish marriage customs by churchmen, some going as far back as the 6th century.

83. Pontificia Hibernica, i. 15-16. Gerald's text is in Exp., pp. 317-18; Ralph of Diceto's in his Opera Historica, ed. W. Stubbs (RS, 1876), i. 300-1.

84. Ibid., i. 350-1.

85. Pontificia Hibernica, i. 21-3.

86. The phrase is taken from N.P. Canny, 'The Ideology of English Colonisation: from Ireland to America', William and Mary Quarterly. 3rd ser., xxx (1973). The characterization of the Irish by the English in the 16th century and its function as a justification for conquest, as discussed by Canny, have striking resemblances to the 12th-century situation.

87. Richter, Giraldus Cambrensis.

88. 'Canterbury's Primacy in Wales and the First Stage of Bishop Bernard's Opposition', Journal of Ecclesiastical History, xxii (1971); 'Professions of Obedience and the Metropolitan Claim of St. David's', National Library of Wales Journal, xv (1967-8).

89. The De Rebus a se Gestis received its final form after 1208, since Meiler fitzHenry is refereed to as 'Hiberniae tunc justiciarum' (p. 7) and he was replaced as justiciar in that year (Richter, Giraldus Cambrensis, p. 95 n. 1).

90. De Reb., pp. 32-9.

91. Ibid., pp. 40-1, 48-9.

92. Ibid., p. 44.

93. Ibid., p. 55.

94. Ibid., p. 111, as translated by H.E. Butler, in The Autobiography of Giraldus Cambrensis (London, 1937).

95. Itin., pp. 15-16. This passage is not in the first recension of c.1191, but is in the second recension of c.1197. It is an indication that Gerald became more alive to the issue of the rights of St. David's during the 1190s, after his retirement from royal service.

96. Inv., p. 213. See Richter, Giraldus Cambrensis, p. 87. The last books of the Invectiones, which contain this passage, were certainly not written until after 1208 and probably not until after 1216: see Spec. Duorum, pp. xix-xxi.

97. Inv., pp. 193-5; De Jure, pp. 337-9; De Reb., pp. 85, 87. Cf. his remarks on the renewed offer of St. David's in 1215, which he says he refused because of the poverty of the diocese, De Jure, p. 133. Gerald claimed to have been offered Llandaff by Count John and Bangor by William de Longchamp (both c.1191); Wexford (Ferns) with Leighlin by John in 1185; Waterford in 1204 and the archbishopric of Cashel in 1206 by his cousin Meiler fitzHenry, Justiciar of Ireland.

98. e.g. Itin., pp. 7-8; Descr., p. 162; Top., p. 4; Prin., p. 6.

99. See Richter, Giraldus Cambrensis, pp. 29-38; id., 'Canterbury's Primacy'; id., 'Professions of Obedience'; also his editorial introduction to Canterbury Professions, Canterbury and York Society, lxvii (1973), esp. pp. lxxxvi-xcvi.

100. Episcopal Acts, i. 91-7; Richter, Giraldus Cambrensis, p. 30.

101. Ibid., p. 35, quoting from Brut y Tywysogyon, p. 83.

102. K. Williams-Jones, 'Thomas Becket and Wales', Welsh History Review, (1970-1), 83.

103. Inv., p. 85 (Butler's tr.).

104. De Jure, pp. 340-1.

105. Ibid., p. 133.

106. Ryan, 'Historical value', suggests that Henry II opposed Gerald's election in 1176 because he had no wish to see a strong bishop of St. David's related to the fitzGeralds at a time when Raymond le Gros, a fitzGerald, might well be in line to take over the Norman enterprise on Strongbow's death. In 1199 Gerald visited his Marcher relatives in Ireland to obtain support for his fight over St. David's (De Reb., p. 112). He wrote that Hubert Walter was hostile to his election 'because he knew that I was nobly born from both races of our land', Inv., p. 106. Often Gerald wrote in general terms that it was relationship with 'the chief men of Wales' that jeopardized his chances—this could apply equally well to the Marchers or the Welsh princes.

107. De Reb., pp. 42-3; cf. Inv., pp. 188-9.

108. Inv., pp. 94-6, 116, 118-20, 153-4; De Jure, pp. 193, 195, 240-2, 253, 287. See Episcopal Acts, ii. 435-6. R.W. Hays, 'Rotoland, Subprior of Aberconway, and the Controversy over the See of Bangor 1199-1204', Journal of the Historical Society of the Church in Wales, xiii (1963), summarizes the details.

109. Letters of Henry III, ed. W.W. Shirley (RS, 1862-6), i, 4. Cf. The Black Book of Limerick, ed. J. MacCaffrey (Dublin, 1906), pp. xxx-xxxi, xc. This letter is put in context by Watt's discussion of 'The Anglicisation of the Episcopate' in Church in Medieval Ireland, pp. 87-109. See also ch. 3 of his Church and Two Nations.

110. His hostility is described fairly indiscriminately as being towards either any Walensis or anyone de Wallia oriundus, e.g. De Reb., pp. 95, 103; cf. De Jure, p. 120.

111. Inv., p. 93.

112. Ibid., p. 106: 'Quia Walensis eram ut dixit (i.e. Hubert Walter)'—hardly a self-
    identification. Gerald preferred the terms Kambria and Britones to Wallia and Wallenses
    (see pp. 151-2).

113. De Reb., p. 43.

114. Inv., p. 186.

115. Ibid., pp. 91-2. Gerald says that Hubert Walter was still justiciar, but in fact he had
    resigned the month before the battle. Most chroniclers attribute the victory to Geoffrey
    fitzPeter, Hubert Walter's successor. See J.T. Appleby, England without Richard 1189-1199
    (London, 1965), pp. 228-9; C.C. Young, Hubert Walter (Durham, N.C., 1968), pp. 121-1.

116. Inv. pp. 187-. Gerald claimed that Henry II sought papal permission for his bishops to
    excommunicate rebels solely on account of the Welsh.

117. Descr., p. 180. This dates from c. 1194 and is an early indication of sympathy with the
    Welsh.

118. Ibid., p. 183.

119. Ibid., pp. 179-84, 186, 192-4. Cf. below, p. 162.

120. Inv., pp. 137, 162-4; De Jure, pp. 109-10, 168, 229.

121. Gemma Eccl., p. 330.

122. De Jure, p. 135.

123. Ibid., pp. 338-9.

124. Ibid., p. 153; Itin., p. 106.

125. Gemma Eccl., p. 331. The word scurra, which I have translated freely as 'paid look-out',
    can mean 'buffoon', 'parasite', 'servant,' or 'mercenary'.

126. Symb. Elect., p. 302.

127. Inv., p. 86.

128. Symb. Elect., p. 306.

129. Inv., p. 163. Cf. Bishop Bernard's similar argument, ibid., p. 142.

130. De Jure, pp. 244-6.

131. Ibid., p. 210.

132. Ibid., p. 226.

133. Inv., p. 94.

134. Ibid., pp. 142-3, 146-7.

135. Inv., p. 34. C. Brooke, discussing Bernard's campaign, makes the point that 'it is salutary
    to remember when studying this period of Welsh history that a Welshman is not always
    consistently a Welshman, and a Norman almost never consistently an Englishmen',
    'The Archbishops of St. David's, Llandaff and Caerleon-on-Usk', in Studies in the Early
    British Church, ed. N.K. Chadwick et al. (Cambridge, 1958), p. 217.

CHAPTER III

1. Gerald entered royal service at the request of Henry II 'who was then in the March
    busy over the pacification of Wales' (De Reb., p. 57). This was in 1184 (R.W. Eyton,
    Court, Household and Itinerary of King Henry II (London, 1878), p. 256). The date of
    his retirement from court is not certain. He went to Lincoln in 1196 (Op. v, p. liii, n.
    2) but it has been suggested that he had spent the period 1194-6 away from court too,
    perhaps at Hereford (M. Richter, Giraldus Cambrensis, pp. 7, 88). Gerald himself said he
    spent ten years at court (Op. viii, p. lvii) but he is notoriously unreliable in matters of
    chronology.

2. See above, pp. 45-6.

3. Top., pp. 189-93. Gerald also included the passage in his Symbolum Electorum, a selection

of his best pieces (p. 391), and part of it is in Prin., pp. 199-200.

4. On Gerald's concept of 'the lettered prince', and on the reaction of literary clerics to court life in general, see E. Türk, Nugae curialium, le regne d'Henri II Plantagenêt, 1154-1189, et l'éthique politique (Geneva, 1977). Gerald is discussed on pp. 95-124.

5. Top., p. 4.

6. Map, p. 237; Peter of Blois, ep. 66 (Becket Materials vii. 573).

7. W. Stubbs, 'Learning and Literature at the Court of Henry II', Seventeen Lectures on the Study of Medieval and Modern History (3rd edn., Oxford, 1900); C.H. Haskins, 'Henry II as a Patron of Literature', in Essays in Medieval History Presented to T F Tout, ed. A.G. Little and F.M. Powicke (Manchester, 1925); V.H. Galbraith, 'The Literacy of the Medieval English Kings', Proceedings of the British Academy, xxi (1937), reprinted in Studies in History, selected by Lucy S. Sutherland (London, 1966), pp. 92-3; P. Dronke, 'Peter of Blois and Poetry at the Court of Henry II', Mediaeval Studies, xxxviii (1976).

8. Galbraith, 'Literacy', p. 93.

9. Itin., p. 4.

10. The first edition of the Itin. (1191) dedicated to Longchamp (see above p. 56); the first edition of the Descr. (1194) to Hubert Walter, who also received a presentation copy of the Itin. in the 1190s; the second edition of the Itin. (1197) to Hugh of Lincoln, who also received a presentation copy of the Descr. about the same time; the second edition of the Vita Rem., the Vita Hug., the third edition of the Itin. (all c. 1214), the second edition of the Descr. and the De Jure (1215-16) and the Spec. Eccl. (c.1220) to Langton.

11. See above, p. 86, p. 24.

12. See above, pp. 17-18, 19.

13. Exp., pp. 405-11. The letter refers to Map as dead (p. 410) and must therefore be after 1208, and mention of John's 'many sons, both natural and legitimate' (p. 407) might date it after the birth of Richard, John's second legitimate son, in 1209. It was clearly written before John's Irish expedition of 1210. But a composition date of 1209-10, during the Interdict, gives a strange ring to Gerald's exhortations to John to 'exalt the Church of God in those parts and to give the annual tithe from every house to St. Peter in Ireland, as in England' (p. 409).

14. The only manuscript of the first edition with a dedication is Bodl. MS Rawlinson B. 188 and here it is placed at the end of the work (ff. 96ᵛ-97) and is incomplete. This does seem to suggest attempted suppression, as presumed by the Rolls Series editors (Op., vi, pp. xxxiv-xxxvi; Itin., p. 3 n. 1). Longchamp is savagely denounced in the Vita Galf, esp. pp. 420-1.

15. Prin., p. 198.

16. Ibid., p. 213.

17. Top., p. 192 (cf. p. 199); Exp., p. 303.

18. Exp., pp. 304-5.

19. Describing both vices and virtues was behaving 'more historico'; see above, p. 150.

20. Adam of Eynsham, Magna Vita Hugonis, ed. D.L. Douie and Dom H. Farmer (London, 1961-2), ii. 68-72. 'Hugh frequently reproved him for his various sins and constantly urged him to make amends' (ibid., 71). Cf. Hugh's rebuke to Henry over the Forest Law (Map, p. 5).

21. In 1213 King John had Peter of Pomfret hanged for making unsettling prophecies: Ralph of Coggeshall, Chronicon Anglicanum, ed. J. Stevenson (RS, 1875), p. 167; Roger of Wendover, Flores Historiarum, ed. H.G. Hewlett (RS, 1886-9), ii. 76-7. In 1225 a man was exiled 'pro falsa predicatione et aliis stulticiis': Curia Regis Rolls, xii (HMSO, 1957), 328.

22. Henry I blinded a knight 'pro derisioriis cantionibus'. 'This facetious joker', the King said, 'composed dirty songs about me, sang them publicly, to my injury, and often gave my enemies, who wished me evil, cause for a good laugh.' Ordericus Vitalis, *Ecclesiastical History*, Book XII, c. 39 (ed. M. Chibnall, vi (Oxford, 1978), 354).

23. Exp., p. 404. It is not clear if Book III was ever written.

24. Prin., p. 149 (cf. ibid., p. xix).

25. Vita Galf., p. 359; De Jure, p. 116; cf. Top. 199: 'it is dangerous to write against a man who can write you off' (periculosum quippe est quantalibet occasione in illum scribere qui potest proscribere).

26. Spec. Duorum, p. 144 (transl. p. 145).

27. See above, p. 204, n1.

28. See above, p. 24.

29. Longchamp is also criticized in Gemma Eccl., pp. 302, 348.

30. Hubert Walter is represented as an important figure in the attempt to block Geoffrey's appointment as archbishop (Vita Galf., pp. 373, 376-8) and Hugh de Puiset is shown as involved in simony and nepotism (ibid., p. 377).

31. De Reb., p. 86; see Richter, Giraldus Cambrensis, pp. 85-6.

32. Above, pp. 24-9.

33. Prin., p. 160; Exp., p. 304. Gerald characterizes Dermot of Leinster's 'heavy and intolerable tyranny' in the same way; Exp., p. 225.

34. Top., p. 199.

35. Exp., p. 304: cf. Prin., p. 160 (justitiae venditor et dilator).

36. e.g. Prin., p. 250; Vita Galf., p. 418.

37. W.L. Warren, King John (London, 1961), p. 179. Warren is more tentative in his Henry II (London, 1973), pp. 382-3, where these proposals only 'dimly foreshadow clauses of Magna Carta'. Cf. J.C. Holt, Magna Carta (Cambridge, 1965), pp. 60-2.

38. Prin., pp. 183-6 (quotation at p. 186).

39. It is not quite clear what is meant by 'tria quae juravit in coronatione sua de ecclesia Dei manutenda'. The English coronation oath was a threefold oath, but only the first part related to the Church. The reference may be to Henry II's coronation charter, which simply confirmed Henry I's promises concerning selling and farming out Church property and revenue during vacancies.

40. Roger of Asterby's widow, Constance, and son, John, alienated property to the Gilbertine home of Alvingham. Constance was a member of the Meaux family who were also entangled in debts to the Jews. Constance's sister-in-law, Beatrice, alienated half her demesne to Alvingham in return for 87 silver marks to pay debts to the Jews incurred by her husband, Peter of Meaux, her son, John, and herself (Alvingham cartulary, BodL MS Laud Misc. 642, ff. 10ʳ-12aᵛ). Details of the Meaux family can be found in Early Yorkshire Charters, xi, ed. C.T. Clay (Yorkshire Archaeological Society Record Series, 1963), pp. 261-4. There was another late 12th-century Roger of Asterby, one of the six sons of Thorald of Asterby (Charters of Gilbertine Houses, ed. F.M. Stenton (Lincoln Record Society, xvii, 1922), pp. xxiv, 106, 111). I would like to thank Brian Golding for help with these references.

41. Itin., pp. 21-2; Vita Rem., p. 70.

42. Exp., pp. 304-5.

43. Vita Hug., p. 103.

44. 'Insular tyranny' was one of Gerald's favourite descriptions of the regime under which England suffered (e.g. Vita Galf, p. 388; Vita Rem., p. 71; Itin., p. 149; Spec. Eccl., p. 337). It is based on the idea that islands are particularly prone to tyranny. Gerald quotes the

phrase 'Britannia occidentalis insula fertilis est tyrannorum patria' (Prin., pp. 76, 303)
from Gildas, where we find 'Britannia fertilis provincia tyrannorum' (MGH, Auctores
Antiquissimi xiii. 29). Gildas himself is quoting Porphyry, probably via Jerome, Epistolae,
132 (PL, xxii, col. 1157). Gerald also quotes 'reges insularum omnes tyranni sunt' (Prin.,
pp. 75, 303), which he attributes to Boethius.

45. See above, pp. 33-4.

46. De Jure, p. 164.

47. Discussed in Ch. 4.

48. Exp., p. 305; Itin., p. 145; Inv. 104. Henry II's policy towards episcopal vacancies is
discussed by Margaret Howell, who concludes 'The reign of Henry II, then, saw not
only the reassertion of regalian right but also a steady development and consolidation in
the method of exercising it.' Regalian Right in Medieval England (London, 1962), p. 44.

49. Catalogus Brevior (Op., i. 423).

50. Itin., p. 53.

51. Prin., p. 149, and intro., pp. xviii-xx.

52. e.g. on p. 308 the sentences 'De tribus autem... in tempora longa' were clearly written early
in John's reign, while the following sentence, 'Vide lector coeperat et evanescere' must date
from 1216. The reference to 'tempus Johannis' on p. 310 might imply John is dead.

53. Prin., pp. 133, 140-1.

54. It is discussed as an example of the genre in Berges, Die Führstenspiegel, pp. 143-50.

55. Ed. J. Holmberg (Uppsala, 1929). Its authorship is debated. It has been attributed to
William of Conches. See T. Gregoty, Anima Mundi. La Filosofia di Guglielmo di
Conches e la Scuola di Chartres (Florence, 1955), pp. 19-26; J.R. Williams, 'The Quest
for the Author of the Moralium Dogma Philosophorum, 1931-56', Speculum, xxxii
(1957).

56. Only excerpts of this are printed in MGH, Scriptores, ix, and PL, clxiii, but the Rolls
Series editors of Gerald have collated Book I of the Prin. with the complete work.

57. Prin., pp. 24-5 consists of Hildebert, Epistolae, xv (PL, clxxi, col. 181); Prin., pp. 25-7
consists of Hildebert, Ep. iii (PL, clxxi, col. 144).

58. Prin., pp. 106-12 consists of Gemma Animae, i, cap. 180-8 (PL, clxxii, cols. 599-602).

59. Prin., pp. 114-17 consist of extracts from the Codex, pp. 112-14 of extracts from canon
law texts.

60. Prin., pp. 94-8, 126-9.

61. Ibid., p. 19.

62. See J.E.A. Jolliffe, Angevin Kingship (2nd edn., London, 1963).

63. Prin., p. 76.

64. Ibid., p. 6.

65. Ibid., p. 154.

66. Ibid.

67. The general medieval background for these two frameworks can be approached via P.
Courcelle, La Consolation de Philosophie dans la tradition littéraire (Paris, 1967).

68. Exp., pp. 383-5.

69. Prin., p. 172.

70. Exp., pp. 379-80 (repeated in Prin., p. 220).

71. Exp., p. 378 (repeated in Prin., p. 219).

72. Prin., pp. 153-4.

73. Ibid., p. 163.

74. A similar integration is found at Prin., p. 225, where divine grace carries Henry to the
top of the wheel and his own obstinate malice takes him to the bottom.

75. The use of phrases such as 'Deus et fortuna secunda' (e.g. Exp., p. 407; Prin., p. 287) or 'Volvitur interea Fortunae rota...' (e.g. Prin., p. 234) are often purely conventional.

76. Becket Materials, v.377-9; for the exactions of 1159 see J.H. Round, Feudal England (London, 1895, repr. 1964), pp. 214-21.

77. In the late 1170s and early 1180s Henry was an international arbiter, as Gerald himself witnesses (Prin., pp. 159, 188-90). The appeal of the Patriarch Heraclius in 1185 is another indication of his prestige.

78. Prin., p. 297.

79. As in the passage quoted above, p. 66.

80. William of Newburgh, Historia Rerum Anglicarum, ed. R. Howlett, Chronicles of the Reigns of Stephen, Henry I and Richard I (RS. 1884-9), i 281.

81. Gerald carried a 'Becket token' around his neck and addressed his prayers to the saint in times of urgent need (De Reb., pp. 49, 53).

82. e.g Gemma Eccl., p. 360; Itin., p. 149; Vita Rem., p. 50.

83. Exp., p. 289; in the same work Gerald gave an account of Becket's death and praised him as a martyr, but avoided any mention of the King's role, ibid., pp. 259-62 (repeated in Prin., pp. 161-2).

84. There were two editions of the Vita, one c.1197 the other c.1214, but no copy of the former survives. It is, therefore, not normally possible to tell what material was added in the second edition (but see n. 85 below).

85. Vita Rem., pp. 60-1. There is an inconsistency in the story as told by Gerald. The knight is supposed to have come to Bartholomew, Bishop of Exeter, 'straightaway after the murder', but the Bishop is also said to have believed that Henry was innocent 'for a long time' before the confession changed his mind. The last comment is a marginal addition.

86. Ibid., pp. 70-1.

87. Ibid., p. 62.

88. De Reb. pp. 73-79, 84-5; Itin., p. 14. Cf. Inv., pp. 158-9.

89. In his preface to Book II (Exp., pp. 307-8) Gerald explained that his preoccupation with the Crusade meant that this book could not be as polished as Book I. Events in the Holy Land and preparations for the Crusade are described (e.g. Exp., pp. 365-72).

90. Something like a quarter of the text of Books II and III is directly concerned with the Crusade.

91. Exp., pp. 369-72 (repeated in Prin., pp. 264-6, but with a revised interpretation, pp. 266-7).

92. 'Sicut depingi solet'—an interesting example of the way dream imagery draws on contemporary artistic reproductions.

93. Newburgh, Historia, i. 271.

94. Marc Bloch quotes a troubadour song that illustrates how the Crusade fulfilled both the religious and military aspirations of the aristocracy: 'No need is there now to endure the monk's hard life in the strictest of orders... To accomplish honourable deeds and thereby save oneself from hell—what more could one wish?' (Feudal Society, tr. L.A. Manyon (2nd edn., London, 1962), pp. 295-6). For an isolated critic of the Crusade see G.B. Flahiff, 'Deus non vult: A Critic of the Third Crusade', Mediaeval Studies, ix (1947) on Ralph Niger.

95. Top., p. 190.

96. Ibid., p. 192 (an addition of the 2nd edn. of 1189).

97. Exp., pp. 388-9 (cf. Prin., p. 221).

98. Exp., pp. 367

99. Ibid., p. 368.

100. Gerald's ideal king, who relies solely upon God and therefore does not have to burden his people with taxes, is shown in the story he tells about Edward the Confessor (Prin., pp. 130-1). The King remitted the Danegeld, collected to meet a threatened invasion, and the hostile fleet was destroyed by a storm sent by God. Peter of Blois, too, criticized the reliance of the western crusading kings on resources and numbers. 'Repeated experience', he wrote, 'teaches that victory is given to the soldiers of Christ not through money or masses of armed men or the courage of the fighters, but from the power of the Lord of powers' (De Hierosolymitana Peregrinatione Acceleranda, PL, ccvii, col. 1068).

101. Prin., p. 166.

102. Ibid., p. 170.

103. Ibid., pp. 171-2.

104. Ibid., pp. 202-12. Some of this accont was transferred directly from the Exp., but Gerald made large additions. Exp., pp. 360-2 is the same as Prin., pp. 203, 206. Later editions of the Exp. contain much of the longer account in the Prin.

105. Ibid., p. 200.

106. Gerald dramatizes the urgency of Heraclius's mission by reversing chronological order. He first discusses the state of near civil war in Outremer (1186-7) and gives the text of a supposed letter of Urban III describing the massacre of the Templars at the springs of Cresson on 1 May 1187 (Prin., pp. 201-2; the letter is dated 3 Sept.). Gerald then goes on to Heraclius's visit (1185) and the letter of Lucius III (1184).

107. Henry II was descended from the first marriage of Fulk V, count of Anjou and King of Jerusalem (d. 1143), the kings of Jerusalem from the second.

108. Prin., p. 206.

109. Ibid., pp. 207-8.

110. Wareen, Henry II, pp. 605-8 (quotation at p. 605).

111. Prin., p. 209.

112. Above, p. 75.

113. Prin., p. 209.

114. Ibid., pp. 210, 211-12 (also in later editions of the Exp., pp. 363-4).

115. The urge to adopt a Becket-like pose was not uncommon at this time. Archbishop Richard also professed willingness to suffer Becket's fate for the defence of the Church, but was given the cool advice, 'God did such a work through the holy martyr that the king, even if he wished, would not find a rogue in the land who would dare to lay a finger on you. The war is over. Hold firmly, if you will, what the martyr had conquered.' (Vita Rem., p. 69.)

116. Prin., p. 212 (also Exp., p. 364).

117. Warren, Henry II, p. 618 n. 3.

118. Gerald's account of Barbarossa's Crusade is taken from Book I of the Itinerarium Regis Ricardi, attributed to Richard of Aldgate ed. W. Stubbs, Chronicles and Memorials of the Reign of Richard I (RS, 1864-5), i. (Prin., pp. 267-73, 273-6, 277-80, 280-1 consists of Itin. Reg. Ric., pp. 35-43, 45-9, 51—5, 57 respectively.)

119. Prin., p. 241.

120. Ibid., pp. 234, 235-6; cf. p 221 for the recurrent theme that John's Irish expedition of 1185 should have been sent against the infidel.

121. Ibid., p. 235.

122. Ibid., pp. 244-5; cf. p. 255.

123. Ibid., p. 250-1.

124. Ibid., p. 256.

125. Ibid., p. 283.
126. Ibid., pp. 257, 283-4.
127. Ibid., pp. 251-2.
128. Ibid., p. 287. The most dramatic clash over these reservations occurred at Montmirail in 1169 (Becket Materials, iii. 418-28) but Becket employed them on many occasions in the 1160s.
129. Prin., p. 288.
130. Ibid., p. 159; cf. Exp., p. 306.
131. Newburgh, Historia, i. 281.
132. Cf. Adam of Eynsham, Magna Vita Hugonis, pp. 184-5, where St. Hugh prophesies, on his death-bed, the downfall of the Angevins at the hands of the Capetians as retribution for Eleanor and Henry's adulterous union.
133. Prin., p. 282.
134. Ibid., pp. 288-94.
135. Warren, Henry II, p. 626.
136. Prin., p. 295.
137. Ibid., pp. 296-7.
138. Ibid., pp. 304-6. William of Newburgh's account of the funeral is quite different (Historia, i. 278-9).
139. Prin., p. 304.
140. Ibid., pp. 261-2, 307.
141. Ibid., pp. 312-13.
142. Ibid., pp. 314-15.
143. Ibid., p. 313 (twice).
144. Ibid., p. 315.
145. Ibid., p. 314.
146. Ibid., p. 308.
147. Ibid., p. 312.
148. Caesarius of Heisterbach, Dialogus Miraculorum, ed J. Strange (Cologne, etc., 1851), i. 21; cf. Ibid., ii. 20, 'daemones vero in effigie corvorum'.
149. Prin., p. 301. This is a variant of the Mélusine story discussed by J. Le Goff and E. LeRoy Ladurie, 'Mélusine maternelle et défricheuse', Annales, xxvi (1971), although the authors limit themselves to the femme serpent version. Reprinted (in part) in Le Goff's Pour un autre moyen âge (Paris, 1977).
150. Prin., pp. 309, 211, 301; cf. Caesarious, Dialogus Miraculorum, i. 124.
151. Prin., pp. 301-2.
152. Ibid., p. 302.
153. Ibid., pp. 301-2.
154. Ibid., p. 300; this is the strange story of how the Emperor Henry V, Matilda's first husband, did not die in 1125, but lived on as a hermit near Chester, recounted in Itin., pp. 139-40.
155. Prin., pp. 298-301.
156. Spec. Duorum, pp. 38, 40.
157. Ibid., p. 38.
158. Ibid., p. 30.
159. Prin., p. 299. Of Eleanor's five sons, one died in infancy and two, Henry and Geoffrey, died before their parents, while in their twenties. Only Geoffrey and John had surviving sons, and Geoffrey's son Arthur left no line.
160. Exp., pp. 345, 409.

161. e.g. Inv., pp. 93-4 (also in De Jure, pp. 193-4), 202 (also in De Jure, p. 223).

162. Gerald's picture of Edward the Confessor (Prin., pp. 129-31) is very favourable. This is not surprising in the light of the elevation of the King, culminating in the canonization of 1161, but it also fits in very well with Gerald's criticisms of the Norman-Angevin line, especially their acquisition of the kingdom 'quasi per hysteron proteron'.

163. Prin., pp. 302-3, 327.

164. Ibid., pp. 289-91.

165. Ibid., p. 326.

166. Ibid., p. 324.

167. Ibid., p. 322; cf. p. 324. The New Forest was actually created by William I. Early twelfth-century writers (e.g. Ordericus Vitalis, William of Malmesbury, 'Florence of Worcester') are accurate about this, while they still attribute Rufus's death to divine punishment for the afforestation. Other contemporaries of Gerald thought Rufus had made the Forest (Map, p. 232).

168. Prin., pp. 315-16.

169. Ibid., pp. 322-3.

170. Ibid., pp. 324-5.

171. Ibid., pp. 324, 180.

172. Ibid., p. 76.

173. Ibid., p. 37.

174. Gemma Eccl., pp. 125-6.

175. Prin., pp. 140-1.

176. On this subject see R.W. Southern, 'England's First Entry into Europe', Medieval Humanism and Other Studies (Oxford, 1970).

177. Becket Materials v. 98 (translated in Southern, Medieval Humanism, p. 145).

178. Map, pp. 222-7.

179. De Reb., p. 93.

180. Prin., p. 8. The development of this concept is discussed by F.J. Worstbrock 'Translatio Artium', Archiv für Kulturgeschichte, xlvii (1965).

181. Ibid., pp. 131-2 (also in Gemma, pp. 216-17), 133, 134, 318-22.

182. Ibid., pp. 318, 319.

183. Ibid., p. 138.

184. Ibid., p. 320.

185. Ibid., pp. 231, 253; cf. p. 211.

186. Ibid., p. 258.

187. See above, p. 162.

188. Prin., pp. 138, 227-8, 288-90, 291-4.

189. Ibid., p. 138.

190. Corpus Christi College, Cambridge, MS. 400, f. 115. Printed from an imperfect copy in British Library, Cotton MS, Vitellius E. v. in Symb. El., pp. 374-7 (consisting of poems xxiii and xxxiv, wrongly separated). See Appendix II.

191. ll. 1-2.

192. e.g. Prin., pp. 149, 328.

193. Ibid., p. 328.

194. Line 4 in the 1216 poem.

195. ll. 5-6.

196. 'Francia flos orbis', ll. 74, 76-9.

197. l. 35.

198. ll. 38-41.

199. ll. 30-3.

200. ll. 42-3.

201. See J.R. Strayer, 'France: The Holy Land, the Chosen People, and the Most Christian King', Medieval Statecraft and the Perspectives of History (Princeton, 1971).

202. Prin., pp. 291, 303, 322, 328-9.

203. 'ad cultum Dei ampliandum,' ibid., p. 291.

204. Ibid., p. 310.

205. Ibid., pp. 6-7.

206. Ibid., p. 133.

207. Ibid., pp. 322, 328-9.

208. Ibid., pp. 328-9.

209. Ibid., p. 311.

210. Ibid., pp. 322, 328-9.

211. Gerald was probably at Lincoln during this period, which included the battle of Lincoln.

212. See esp. the work of J.E.A. Jolliffe and J.C. Holt.

213. Prin., pp. 328-9.

214. Itin., p.7; cf. Top., pp. 3, 5-6; Exp., pp. 213 (also in Descr., p. 164), 222; Prin., p. 6; Gemma, pp. 4-5.

PART II

INTRODUCTION

1. Top., pp. 7-8.

2. Different appreciations of twelfth-century naturalism can be found in such works as M.-D. Chenu, Nature, Man and Society in the Twelfth Century, tr. J. Taylor and L.K. Little, (Chicago, 1968), selections from his La Théologie au douzième siècle (Paris, 1957); T. Gregory, 'L'Idea di Natura nella Filosofia Medievale prima dell'Ingresso della Fisica di Aristotele—Secolo XII', La Filosofia della Natura nel Medioevo. Atti del Terzo Congresso Internazionale di Filosofia Medioevale, 1964 (Milan, 1966); C. Morris, The Discovery of the Individual (London, 1972); Southern, Medieval Humanism, esp. the title essay. There is an interesting interpretation of 'naturalism' and 'supernaturalism' in legal processes by Peter Brown, 'Society and the Supernatural: A Medieval Change', Daedalus, civ (Spring 1975).

CHAPTER IV

1. e.g. Gemma, p. 55; Itin., p. 57-61.

2. e.g. Top., pp. 129-36; Itin., pp. 23-6; Gemma, pp. 104-9.

3. Map, pp. 65-6.

4. 'Ecce qualia sunt miracula Sanctae Fretheswidae!'

5. Gemma, pp. 153-4. Frideswide's translation took place in 1180. Philip, Prior of St. Frideswide's, compiled an account of the miracles that followed her translation, Historia Miraculorum Sanctae Frideswidae, AASS, October, viii. 567-90.

6. Map, pp. 37-9.

7. Top., pp. 7-8.

8. Ibid., p. 74.

9. 'Nunc ad miracula transeamus.' Ibid., p. 113.

10. Ibid., p. 119.

11. Ibid., p. 125.

12. Itin., pp. 67-9.

13. This aspect of miracles is strikingly exemplified in the chronicle of a contemporary French Cistercian house. After a saintly monk was buried in the grounds of the abbey, his tomb became a centre for miraculous cures. Disturbed by the crowds who flocked to the place, the Abbot and monks went to the tomb and addressed the departed monk: 'What is this, brother? We do not doubt the sanctity of your life and conduct. Why then these miracles? Do you not see that laymen coming to your tomb disturb the quiet of the monastery? In the name of our lord Jesus Christ, we order you to stop performing miracles. Otherwise, we will bury your body outside the monastery, so that the laity can have free access to your tomb and the brothers will be disturbed no more.' The miracles stopped. This story highlights the role of miracles as signs of saintly virtue; their beneficent effects are quite unimportant. (The Chronicle of Signy, ed. L. Delisle, Bibliothèque de l'École des Chartes, lv (1894), 649.)

14. '...saltu mirabili transferuntur, et, nisi piscis proprietas hoc exigeret, miraculoso. Hoc etenim piscium genus saltum appetit ex natura.' Top., p. 126; Itin., p. 114.

15. Top., p. 88.

16. Gerald equated proprietas and natura; some other twelfth-century writers distinguished between them, e.g. Marius, On the Elements, ed. R.C. Dales (Berkeley, 1976), pp. 12, 47, 53-4.

17. Itin., p. 28.

18. Ibid., p. 17.

19. Ibid., pp. 16-17.

20. Top., pp. 74-6.

21. Exp., pp. 209-11.

22. 'Nec mirum tamen, si circa ejus opera, qui omnia quaecunque voluit fecit, mira reperiantur, referantur et scribantur; apud quem nihil impossibile; quique naturam, utpote naturae dominus, quo vult inflectit, et quasi de non natura naturam facit. Praeterea, contra primaevam et veram, quae Deus est, naturam, qualiter vere fieri quicquam dicetur, quod ipso constat auctore patratum? Contra naturam igitur usuali sermone quam proprio magis ea sola fieri dicuntur, quae contra ejusdem non potentiam sed frequentiam prodire videntur' Top., p. 75.

23. He used similar arguments in defending the Irish works against the charge of indecency, Spec. Duorum, p. 168. It was not uncommon to appeal to the Bible or the Fathers to justify marvellous or miraculous stories (see B. de Gaiffier, Études critiques d'hagiographie et d'iconologie (Subsidia Hagiographica xliii (Brussels, 1967), 60-1).

24. Exp., p. 210; cf. ibid., p. 356; Itin., p. 78; Vita Dav., p. 395; Vita Ethel., p. 234.

25. Civitas Dei 21.8 (Corpus Christianorum, Series Latina, xlviii (1955), 771); Exp., p. 210.

26. Civitas Dei 21.8 (p. 773); Exp., p. 210.

27. See R.M. Grant, Miracle and Natural Law in Graeco-Roman and Early Christian Thought (Amsterdam, 1952), pp. 24, 193-6.

28. Liber contra Wolfelmum, ch. xxii, ed. W. Hartmann (MGH, 1972), p. 96.

29. T. Gregory, 'L'idea di Natura', discusses Manegold (p. 36) and refers to 'una concezione miracolistica della natura' (p. 39).

30. The example is Augustine's: De Genesi ad Litteram, 9.17 (ed. J. Zycha, CSEL xxviii, pt. I (1894), p. 292).

31. 'God established the order of nature, therefore, if he does anything outside the natural

order, it would seem that he is changeable', Thomas Aquinas, Summa Theologica I, q. 105, art. 6, obj. 3 (ed. P. Caramello (Rome, 1948), i. 499-500).

32. Contra Celsum, 5.23 (PG, xi, cols. 1215-18; or ed. M. Borret (Paris, 1967-76), iii. 70-3).

33. H. de Lubac, Surnaturel, Études Historiques (Paris, 1946), pp. 323-428.

34. Contra Faustum, 26.3 (ed. J. Zycha, CSEL, xxv (1891), 731).

35. Ibid.

36. Policraticus 2.12 (ed. C.C.J. Webb (Oxford, 1909), i. 85-6; cf. his Entheticus, ll. 607-30 (ed. R.E. Pepin, 'The "Entheticus" of John of Salisbury: A Critical Text', Traditio, xxxi (1975)).

37. 'The distinction between a natural order and a departure from it is here obliterated in the identification of all happenings as willed by God; and we are left with a conception of "nature" as compatible with any possible happening, contrasted with a "nature as known", a limited understanding, almost a human prejudice, based on experienced normality', R.A. Markus, 'Augustine, God and Nature', Cambridge History of Later Greek and Early Medieval Philosophy, ed. A.H. Armstrong (Cambridge, 1967), p. 401.

38. Contra Faustum, 26.3 (ed. Zycha, pp. 730-1).

39. Markus, 'Augustine', p. 398.

40. De Genesi ad Litteram, 6.14 (ed. Zycha, pp. 290-2) seems consistent with this view.

41. Ibid. (p. 189) seems to support this interpretation. The debate is summarized by P. de Vooght, 'La Notion philosophique du miracle chez S. Augustin dans le De Trinitate et De Genesi ad Litteram', Recherches de Théologie Ancienne et Médiévale, x (1938), 317-23.

42. Sententiae in IV Libris Distinctae, II. 18.6 (Spicilegium Bonaventurianum iv (Grottaferrata, 1971), i. 419-20).

43. Life and Works of Clarembada of Arras ed. N.M. Häring (Toronto, 1965), pp. 233, 236, 238.

44. Summa Theologica II, tr. viii, q. 31, m. 1 (ed. A. Borgnet, Opera Omnia, xxxii (Paris, 1895), 329-37).

45. De Genesi ad Litteram 9.17 (ed. Zycha, p. 291).

46. Summa Theologica I, q. 105, art. 6, resp. (ed. Caramello, i. 499-500).

47. There is a striking demonstration of this in the historiography. P. de Vooght has written two essays on Augustine's theory of miracle, 'La Notion Philosophique', which involves technical discussion of the seminales rationes; and 'La Théologie du miracle selon S. Augustin', Recherches de Théologie Ancienne et Médiévale, xi (1939), discussing Augustine's more general reflections. It is significant that all the material Gerald borrowed from Augustine on the subject of miracle is covered in the latter treatment.

48. Top., p. 49.

49. Ibid., p. 54.

50. Civitas Dei, 21.7 (Corp. Christ. ed., p. 768).

51. Top., p. 49; cf. Vita Ethel., pp. 233-4.

52. Civitas Dei, 21.7 (Corp. Christ. ed., p. 768).

53. Ibid., 21.4 (p. 763); Exp., p. 210.

54. Top., p. 75.

55. Ibid., pp. 7 and 49; cf. Bernard Silvester's epithet for the peacock, 'Nature ludentis opus, Iunonius ales', Cosmographia, I. iii. l. 459 (ed. P. Dronke (Leiden, 1978), p. 116); Alexander Nequam's 'opus est naturae aut ludentis aut prodigiosae aut providae', De Naturis Rerum, ed. T. Wright (RS, 1863).

56. Top., p. 21.

57. Entheticus, l. 609, 'Causarum series natura vocatur'.

58. Gerald wrote five saint's lives, all inspired by local attachments. The lives of David and

Caradoc of Llancarfan (the latter lost, apart from the prologue) reflect his involvement with south-west Wales. The lives of Hugh and Remigius, bishops of Lincoln, and of Ethelbert, patron saint of Hereford, were probably written while he was resident in those cities. It is likely that Gerald drew on records kept at the tombs of Remigius and Hugh for his account of their miracles (Vita Rem., pp. 22-31; Vita Hug., pp. 113-47). He recorded the 'ancient miracles' of Ethelbert, from earlier Lives, and promised to add accounts of more recent miracles (Vita Ethel., p. 236), although he did not do so. He left the account of David's miracles to 'the diligence of someone in the future' (Vita Dav., p. 404).

59. Top., p. 179; Itin., p. 27. These staffs could possess important ecclesiastical-political significance. It has been suggested that the capture of the 'Staff of Jesus' (traditionally St. Patrick's own) from Armagh in 1177 and its transference to Dublin was part of a move to claim ecclesiastical supremacy for Dublin (see the references in J.A.Watt, The Church and the Two Nations, p. 110 n. 5: Watt himself does not adopt this interpretation).

60. e.g. Top., p. 180; Inn., pp. 17-18.

61. Gemma, p. 103.

62. Itin., pp. 23-4.

63. Ibid., p. 25.

64. Ibid., pp. 17-18.

65. Gemma, pp. 40-2.

66. AASS, October, viii. 568.

67. See B. Smalley, The Becket Conflict, pp. 75-6, n. 69.

68. e.g. Gerald repeated a story from the Life of St. Basil of Caesarea of how the miraculous transformation of the boat had converted a household of Jews, Gemma, p. 39. Verbal similarities suggest that, of the three Latin translations of the Pseudo-Amphilochius' Life, Gerald was using the Vita Sancti Patris Basili Magni printed in L. Surius, De Probatis Sanctorum Historiis (Cologne, 1576-81), i (this story is at pp. 8-9); the Bollandists suggest that the author of this Life was a certain Ursus (Bibliotheca Hagiographica Latina, ed. Socii Bollandiani (Brussels, 1898-9), p. 154).

69. Gemma. p. 40.

70. Ibid., p. 39.

71. Itin., pp. 23-4.

72. Gemma, pp. 106-8; or a holy place, Top., p. 134.

73. Itin., pp. 32-3; Gemma, pp. 162-3.

74. Gemma, pp. 105-6.

75. e.g. Top., pp. 129-36; cf. Gemma, pp. 155-7.

76. Gemma, pp. 108-9.

77. Top., p. 137.

78. Gemma, p. 157. Cf. above, p. 35-6.

79. Itin. 27; Top. p. 179.

80. Top., p. 130; repeated in Gemma, p. 157.

CHAPTER V

1. With certain exceptions, e.g. Constantine the African's translation of Haly Abbas and Isaac Judaeus.

2. De Naturis Rerum, pp. 2-3.

3. Ibid.

4. This theme is discussed by Chenu, 'The Symbolist Mentality', chapter 3 of Nature, Man and Society, esp. pp. 27-38.

5. There is a large literature on the translation movement. C.H. Haskins, Studies in the History of Medieval Science (2nd edn., Cambridge, Mass., 1927) is a standard work. Translations of Aristotle's works are listed in G. Lacombe, Aristoteles Latinus (Rome, 1939-61) and are being printed in Aristoteles Latinus (Union Académique Internationale. Corpus philosophorum medii aevi, Rome, 1951-). L. Minio-Paluello's studies on the subject are collected in Opuscula: the Latin Aristotle (Amsterdam, 1972). There are good studies of the influence of individual authors, notably Richard LeMay, Abu Ma'shar and Latin Aristotelianism in the Twelfth Century (Beirut, 1962).

6. Haskins, Studies, pp. 14-15.

7. See above, p. 106.

8. Haskins, Studies, ch. 2. For the significance of 'claimed', see B. Lawn, The Salernitan Questions (Oxford, 1963), pp. 20-30.

9. For the following, see the preface to Daniel's Philosophia or Liber de Naturis Inferiorum et Superiorum, ed. K. Sudhoff (Archiv für die Geschichte der Naturwissenschaften, viii, 1918); the preface alone is in Oxford Historical Society, Collectanea, ii (1890), 171-3.

10. Mathematicus, PL, clxxi, cols. 1365-80, there attributed to Hildebert of Le Mans.

11. Experimentarius, ed. M.B. Savorelli in Rivista Critica di Storia della Filosofia, xiv (1959).

12. T. Silverstein, 'Daniel of Morley, English Cosmologist and Student of Arabic Science', Mediaeval Studies, x (1948).

13. For these scholars see R.W. Hunt, 'English Learning in the Late Twelfth Century', Transactions of the Royal Historical Society, 4th ser., xix (1936), reprinted in Essays in Medieval History, ed. R.W. Southern (London, 1968); D.A. Callus, 'The Introduction of Aristotelian Learning to Oxford', Proceedings of the British Academy, xxix (1943); on Alfred, J.K. Otte, 'The Life and Writings of Alfredus Anglicus', Viator, iii (1972).

14. Op., i. 414, 421; De Jure, p. 372.

15. Symb. El., pp. 341-9.

16. Gerald ascribed the Cronographia and Cosmographia to his own annis adolescentiae (Op. i. 421) and, elsewhere, to anno aetatis nostrae quasi vicesimo. Since he regarded himself as having written the Irish works (published 1188-9, but material collected from 1185 or 1183) in anno quasi tricesimo and the Welsh works (1191-4) in anno quasi quadragesimo, it is likely that anno quasi vicesimo means 'in my twenties' (De Jure, pp. 372-3).

17. Top., p. 79.

18. Ed. P. Dronke, tr. W. Wetherbee (New York, 1973). There are studies by B. Stock, Myth and Science in the Twelfth Century: a Study of Bernard Silvester (Princeton, 1972), and in W. Wetherbee, Platonism and Poetry in the Twelfth Century (Princeton, 1972).

19. He quoted Bernard explicitly only once (p. 117, repeated in Descr., p. 175, from the Cosmographia, I. iii, ll. 229-30); moreover, this was an addition of the period 1197-1214 and could well have come via Nequam (De Naturis Rerum, pp. 76, 81). Hence there is no evidence in Gerald's later works of direct familiarity with Bernard's Cosmographia. Dronke's claim that Gerald's work is 'little more than a plagiarism' of Bernard's (Cosmographia, p. 12) is extreme and indefensible.

20. I. iii, ll. 61-5.

21. p. 345, ll. 3-6, 9.

22. II. x, ll. 45-8.

23. p. 346, ll. 15-18. There are other examples, e.g. Bernard I. iii, 265-6, and p. 19-20; I. iii, 321-2 and p. 346, ll. 28-9.,

24. Glosae super Platonem, ed E. Jeanuneau (Paris, 1965).

25. Commentaries on Boethius by Thierry of Chartres and His School, ed. N.M. Häring (Toronto, 1971).

26. p. 341, ll. 11-12; p. 342, ll. 7-8.

27. p. 341, ll. 21-2; p. 342, ll. 1-4.

28. The Consolation of Philosophy, III, metre ix, ll. 4-9, ed. S.J. Tester (Loeb Classical Library, 1973), pp. 270-1.

29. 'Optimus erat, ab optimo porro invidià longe relegate est', Timaeus 29E (Calcidius, Timaeus Calcidius, ed. J.H. Waszink (Corpus Platonicum Medii Aevi, iv, London and Leiden, 1962), p. 22).

30. De Diversibus Quaestiones LXXXIII, q. 46, 'De Ideis' (ed A. Mutzenbecher (Corpus Christianorum, Series Latina, xliv A, 1975), p. 71).

31. p. 342, ll. 19-22.

32. Stock, Myth and Science, p. 94.

33. This conception is thoroughly discussed in Gregory, Anima Mundi.

34. p. 341, 1.17.

35. I. i, ll. 1-2. Silva is the principle of raw matter.

36. The question is discussed by T. Silverstein, 'The Fabulous Cosmogony of Bernard Silvestris', Modern Philology, xlvi (1948-9), 100-3. Peter Comestor wrote, 'Plato dixit tria fuisse ab aeterno, scilicet Deum, ideas, ile, et in principio temporis, de ile mundum factum fuisse... Moyses vero solum Deum aeternum prophetavit et sine praejecenti materia mundum creatum', Historia Scholastica, Gen. I (PL, cxcviii, cols. 1055-6).

37. S. Viarre, La Survie d'Ovide dans la littérature scientifique des XII⁰ et XIII⁰ siècles (Poitiers, 1966), pp. 49, 92-3, 94.

38. Metamorphoses I, ll. 5-9.

39. p. 347, ll. 21-31; Bedae Opera de Temporibus, ed. C.W. Jones (Medieval Academy of America, Publication xli, 1943), pp. 246-7.

40. It seems probable that Thierry, William, and Bernard all died some time during the 1150s. The dates of Bernard's active life depend upon the interpretation of the Experimentarius; cf. Wetherbee's introduction to his translation of the Cosmographia.

41. Le May, Abu Ma'shar, 258-64; Stock, Myth and Science, p. 27.

42. Top., pp. 40-1.

43. Op., i. 414-15, 422; see below, p. 228, n. 83.

44. A. Gransden, 'Realistic Observation in Twelfth Century England', Speculum, xlvii (1972), 42-4, 48-50.

45. U.T. Holmes, 'Gerald the Naturalist', Speculum, xi (1936), 111, 120.

46. Exp., p. 381.

47. Top., pp. 27-8.

48. Otia Imperialia I, xii (ed. G.G. Leibnitz, Scriptores Rerum Brunsvicensium (Hanover, 1707-11), i. 893); cf. John of Garland, De Triumphis Ecclesiae, ed. T. Wright (Roxburghe Club lxxii, 1856), pp. 53-4, six lines beginning 'Aere surgentes tenues...'

49. Top., pp.77-80. J.K. Wright, Geographical Lore at the Time of the Crusades (New York, 1925), praises the acuteness of Gerald's observations on the tides (pp. 194-6).

50. 'Quos ultra fines nec terra subsistit, nec hominum vel ferarum habitatio est ulla: sed trans omnem horizontem in infinitum per investigabiles et occultas vias solus oceanus circumfertur et evagatur', Top., p. 20.

51. Ibid., p. 7.

52. Ibid., p. 97. Paul the Deacon referred to two whirlpools, one in the ocean west of Scandinavia, the other between Britain and France, to which he attributed the tides, Historia Langobardorum, I. vi (MCH, Scriptores Rerum Langobardorum, pp. 50-1). On medieval tidal theories, see Wright, Geographical Lore, pp. 26-7, 84-5, 190-6.

53. Top., p. 98.

54. Ibid., p. 37.

55. Ibid., pp. 47-8.

56. This information is derived from E. Heron-Allen, Barnacles in Nature and in Myth (London, 1928).

57. De Arte Venandi cum Avibus, ed. C.A. Willemsen (Leipzig, 1942), i. 55. Also quoted in Haskins, Studies, p. 321.

58. Itin., p. 131.

59. Ibid., P. 132.

60. William of Conches, Philosophia Mundi, IV, viii (PL clxxii, col. 88); Albertus Magnus, De Animalibus, XV, ii. 3 (Opera Omnia, xii (1891), 106); Aquinas, Scriptum Super Libros Sententiaram, II, dist. xxx, q. 2, art. 2 (ed. P. Mandonnet and M.F. Moos (Paris, 1929-47), ii. 772); Vincent of Beauvais, Speculum Naturale XXXI, xi (Speculum Maius (Venice, 1591), i, f. 394ᵛ). These references are from C. Zirkle, 'The Early History of the Idea of the Inheritance of Acquired Characteristics and of Pangenesis', Transactions of the American Philosophical Society, xxxv (1946).

61. Entheticus, ll. 603-10.

62. e.g. the various treatises De Elementis; see the introduction to Marius, On the Elements.

63. Top., p. 62.

64. Ibid., pp. 62-3.

65. Ibid., pp. 119-20. Nannan has not been identified; Yvor is probably St. Ibar, who had his monastery near Wexford (AASS, April, iii. 173-4).

66. See his account of Patrick's life (Top., p. 161) and of his translation (ibid., pp. 163-4).

67. AASS, March, ii. 540-80. The story of Patrick's expulsion of poisonous beasts is at p. 574 C-D. The prologue to the Life states that it was written at the request of Thomas, Archbishop of Armagh (1180-1201), Malachy, Bishop of Down (c. 1176-1202), and John de Courcy (d. 1219). It was, therefore, written in the last two decades of the twelfth century. J.A. Watt dates it more precisely, to 1185-6 (The Church and the Two Nations, p. 111).

68. Top., p. 180.

69. Historia Ecclesiastica I, i (ed. C. Plummer (Oxford 1896), i. 12-13).

70. Itin., p. 124.

71. Ibid., pp. 35-6.

72. Top., p. 28; Solinus, Collectanea Rerum Memorabilium 22, 2 (ed. T. Mommsen (Berlin, 1895), p. 100); Isidore of Seville, Etymologies, XIV, vi, 6 (ed. W.M. Lindsay (Oxford, 1911), no pagination); Bede, Historia Ecclesiastica I, i (ed. Plummer, i. 13).

73. Top., pp. 28-9. St. Dominic of Ossory is identical with Modomnoc, St. David's disciple and bee-keeper. The story of how his bees followed him to Ireland, where there had been none before, is told in Rhigyfarch, Life of St. David, ed. J.W. James (Cardiff, 1967), pp. 18-19 (cf. Vita Dav., pp. 396-7).

74. 'Distinguantur... tempora, et concordabit scriptura', Descr., p. 209. The phrase appears to have been a standard maxim. It even recurs in the 17th century: 'Distinguenda sunt tempora et concordabunt leges', wrote Sir Edward Coke, Reports, Part 9, ed. Geroge Wilson (London, 1776-7), v. 16. When discussing how to harmonize apparent contradictions in the Fathers, Abelard advised, 'Distinguenda... tempora sunt' (prologue to Sic et Non, ed. Blanche Boyer and Richard McKeon (Chicago, 1976-7), p. 96).

75. Top., p. 29. Isidore and Solinus references as above, n. 72. Rhigyfarch includes this story in his Life of St. David, p. 19, but Gerald omits it from his version.

76. Top., p. 29.

77. Itin., pp. 114-18; cf Top., pp. 58-9; Descr., pp. 173-5.

78. The exact connotations of ingenium are discussed by Silverstein; 'Fabulous Cosmology',p. 98, n. 34, and Wetherbee, Platonism and Poetry, p. 94.

79. De Naturis Rerum, p. 220.

80. Beavers were traditionally associated with the Black Sea, e.g. 'virosaque Pontus/castorea' (Virgil, Georgics, I, ll. 58-9.)

81. Naturalis Historia,VIII. 109; XXXXII. 26 (ed. H. Rackham,W.H.S. Jones, and D.E. Eichholz, Loeb Classical Library, 1938-63), iii. 78; viii. 480).

82. Physiologus, ed. F. Sbordone (Milan, 1936), pp. 82-5; D. Offermans (ed.), Der Physiologus nach den Handschriften G und M (Beiträge zur Klassischen Philologie, xxii, 1966) 86. On the early history of the story see F. Sbordone, Ricerche sulle Fonti et sulla Composizione del Physiologus Greco (Naples, 1936), pp. 54-5.

83. Physiologus Latinus, ed. F.J. Carmody (Paris, 1939), pp. 32-3. There is a facsimile edition of a typical twelfth-century English bestiary,The Bestiary, ed. M.R. James (Roxburghe Club, 1928); the beaver is on f. 8ᵛ.

84. The list of eastern animals that Gerald inserted into the second edition of his Topographia Hibernica is clearly based on bestiaries (Top., p. 69). He had some influence on the bestiary tradition.Two thirteenth-century bestiaries (MS Bodley 764 and its counterpart, British Library MS Harleian 4751) borrowed 4 chapters on the barnacle, osprey, kingfisher, and badger (Top., pp. 47-51, 58 is the same as Bodley 764, ff. 30, 36-8, and Harleian 4751, ff. 50ᵛ, 58ᵛ-60. They are based on the 1st edition of the Top.). Gerald's importance for the transmission of the barnacle story is mentioned by F. McCulloch, Medieval Latin and French Bestiaries (Chapel Hill, N. Carolina, 1960), pp. 36, n. 42, 199.

85. This is from the Pro Scauro, which survives only in fragments and was unknown in the twelfth century.

86. Satire, XII, 1.34.

87. Etymologies, XII, ii. 21.

88. The working text of the Speculum Duorum has survived to show this process frozen in midstream, while one of Gerald's letters of c.1218 (Op. i. 409) refers to a continuing emendation and expansion of his works (including the Topographia Hibernica). His account of beavers underwent this process of expansion. A short passage in the Topographia Hibernica was greatly expanded in the first edition of the Itinerariam Kambriae. This was copied into the Descriptio Kambriae, with additions which were, in turn, incorporated into later versions of the Itinerarium Kambriae. Material was also reapplied. The phrase 'mirabili, ne dicam ingenio, vi quadam ingenita et quasi discrativa' was originally applied to the weasel in the Topographia Hibernica (Top., p. 60). A description in the Topographia Hibernica of how badgers use each other as carts was reapplied, in the Itinerarium Kambriae, to beavers (Top., p. 58; Itin., p. 115).

89. Commentary on Virgil's Georgics, I, ll. 58-9, in Servii Grammatici qui Feruntur in Vergilii Carmina Commentarii, ed. G. Thilo and H. Hagen (Leipzig, 1878-1902), III, i, pp. 147-8.

90. Top., p. 39.

91. Ibid., p. 51.

92. Spec. Duorum, pp. 170-72; De Jure, pp. 334-5; Op. i. 410.

93. The phrase is Seneca's (Ad Lucilium, Ep. 49) and is used by Alanus in his Sermo de Clericis ad Theologiam non Accedentibus, by Stephen of Tournai and an anonymous porretanus (Alain de Lille,Textes Inédits, ed. M.-T. d'Alverny, Etudes de Philosophie Médiévale, lii (1965), 146 n. 67, 274-8).

94. Descr., p. 156.

95. Spec. Duorum, p. 168.

96. Ibid., pp. 170-2.

97. It would seem, from the description of his works, that William would be very vulnerable to these criticisms; see H. MacKinnon, 'William de Montibus: A Medieval Teacher', Essays in Medieval History Presented to Bertie Wilkinson, ed. T.A. Sandquist and M.R. Powicke (Toronto 1969). Some of Gerald's works, of course, especially the Gemma Ecclesiastica, could be criticized in just the same way.

98. Spec. Duorum, pp. 170-2.

99. Descr., pp. 157-8.

100. Part of it comes from Gregory of Nazianzus, Oratio Apologetica 16 (PG, xxxv, cols. 425-6).The phrase 'ars est artium regimen animarum' was borrowed by Gregory the Great, Regula Pastoralis, I, i (PL, lxxvii, col. 14), but Gerald's quotation seems to have been direct.There was a translation by Rufinus, Orationum Gregorii Nazianzeni Novem Interpretatio, ed. A. Engelbrecht (CSEL, xlvi, 1910), p. 18. Gerald gave a fuller quotation in Symb. El., p. 272.

101. Ibid.

102. Ibid., p. 284.

103 Ibid., pp. 285, 287, 288. Peter of Blois wrote a remarkably similar letter (Ep. 76, PL, ccvii, cols. 231-7).

104.T. Stiefel, 'The Heresy of Science: A Twelfth Century Conceptual Revolution', Isis, lxviii (1977);T. Gregory, 'La nouvelle idée de nature et de savoir scientifique au XIIe siècle', in The Cultural Context of Medieval Learning, ed. J.E. Murdoch and E.D. Sylla (Dordrecht and Boston, 1975).

105. Quaestiones Naturales, c. 32, ed. M. Müller, Beiträge zur Geschichte der Philosophie des Mittelaltters, xxxi (1934-5), 37.

106. Philosophia Mundi, I. 23 (PL,clxxii,col.56).

107. Ibid.

108. Adelard, Quaestiones Naturales, c. 4 (ed. Müller, p. 8);William of Conches, In Boethium, ed. J.M. Parent, in his La Doctrine de la Création dans l'École de Chartres (Paris, 1938), p. 126.

109.William, Dragmaticon, quoted in Gregory, Anima Mundi, p. 243;William, Philisophia Mundi, II.3 (PL,clxxii, col. 58); Adelard, Quaestiones Naturales, cc. 1, 4 (ed. Müller, pp. 6, 8).

110. Ibid., c. 64 (p.59).

111. Philosophia Mundi, I. 23 (PL, clxxii, col. 56).

112. De Erroribus Guillelmi de Conchis (PL, clxxx, cols. 339-40).

113. Contra Quatuor Labyrinthos Franciae, ed. P. Glorieux, Archives d'histoire doctrinale et littéraire du moyen âge, xix (1952), 273-4, 289.

114. Op. i. 421.

115. Above, p. 117.

116. See the articles by Callus and Hunted cited in n. 13.

117. See, for example, the systematic introduction to his book on birds, which derives its order largely from Aristotelian models, De Proprietatibus Rerum (Lyons, 1480), intro, to Book XII.

118. The preface was badly damaged in the Cottonian fire but has been substantially reconstructed from seventeenth-century transcripts; R.W. Hunt, 'The Preface to the Speculum Ecclesiae of Giraldus Cambrensis',Viator, viii (1977).This quotation is at p. 209.

119. E.g. John Blund,Tractatus de Anima, ed. D.A. Callus and R.W. Hunt, Auctores Britannici Medii Aevi, ii (London, 1970).

120. Hunt, 'Preface', p. 210; Avicenna Latinus, ed. S. Van Riet (Louvain, 1968–72), I. 3.

121 Hunt, 'Preface:, p. 210; Eccl. 3:22.

122. Top., p. 40.

123. Ibid., p. 43.

124. 'De Naturis Rerum et Super Ecclesiasten', 3. 10, quoted in R. W. Hunt, 'Alexander Nequam' (Oxford University D. Phil. thesis, 1936), p. 243.

125. Top., p.42.

126. Ibid., p. 45. The story is from the Confessions, 11. 12, ed. P. Knöll (CSEL, xxxii 1896), p. 290. It is repeated in the Speculum Ecclesiae, Hunt, 'Preface', p. 210.

127. Gemma, p. 28; Augustine, Sermones, 117 (PL, xxxviii, col. 663).

128. Op, i. 348.

CHAPTER VI

1. Gesta Hammaburgensis Ecclesiae Pontificum, ed. B. Schmeidler, Scriptores Rerum Germanicarum in Usum Scholarum (Hanover, 1917); new version of Schmeidler's text, with German translation, ed. W. Trillmich, in Quellen des 9. und 11. Jahrhunderts zur Geschichte der Hamburgischen Kirche und des Reiches (Berlin, 1961).

2. Cronica Slavorum, ed. B. Schmeidler, Scriptores Rerum Germanicarum in Usum Scholarum (Hanover, 1937); new version of Schmeidler's text, with a German translation, Slawenchronik, ed. H. Stoob (Darmstadt, 1963).

3. Adam, IV, 1 (p. 227–8); there is a biblical echo here (Deut. 32:10).

4. Ottonis et Rahewini Gesta Friderici I Imperatoris, ed. G. Waitz, Scriptores Rerum Germanicarum in Usum Scholarum (Hanover, 1912), pp. 49–51; new version of Waitz's text, with a German translation, Die Taten Friedrichs, ed. F.-J. Schmale (Berlin, 1965).

5. Descr., pp. 180, 200; Top., p. 152.

6. Helmold, c. 38 (p. 77): 'apud Ranos non habetur moneta nec est in comparandis rebus nummorum consuetudo'.

7. Otto, p. 50.

8. Historia, i. 165–6.

9. Gesta Regum, ed. W. Stubbs (RS, 1887–9), ii. 485.

10. Top., pp. 151–2.

11. Gesta Stephani, ed. K. R. Potter, new edn. with intro and notes by R. H. C. Davis (Oxford, 1976), pp. 14, 54.

12. Descr., pp. 179–80, 201. For further details see p. 159

13. Top., p. 151.

14. Historiarum Sui Temporis Libri V, II, iii, ed. M. Prou, Les Cinq Livres de Ses Histoires (Paris, 1886), pp. 30–2; this passage was copied into the Chronica de Gestis Consulum Andegavorum, ed. P. Marchegay and A. Salmon, Chroniques d'Anjou, i (Paris, 1856), 94.

15. Adam, IV, 31–2, 36 (pp. 263–5, 272).

16. Ligurinus, ed C. G. Dümge (Heidelberg, 1812), VI, ll. 37–43 (PL, ccxii, col. 405). Scandinavia was regarded as an 'island of the Baltic' according to twelfth-century geography.

17. Adam, IV, 31 (pp. 263–4).

18. Ibid., IV, 32 (p. 265).

19. See p. 145.

20. Gesta Willelmi, I, 44 (ed. R. Foreville, Histoire de Guillaume le Conquérant (Paris, 1952), pp. 108–10).

21. Top., pp. 170–1.

22. Quoted by W.R. Jones, 'The Image of the Barbarian in Medieval Europe', Comparative Studies in Society and History, xiii (1971), from S.N. Kramer, The Sumerians (Chicago, 1963) p. 63.

23. L. Alcock, 'Some Reflections on Early Welsh Society and Economy', Welsh History Review, ii (1964-5), 4-5.

24. Adam, IV, 6 (p. 233).

25. Helmold, c. 51 (p. 102); cf. c. 65 (p. 122); c. 70 (p. 136); c. 85 (pp. 165-8).

26. Descr., pp. 207, 211-12; see pp. 163-4.

27. Gesta Stephani, p. 20.

28. Descr., p. 225.

29. Adam, IV, 18 (p. 246).

30. Ibid., IV, 22 (pp. 252-3).

31. Historia, i. 166.

32. On the free clans (gwelygorddau) see Pierce, Medieval Welsh Society, pp. 23-6, 49-51, 251-87, 329-37, 339-51, although his views must be modified by those of G.R. Jones, 'The Tribal System in Wales', Welsh History Review, i (1961), and 'The Distribution of Bond Settlements in North-West Wales', ibid., ii (1964-5).

33. Pierce, pp. 20-3 and chapter X, 'The Laws of Wales—the Kindred and the Blood Feud', for a discussion of the survival of the feud see R.R. Davies, 'The Survival of the Blood Feud in Medieval Wales', History liv (1969).

34. Descr., p. 200.

35. Top., p. 188.

36. Adam, I, 52 (p. 53); 61 (p. 59); Helmold c. 5 (p. 15); c. 70 (p. 136); c. 85 (p. 165).

37. Otto, pp. 50-1.

38. Ligurinus, VI, ll. 26-34 (PL, ccxii, col. 405).

39. Henry II, p. 158.

40. Descr., p. 207; cf. De Jure, p. 114, 'gens inquieta, rapinis et rebellioni semper accommoda'.

41. Helmold, c. 109 (p. 216). The Germanizing Abodrite prince, Henry, 'ordered the Slavs that each man should cultivate his field and engage in useful and suitable work, and he extirpated raiders and devastators from the land', c. 34 (p. 68); Helmold uses viri desertores to mean 'devastators', although in its biblical context (I Mac. 7:24) it means 'deserters'. On Slav raiding and slaving cf. c. 35 (p. 69); c. 38 (p. 77); c. 65 (p. 123); c. 68 (p. 129); c. 83 (p. 159). According to Helmold, the Nordalbingians' tendency to furta and latrocinia was 'proprer barbarorum viciniam', c. 47 (p. 92).

42. Helmold, c. 84 (p. 165).

43. Exp., pp. 395-6; Descr., p. 220. For further discussion see pp. 159-62.

44. Helmold, c. 25 (pp. 47-8).

45. Adam, II, 57 (p. 117).

46. Ibid., IV, 16 (p. 244).

47. Ibid., IV, 32 (pp. 265-6).

48. Ibid., II, 48 (p. 108).

49. Ibid., II, 35 (p. 96); 'barbari suo more signum quaererent'; cf Matt. 16:4, 'Generatio mala et adultera signum quaerit'.

50. Ibid., IV, 16 (p. 244).

51. Helmold, c. 108 (p. 212). On the link between paganism and ferocity, see c. 36 (p. 70).

52. Adam, IV, 17 (p. 244) (Estonians); IV, 27 (p. 260) (Swedes); Helmold, c. 52 (pp. 102-3) (Slavs); c. 108, (p. 213) (Rani).

53. Top., p. 164. See also above, pp. 38-9.

54. Letters of John of Salisbury, Letter 87, (ed. Millor and Butler, i. 135).

55. Vita Sancti Malachiae, p. 325.

56. Pontificia Hibernica, i. 19.

57. Adam, IV, 21 (pp. 251-2).

58. Above, pp. 39-42. Adam also criticized the Danish habit of allowing bastards to inherit, 'ut mos est barbaris', II, 74 (p. 134).

59. Above, pp. 42-3..

60. Gesta Willelmi, I, 44 (p. 108).

61. Descr., pp. 182-3.

62. Helmold, c. 108 (p. 214). On one of his journeys, Helmold had personal experience of Slav hospitality: 'There I learned by experience what I had known previously by repute, that no people is more distinguished in the courtesy of hospitality than the Slavs', c. 83 (p. 158).

63. Adam, IV, 21 (p. 252); cf. II, 22 (p. 79) regarding the Slavs of Jumne, 'hospitalite nulla gens honestior aut benignior'.

64. Map, p. 89.

65. The 'moral', 'political', and 'ethnographic' explanations of the Germania are summarized in J.G.C. Anderson's introduction to his edition (Oxford, 1938). R. Syme, Tacitus (Oxford, 1958), i. 46-8, 126-9, discusses the work. I have treated the Germania as reliable ethnography, although controversy on this issue continues. Contrast J.M. Wallace-Hadrill's 'the Germania... affords no solid ground for generalisation about Germanic society at large', Early Germanic Kingship (Oxford, 1971), p. 2, with E.A. Thompson's 'in general I accept the uncommon view that the explicit assertions of... Tacitus are credible' (unless self-evidently wrong or controverted by archaeology), The Early Germans (Oxford, 1965), p. viii.

66. Adam, IV, 36 (pp. 272-3).

67. Descr., p. 213.

68. Adam, IV, 18 (pp. 245-6).

69. Descr., p. 210; cf. ibid., p. 182.

70. Adam, IV, 31 (p. 264).

71. Pierce, Medieval Welsh Society, 1, 'The Age of the Princes'; ibid., ch; 10, 'The Laws of Wales—the Kindred and the Blood feud'; and, for 'proto-urban development', ibid., pp. 120-4, 141-4.

72. Adam, I, 4-7, borrows from the 9th-century Translatio S. Alexandri (MGH, Scriptores ii, 674-6), which incorporates parts of Germania IV, IX-XI.

73. Adam, IV, 19 (pp. 246-8).

74. Ibid., IV, 19 (p. 248).

75. e.g. Abbot Suger, Vie de Louis VI le Gros, ed. H. Waquet (Paris, 1929), p. 222; John of Salisbury, Historia Pontificalis, ed. M. Chibnall (London, 1956), p. 55.

76. These achievements, as exemplified in Gerald's works, are the subject of the next chapter.

77. Above, p. 170; the Sallust reference is to Bellum Iugurthinum 80, 6 (ed. J.C. Rolfe (Loeb Classical Library, London, revised edn., 1931), p. 302).

78. Adam, IV, 31, scholium 144 (140) (p. 265); the Servius reference is to the Commentary on Aeneid V, 95 (ed. Thilo and Hagen, i. 604).

79. Adam, I, 7 (p. 9).

80. Above, p. 163.

81. Top., p. 151.

82. Canny, 'The Ideology of Colonisation'.

CHAPTER VII

1. See Appendix I.
2. Ibid. for Latin and Provençal abridgements of the Top. and Anglo-Irish translations and an Irish version of the Exp. Jean de Meung is said to have translated the Top.
3. Translations of the Exp. appeared in Holinshed's Chronicles in abridged form in the 1577 edition, complete in the 1587 edition. Extracts from the Top. were published by Richard Stanihurst, De Rebus in Hibernia Gestis (1584). The Welsh works (excluding Descr., Bk. II) were published by David Powel (1585). Camden's Anglica, Hibernica, Normannica, Cambrica a Veteribus Scripa (1602) includes all four works (again, excluding Descr. Bk. II, which was not printed until its appearance in Wharton's Anglia Sacra of 1691).
4. J.J. O'Meara edited 'Giraldus Cambrensis in Topographia Hibernie. Text of the First Recension', Proceedings of the Royal Irish Academy, lii, sect. c. (1948-50), and translated it as The Topography of Ireland (Dundalk, 1951). A new edition of the Expugnatio Hibernica by A.B. Scott and F.X. Martin and a translation of the Welsh works by Lewis Thorpe for Penguin Classics appeared in 1978.
5. J.F. O'Doherty, 'A Historical Criticism of the Song of Dermot', Irish Historical Studies, i (1938), regards the Exp. as superior to this other main narrative source. Ryan, 'The Historical Value of Giraldus Cambrensis' Expugnatio Hibernica' (thesis), also comments on Gerald's reliability and his closeness to eyewitness.
6. Classical ethnography has been studied intensively from the pioneering E.E. Sikes, The Anthropology of the Greeks (London, 1914), to the recent Klaus E. Müller, Geschichte der Antiken Ethnographie und Ethnologischen Theoriebildung, i (Wiesbaden, 1972).
7. For the debate on the Germania, see above, p. 224, n. 65.
8. C.J. Glacken, Traces on the Rhodian Shore (Berkeley, 1967), pp. 80-115, discusses classical climatic determinism.
9. For a good analysis of this strand see A.T. Cole, Democritus and the Sources of Greek Anthropology (Middletown, Conn., 1967).
10. tr. J.C. Rolfe, p. 169; see B. Smalley, 'Sallust in the Middle Ages', in R.R. Bolgar (ed.), Classical Influences on European Culture 500-1500 (Cambridge, 1971), esp. p. 171.
11. Gesta Friderici (ed. Waitz, pp. 49-51).
12. A. Borst, Der Turmbau von Babel (Stuttgart, 1957-63) has the subtitle Geschichte der Meinungen über Ursprung und Vielhalt der Sprachen und Völker. It is a good guide to the sources, but is more of a catalogue than an analysis, and concentrates too emphatically on biblically inspired accounts. Gerald is discussed on pp. 694-6.
13. Top., p. 8.
14. Itin., p. 54 (Gwentian archers).
15. Ibid., pp. 87-9 (Pembrokeshire Flemings' scapulomancy).
16. Descr., p. 155.
17. Gerald originally intended to write his Topographia Britannica after the publication of the Irish works in 1188-9 (Exp., p. 403). Instead he wrote the Welsh works. But he still intended to write the Topographia after the Descr. of c.1194 (Descr., p. 158). Some questions which he raised in the Descr. were, he wrote, to be resolved in the forthcoming Topographia. This passage was not changed in the edition of c.1197, if Wharton is accurate, but in the edition of c.1214 the questions are dealt with within the text of the Descr. itself. Gerald therefore abandoned the idea of writing the Topographia between 1197 and 1214 (Descr., pp. 208-9). It is not easy to see what the Topographia Britannica would have contained. Gerald certainly intended to include an account of the Irish invasion and settlement of Scotland (Top., p. 162), and in the Top. mentioned that he would expand on various topics 'cum de utriusque terrae Walliae scilicet et

Scotiae situ et proprietate, de utriusque gentis origine et natura tractabimus' (Top., p. 59).
But it would have dealt with more than just Scotland, since it was intended to include
a discussion on the courage of the Britons (Descr., p. 208). Perhaps Gerald abandoned
his plans for a complete ethnographical-topographical corpus dealing with the Celtic
peoples because he felt his personal knowledge of the Scots was inadequate, or perhaps
the project was conceived too imprecisely.

18. As in the work of Adam of Bremen and Helmold of Bosau discussed in the previous
     chapter.

19. Descr., p. 205; cf. Prin., p. 213.

20. Ibid.; Exp., p. 301.

21. Descr., p. 207. Cf. William of Newburgh's opinion of Gildas: 'Integritatis... ejus non leve
     documentum eat, quia in veritate promenda propriae genti non parcit et cum admodum
     parce bona de suis loquatur, multa in eis mala deplorat' (Historia, ed. Howlett, i. 11).

22. Descr., p. 157.

23. Ibid.

24. Ibid., p. 161.

25. See above, pp. 24-9.

26. Preface to the Historia Rerum Transmarinarum, PL, cci, col. 211.

27. Giraldus Cambrensis, pp. 65-6.

28. Descr., pp. 218-27.

29. A good illustration of this ambiguity, as shown by the suspiciousness of the people being
     studied, can be found in E.E. Evans-Pritchard, The Nuer (Oxford, 1940), where the
     following conversation between the anthropologist and a Nuer is recorded (p. 13):

'I: ...What is the name of your lineage?

Cuol: Do you want to know the name of my lineage?

I: Yes.

Cuol: What will you do with it if I tell you? Will you take it to your country?'

The Nuer had recently been bombed, machine-gunned, and subdued by the Anglo-
     Egyptian government who had sent Evans-Pritchard to study them (pp. 135-7).

30. Ed. P.A. van den Wyngaert, Itinera et Relationes Fratrum Minorum Saeculi XIII et XIV
     (Sinica Franciscana, i (Quaracchi, 1929), 28).

31. The term is J.H. Rowe's: 'a substantial part of the ethnographic reporting done in the
     sixteenth century was a form of applied anthropology, being carried out at the request
     of government officials or in connection with mission programmes.' 'Ethnography and
     Ethnology in the Sixteenth Century', Kroeber Anthropological Society Papers, xxx
     (1964), 3.

32. Exp., pp. 395-9.

33. Top., pp. 148-9 argues the rights of the English crown to Ireland, pp. 189-90 glorifies
     Henry II's conquest.

34. Inv., p. 130; De Jure, p. 170; Spec. Eccl., p. 36; Descr., p. 165; Prin., p. 126.

35. Descr., pp. 178-9.

36. Historia Regum Britanniae, II, i (ed. A. Griscom (London, 1929), p. 253).

37. J.S.P. Talock, The Legendary History of Britain (Berkeley, 1950), p. 62.

38. Descr., p. 155.

39. Ibid., p. 227.

40. Ibid., p. 205.

41. Ibid., p. 213; quoted above, p. 142.

42. See above, p. 64.

43. Descr., p. 215.

44. Ibid., pp. 215-16.

45. Ibid., p. 206.

46. Ibid., p. 213.

47. Ibid., pp. 161-2; see above, pp. 54-7.

48. Descr., p. 220; cf. Exp., p. 396.

49. Descr., p. 177.

50. Ibid.; on language, see below, pp. 170-1.

51. Descr., p. 214; Hildebert is quoted from Epistolae, 30 (PL, clxxi, cols. 253-4).

52. Top., p. 147.

53. The semi-naked Connaughtmen had never seen humanos ... cultus (Top., p. 171); the Welsh have the same cultus by day and by night (Descr., p. 184). When used in a more general sense, it still retains the underlying meaning of physical as opposed to psychological, e.g. 'tam corporum quam mentium compositione' equals 'tam interiore quam exteriore cultu' (Top., p. 149). Mentium cultus is a metaphorical extension, used as a counterpart to vestium cultus (Top., p. 150).

54. See pp 170-1, on language.

55. See   pp. 159-62, on arma and the Welsh.

56. Descr., p. 179.

57. Top., p. 149.

58. Itin., p. 69; Descr., p. 211.

59. Descr., pp. 213-14; Gerald misunderstood this practice. See above, p. 41.

60. Descr., p. 189.

61. Top., p. 170.

62. Descr., p. 185.

63. Ibid., p. 206.

64. Ibid., p. 213.

65. Top., p. 166; cf. Descr., p.207. The phrase 'Neither strong in war nor trustworthy in peace' is from Gildas, De Excidio et Conquestu Britanniae, ch. 6.

66. Verbum Abbreviatum, ch. 70 (PL, ccv, col. 206). This was one of Gerald's favourite phrases (Spec. Duorum, pp. 50, 52, 90, 96; Descr., p. 220; Symb. El., p. Top., p. 168; Exp., 396; preface to the Vita Karadoci in Trinity College, Cambridge, MS R. 7.11, f. 90ᵛ; Vita Rem., p. 11; De Jure, p. 121; Op., viii, p. lviii; De Reb., p. 22).

67. Top., p. 153.

68. Ibid., p. 168. The quotation is biblical, 1 Cor. 15:33, and is also found in Peter the Chanter; cf. Spec. Duorum, p. 52.

69. Top., p. 168. This, too, is a biblical quotation, Ecclus. 13:1, and is also in Peter the Chanter, cf. Spec. Duorum, p. 52; Symb. El., p. 302.

70. Top., p. 150; cf. p. 153.

71. Top., pp. 167, 169.

72. The late Roman grammarian Sextus Pompeius Festus, epitomizer of Verrius Flaccus, defined 'ritus' as 'mos vel consuetudo' (ed. W.M. Lindsay (Teubner, 1913), p. 336).

73. Descr., p. 202.

74. Ibid., p. 192.

75. Ibid., p. 206.

76. Top., p. 168.

77. Ibid.

78. See above, p. 148.

79. Gerald's qualities as a realistic observer prepared to focus on details are discussed in Gransden, 'Realistic Observation in Twelfth Century England'.

80. Descr., p. 185.

81. Ibid., p. 201; the verse quoted is Horace, Ars Poetica, ll. 180-1.

82. Itinerarium, ed. van den Wyngaert, p. 173. A later Dominican account of the Mongols was illustrated: C. Brunel, 'David D'Ashby, Auteur Méconnu des Faits des Tartares', Romania, lxxix (1958).

83. Gerald mentioned this in the Epistola ad Capitulum Herefordense (Op. I. 414-15) and in the Catalogus Brevior Librorum Suorum (ibid., 422). J.C. Davies attempted to reconstruct the content of this map, 'The Kambriae Mappa of Giraldus Cambrensis', Journal of the Historical Society of the Church in Wales, ii (1952).

84. British Library, Royal MS 13. B. viii, an early manuscript of the Top., has ethnographic illustrations. It seems likely that the illustrations in Bodleian Library, Laud Misc. 720, and Dublin, National Library of Ireland 700, derived from this (O. Pächt and J.J.G. Alexander, Illuminated Manuscripts in the Bodleian Library, Oxford (Oxford, 1966-73), iii, no. 462). The illustrations in Cambridge, University Library, Ff. 1.27, show the same iconography, too. A. Gransden ('Realistic Observation', p. 49) has suggested that 'the originals were executed by Gerald himself, or at least under his supervision'. This is an attractive hypothesis, but the one major problem is that Gerald mentioned undertaking such illustrations. There seems no doubt that, if he had executed these drawings, he would have recorded the fact.

85. M.T. Hodgen, Early Anthropology in the Sixteenth and Seventeenth Centuries (Philadelphia, 1964), discusses these categories as employed by their first user, Herodotus (pp. 22-5).

86. Descr., pp. 165-79.

87. See above, pp. 132-4.

88. Descr., pp. 179-80; mention of barley is symptomatic—this is the usual arable adjunct to the predominantly pastoral agriculture of wet uplands.

89. Ibid., p. 201.

90. Ibid., p. 180.

91. Ibid., p. 218; cf. William of Newburgh, Historia., ed. Howlett, i. 107.

92. Descr., pp. 200-1.

93. Ibid., pp. 206, 216.

94. Above, p. 143.

95. Descr., p. 179.

96. For the taeogs, see Pierce, Medieval Welsh Society, references under 'bondsmen' in the index. The view that the bondsmen formed a much higher proportion of the population than previously thought is advanced by G.R. Jones, 'Tribal System in Wales', and 'Distribution of Bond Settlements'.

97. Pierce, Medieval Welsh Society, p. 348.

98. See above, pp. 31-2.

99. Descr., pp. 180-1.

100. Ibid., p. 210.

101. Ibid.

102. Ibid., p. 220; cf. Exp. 396.

103. Coterelli is a common term for mercenaries; Bragmanni seems peculiar to Gerald. It may have some connection with the term Brabantiones, often used of mercenaries.

104. Descr., pp. 220-1; cf. Exp., pp. 395-7.

105. e.g. Bloch, Feudal Society, ii. 290-1; G. Duby, The Early Growth of the European Economy, tr. H.B. Clarke (London, 1974), p. 44.

106. Descr., p. 221.

107. Ibid., p. 180.

108. Ibid., pp. 221-2.

109. Ibid., p. 192. Gerald thought that his own outspokenness towards Henry II might be attributed to a Britannica temeritas (Prin., p. 207).

110. See above, pp. 134-8.

111. Descr., p. 207.

112. Ibid., p. 211.

113. Pierce, pp. 23-4, 379, and ch. 10.

114. Descr., pp. 221-12.

115. See Lloyd, History of Wales, ii. 549-52, 576-8, 580-1, 587-90.

116. Especially Descr., p. 200, quoted above, p. 135.

117. Descr., p. 212; cf. Top., pp. 167-8.

118. See above, p. 135.

119. Descr., p. 165.

120. Ibid., pp. 192-3.

121. See Glacken, Traces on the Rhodian Shore. He discusses medieval climatic theory on pp. 254-87. Thirteenth-century references will be found in M.J. Tooley, 'Bodin and the Medieval Theory of Climate,' Speculum, xxviii (1953), although the author wrongly associates the theory of environmental conditioning specifically with Aristotelian influence.

122. Etymologies, IX (ed. W.M. Lindsay, ii. 105).

123. Top., p. 71.

124. Airs, Waters and Places, caps. 12, 16, 23-4.

125. Politics, VII, 7 (1327b 23); Problemata Bk. XIV.

126. Descr., p. 186.

127. De Natura Locorum, II, i (Opera Omnia, ed. A. Borgnet, ix. 560).

128. De Naturis Rerum, pp. 39-40.

129. D. Jordan, White Over Black (Chapel Hill, 1968), discusses the European theories on this subject at pp. 11-20, 'The Causes of Complexion'. One later seventeenth-century writer declared, 'A negroe will always be a negroe, carry him to Greenland, give him chalk, feed and manage him never so many ways'. (p. 16)

130. See above, pp. 157.

131. De Jure, pp. 222-3.

132. Prin., p. 70.

133. Glacken, Traces on the Rhodian Shore, pp. 255-6.

134. Above, p. 153.

135. Descr., p. 179.

136. Ibid., p. 206.

137. Symb. El., p. 302; also in the original preface to the Prin., Op. viii, p. lviii.

138. Descr., pp. 189-90.

139. See above, p. 154.

140. Top., pp. 154-5.

141. e.g. Itin., p. 127; Descr., p. 169.

142. Top., p. 154.

143. Descr., p. 185; Bellum Gallicum V, 14.

144. Descr., pp. 207-9.

145. Gildas, De Excidio, cap. 6.

146. Pharsalia, II, 572.

147. In the first edition of the Descr., Gerald promised to give 'Hujus… contrarii solutionem'

in the projected Topographia Britannica. By the time of the 1214 edition he had abandoned the plan and thus added the explanation at this point (see above, pp. 225-6, n. 17).

148. Maximus appears as Macsen Wledig in The Mabinogion (tr. J. Gantz (Harmondsworth, 1976), pp. 19, 118-27); his name is preserved in place-names (E. Ekwall, Etymological Notes on English Place Names (Lund, 1959), pp. 26-7); Welsh and Strathclyde dynasties traced descent from him (S. Frere, Britannia (London, 1967), pp. 360-2).

149. Descr., p. 209; see also above, p. 118.

150. Ibid.

151. Descr., pp. 217-18.

152. E.A. Freeman, History of the Norman Conquest, v (Oxford, 1876), 579. Freeman's judgement is over-enthusiastic, if only because a father should have children.

153. Top., pp. 153-5; Descr., pp. 186-7.

154. Top., pp. 155-61.

155. Ibid., pp. 203-4.

156. Ibid., p. 155.

157. Descr., pp. 186-9.

158. Ibid., p. 170: 'Eryri, called Snowdon in English, that is Mountains of Snow'.

159. Ibid., p. 166: 'nobles, called Uchelwr in Welsh, that is higher men'.

160. Ibid., p. 169: 'Cantred, that is Cantref, from cant, a hundred, and tref, a vill, is found in both Welsh and Irish'.

161. Ibid., pp. 177-8; the Old English works of Bede and Alfred are presumably the translation of the Ecclesiastical History and the other Alfredian translations; I do not know what the reference to Rabanus implies.

162. C.C. Coulter and F.P. Magoun, 'Giraldus Cambrensis on Indo-Germanic Philology', Speculum, i (1926).

163. Itin., pp. 77-8; Descr., p. 194.

APPENDIX II/ GERALD'S POEM

1. A pseudo-Virgilian line found in some versions of the Anthologia Latina (ed. A. Riese, Leipzig, fasc. 1 (1869), p. 179) and in the vulgata version of the Vita Virgilii ascribed to Donatus and probably dependent upon Suetonius (C. Suetoni... Reliquiae, ed. A. Reifferscheid (Leipzig, 1860), p. 66).

3. Cf; Eccles. 11:8.

4. Cf; Esther 8:16.

9. 'loð' in the margin, in red, i.e. 'lodovicus'.

* sunt, V.

† ubique, V.

58. Isaiah, 8:6.

59. Ovid, Remedia Amoris, 1. 808.

72. 'augᵒ' in the margin, in red, i.e. 'augustinus'.

73. 'loð' in the margin, in red, again.

* potest, V.

INDEX